International Tax Competition

Globalisation and Fiscal Sovereignty

COMMONWEALTH SECRETARIAT

International Tax Competition

Globalisation and Fiscal Sovereignty

Edited by

Rajiv Biswas

Commonwealth Secretariat
Marlborough House
Pall Mall
London SW1Y 5HX
United Kingdom
Tel: +44 (0)20 7747 6342
Fax: +44 (0)20 7839 9081

The views expressed in this document do not necessarily reflect the
opinion or policy of the Commonwealth Secretariat.

Published by the Commonwealth Secretariat
Designed by Wayzgoose
Printed in the United Kingdom by Formara Limited

Wherever possible, the Commonwealth Secretariat uses paper that is made
from sustainable forests or from sources that minimise the destructive impact
on the environment.

ISBN 0-85092-688-2   Price: £14.99

Contents

Acknowledgements

The comments and advice received from Commonwealth Secretariat colleagues is gratefully acknowledged. I am particularly appreciative of the guidance provided by Dr Indrajit Coomaraswamy and Professor Andreas Antoniou of the Economic Affairs Division in the preparation of this book.

The analyses and assessments in the papers included in the book represent those of the authors. They do not necessarily reflect the views and policies of either the organisations they represent or of the Commonwealth Secretariat.

Rajiv Biswas
Editor

Abbreviations

BIS	Bank for International Settlements
CFC	Controlled Foreign Corporation
CHOGM	Commonwealth Heads of Government Meeting
EPZ	Export Processing Zone
EU	European Union
FATF	Financial Action Task Force
FDI	Foreign Direct Investment
FIR	Financial Inter-relations Ratio
FSF	Financial Stability Forum
GATS	General Agreement on Trade in Services
GATT	General Agreement on Tariffs and Trade
GDP	Gross Domestic Product
IAIS	International Association of Insurance Supervisors
IBC	International Business Company
IFI	International Financial Institution
IMF	International Monetary Fund
IOSC	International Organisation of Securities Commissions
ITIO	International Tax and Investment Organisation
LDC	Least Developed Country
LLC	Limited Liability Corporation
MAI	Multilateral Agreement on Investment
MLEC	Model Law on Electronic Commerce
MOU	Memorandum of Understanding
NBFI	Non-Banking Financial Institution
NCCT	Non-Co-operative Country or Territory
OAS	Organisation of American States
OECD	Organisation for Economic Co-operation and Development
OFC	Offshore Financial Centre
SCM	Subsidies and Countervailing Measures
UNCITROL	United Nations Commission on International Trade Law
WIPO	World Intellectual Property Organisation
WTO	World Trade Organisation

Introduction: Globalisation, Tax Competition and Economic Development

Rajiv Biswas

The Commonwealth Response to the OECD Initiative on Harmful Tax Competition

The publication of the OECD's 1998 Report on Harmful Tax Competition and the threat of sanctions against non-OECD jurisdictions classified as 'no or low-tax jurisdictions' crystallised a long smouldering acrimony by high-taxing social welfare states against many international business service exporting nations with low income tax structures. The primary concern of the OECD countries was that their tax revenue bases were being eroded by what they regarded as 'harmful' tax competition from low-taxing non-OECD countries. From the OECD perspective, the forces of globalisation and the integration of global financial markets has created concerns that the OECD revenue base is being eroded by cross-border tax competition by international financial centres outside the OECD.

Many Commonwealth jurisdictions were identified by the OECD as meeting its criteria of being potentially harmful, based on four key criteria, including no or low income taxes, ring-fencing regimes, lack of transparency and lack of exchange of information. The OECD sought letters of commitment from all targeted non-OECD governments in which they were to agree to comply with the new OECD guidelines, and future detailed standards and regulations to be formulated by the OECD as the project evolved.

Many of the affected Commonwealth jurisdictions reacted with considerable alarm at the highest levels of government to the OECD Initiative, which was seen as an attempt to infringe on national sovereignty in taxation matters. Fiscal sovereignty is a right which has been carefully guarded by sovereign states and protected in international law over hundreds of years; international fiscal disputes have provoked major international political upheavals, including being one of the triggers for the American Revolution against British colonial rule after the British Parliament imposed the Stamp Act (1765) and the Tea Act (1773). Indeed, the American settlers rallied to the cry of 'no taxation without representation' in their struggle for independence, forging a separate nation to establish their right to fiscal sovereignty. In India, Mahatma Gandhi's major campaign of non-violent protest began with the formation of the Non-Co-operation Movement in 1929, which eventually led India to independence. The defining moment of his campaign was the protest march against the British salt tax in March 1930. By the end of April 1930, the British had imprisoned 60,000 Indians for breaking the salt tax laws and mounting civil disobedience on a massive scale, including related charges against Gandhi himself.

If my letter makes no appeal to your heart, on the eleventh day of this month I shall proceed with such co-workers of the Ashram as I can take, to disregard the provisions of the Salt Laws. I regard this tax to be the most iniquitous of all from the poor man's standpoint. As the Independence movement is essentially for the poorest in the land, the beginning will be made with this evil.

Letter from Mahatma Gandhi to Lord Irwin, British Viceroy of India,
2 March 1930

In response to the OECD Initiative, many affected jurisdictions were also concerned that the standards sought from non-OECD jurisdictions were far more demanding than those that were being required of the OECD countries themselves, creating a double standard that would further enhance the competitive advantage of the OECD international business service exporting industries. A particular concern was also that the OECD sought to impose sanctions on other sovereign states without first undertaking the normal process of consultations and negotiations that would be necessary in forging a multilateral agrement of this nature, via the normal process of international treaty negotiations.

Since the launch of the OECD Report in 1998, many Commonwealth developing countries have expressed their concerns about the OECD Initiative in various Commonwealth ministerial meetings. Concerns about the OECD actions were initially raised at the Commonwealth Finance Ministers Meeting in 1999 as well as at the Global Conference on Development – Agenda for Small States Meeting in February 2000. The Meeting of Law Ministers and Attorneys-General of Small Commonwealth Jurisdictions on 15–17 May 2000 considered that the OECD Initiative was in breach of natural justice and impinged on the sovereignty of small jurisdictions. They also argued that the OECD Initiative eroded the rights of all jurisdictions to compete freely in the provision of international financial services, rights recognised by the Commonwealth Heads of Government Meeting held in Durban in 1999. The Meeting called for these deep concerns to be brought to the attention of Commonwealth Finance Ministers and Heads of Government.

As a result of these concerns, the OECD Harmful Tax Competition Initiative was a key focal point for ministerial discussion at the Commonwealth Finance Ministers Meeting held in Malta in September 2000, and was the special theme for discussion at the meeting of Senior Finance Officials held just before the Finance Ministers Meeting. Many developing countries expressed their concerns about the OECD Initiative. A number of Commonwealth countries were particularly concerned about the potential impact of the OECD Initiative on global economic competition and government efficiencies, and the Commonwealth Finance Ministers Communiqué reflected these concerns. Finance Ministers stated:

Ministers recognised that tax competition could in fact be helpful, and not harmful, because it can further spur governments to create fiscal environments conducive to generating growth and employment.

Commonwealth Finance Ministers Communiqué, September 2000

The importance of tax competition between governments has also been emphasised by Professor Milton Friedman, in order to ensure that government services are provided as efficiently as possible. Professor Friedman stated in May 2001:

Competition among national governments in the public services they provide and in the taxes they impose is every bit as productive as competition among individuals or enterprises in the goods and services they offer for sale and the prices at which they offer them. Both lead to variety and innovation; to improvement in the quality of the goods and services and a reduction in their cost. A governmental cartel is no less damaging than a private cartel.

Milton Friedman, Hoover Institution, Stanford University, Professor Emeritus, University of Chicago and Nobel Laureate, May 2001

One of the underlying assumptions that appeared to be implicit in the OECD approach was that jurisdictions with low or no income taxes were viewed as being 'low or no tax' jurisdictions, which is something quite different altogether. The assumption that absence of income tax or having low income tax was synonymous with having 'no or low tax' is dismissive of the right of a jurisdiction to choose to raise revenues through indirect taxation, customs and excise taxes or other similar taxation instruments. Indeed, many OECD countries have been trying to shift their own tax structures away from direct taxation of incomes towards indirect taxation. At the same time, some of the largest EU and OECD members have done little to plug large revenue loopholes in their own domestic legislation prior to embarking on this overseas exercise. For example, France has a loophole that encourages Frenchmen to sell their businesses and shift their capital and residence abroad, while the UK allows these same

French nationals very attractive loopholes also, generating a thriving community of wealthy French emigrés in the UK. Most EU countries also pay massive fiscal subsidies to agriculture, sometimes even for farmers not to grow any crops on their land. The OECD Initiative also ignores major asset classes such as property. The London property market alone is a major tax loophole for foreign investors, including investors from other EU countries. The scale of this loophole far exceeds the total size of assets in any of the listed OFCs, but no steps have been proposed to exchange information on foreign property owners or tax these assets. Large segments of the London property market are foreign-owned and have bid up prices so high that ordinary British workers, such as nurses and teachers, are unable to afford to live in London, creating shortages of many essential public sector workers.

Many Commonwealth developing countries also expressed concerns about the economic development implications of the OECD Initiative, since the key targets were some of the very industries into which international economic advisers had been urging these countries to diversify in order to reduce dependence on primary commodity exports and subsistence farming.

Recognising the need for consensus building, Commonwealth Finance Ministers also mandated the Commonwealth Secretariat to facilitate multilateral dialogue on harmful tax competition. The Commonwealth Secretariat worked urgently with the OECD Secretariat to organise high-level consultations between the OECD and affected Commonwealth jurisdictions in St Michaels, Barbados on 8–9 January 2001. These consultations were made possible by the gracious invitation of the Prime Minister of Barbados, The Right Honourable Owen Arthur.

The Barbados consultations were the first multilateral discussions on the OECD Initiative held by affected non-OECD jurisdictions. The process of multilateral consultation improved the transparency of the OECD process and also assisted jurisdictions on both sides to achieve a better understanding of the concerns and perspectives of the other side. One of the main outcomes of the Barbados consultations was the creation of a Joint Working Group of OECD and non-OECD jurisdictions to try to find a mutually acceptable way forward. Importantly, agreement was also reached at the Barbados meeting by the non-OECD jurisdictions to commit to three broad principles of transparency, exchange of information and non-discrimination.

The newly created Joint Working Group, comprising six OECD and seven non-OECD jurisdictions, met twice in subsequent weeks in order to negotiate a suitable way forward. The meetings, for which the

Commonwealth and OECD Secretariats provided administrative support, resulted in detailed technical discussions of the OECD requirements. While there was significant progress towards greater agreement, there were still many aspects of the OECD Initiative which the non-OECD jurisdictions felt required greater transparency. As a result, the second meeting of the Joint Working Group held on 1–2 March 2001 included substantial discussion of a list of 17 technical questions which the non-OECD jurisdictions put to the OECD, and which were discussed verbally. However, at the conclusion of the meeting, the OECD undertook to respond to these 17 technical questions in writing, and provided technical responses in mid-July 2001.

Economic Development Perspectives

The issue of international tax competition and economic development strategies for industries are inextricably linked, since fiscal incentives and the tax environment are often critical ingredients in corporate decisions on where to locate investment. As a result of the favourable business environment that they have created in recent decades, international financial and business centres like the Cayman Islands, Bermuda and Barbados today offer many opportunities to their young people for careers in areas such as law, accountancy, banking, fund management, company administration or insurance.

Their island lifestyles seem idyllic, and are undoubtedly the envy of many in more inhospitable regimes, whether geographic, political or fiscal. However, their development into international business centres is relatively recent, taking place mainly in the 1960s and 1970s. Prior to that, most Caribbean islands, and many other islands of the Commonwealth, such as Mauritius, Seychelles, Vanuatu and Fiji, were predominantly colonial outposts, either serving as administration centres, ports or agricultural economies dominated by plantation crops such as sugar, coffee or cocoa. Indeed the British Virgin Islands was at risk of being turned into a bird sanctuary, with a proposal by colonial advisers for its population to be relocated elsewhere, as colonial administrators could think of no sustainable economic activity for long-term employment of the local population.

In seeing the recent economic achievements and the highly skilled professional workforce that exists today in many Caribbean countries, such as the Bahamas, Cayman Islands, Bermuda and Barbados, it is also easy to forget the region's history of African slavery. An estimated 12 million African men, women and children were enslaved and shipped to the Americas, the largest forced migration in world history, with 2 million dying in the slave ships. Of this total, an estimated 5 million enslaved

African people were imported into the Caribbean to work on European colonists' plantations, after the Spanish genocide of an estimated 3–5 million indigenous Taino people. Indentured Indian labour was also transported to Guyana, Jamaica and Trinidad between 1844 and 1917. Even in the 1950s, many islands remained essentially rooted in the plantation economies they had inherited. It is important to recognise this historical background in order to understand the very substantial human development and capacity-building task that was required to transform these jurisdictions into centres of excellence in new growth industries and formation of skilled human capital.

Against this historical background, the achievements of many of the small island states through diversification into international business services and tourism during the last few decades are remarkable. Economic diversification has occurred mainly since the 1960s, as governments sought to attract new industries such as financial services and tourism. Much of the development that has occurred in the Caribbean has reflected these strategies, and has led to the success of some of the island states that is evident today. These strategies were successful because they focused on several of the world's most rapidly growing industries in the late twentieth-century in international business services, where small island states could be internationally competitive.

The world offshore financial services industry has shown rapid growth in the last two decades. This reflects a number of global trends, including the deregulation of domestic financial markets in many countries, rapid growth in world trade and investment, and the globalisation of the financial services industry. The size of the offshore financial services industry is estimated to be US$5–6 trillion, reflecting rapid growth in global foreign investment and trade flows, and the resultant growth in demand for international financial services.

The rapid growth in this industry has resulted in efforts by many nations to compete in this industry sector, with around 70 offshore centres now established worldwide. The term 'offshore' refers to the nature of the client rather than the location of the service. Hence foreign clients using London, Frankfurt or Tokyo for their financial services are making use of an 'offshore' financial services provision in the same way as those who are using services in far-flung islands in the Caribbean or Pacific.

The global offshore financial services industry is in fact dominated by the major financial centres of OECD countries. Indeed, recent estimates by the IMF of global offshore financial services activity indicate that around 60 per cent of total global offshore centres activity is carried out in London, the USA and in the Japanese offshore market. Overall, an estimated 80 per cent of the total offshore financial services industry is located in OECD countries, excluding their colonies. The remaining 20 per cent is outside the OECD, with even this segment dominated by a few very large centres such as Hong Kong.

It is the smallest, non-OECD providers of offshore financial services that are currently facing considerable pressures for change by a number of initiatives coming from the OECD countries, including the Harmful Tax Competition Initiative. This Initiative is focused on eliminating what the OECD determines to be harmful practices in all geographically mobile services. This includes not just to financial services, but all geographically mobile services, including, but not limited to, shipping, distribution services, service industries, and the provision of company headquarters. The OECD is already taking steps to extend its work to e-commerce in developing countries, and its 1998 Report flagged that it would later turn its attention to manufacturing industries in developing countries. Hence the OECD moves to eliminate harmful tax competition in financial services in non-OECD countries is part of a broader initiative to remove harmful competition in a wide range of industry sectors, including e-commerce and manufacturing.

The OECD has indicated that some form of sanctions might be used against those financial services centres which are regarded by the OECD as 'non-co-operating'. Consequently, considerable uncertainties are being created in the near term in relation to the future role of the offshore centres.

With many of the small, developing members of the Commonwealth having concentrated on an economic development strategy focused on exports of international services, the implications of recent initiatives are potentially very adverse for many of the countries most dependent on exports of services. This, in turn, could have far-reaching implications for the political, economic and social stability of many Commonwealth jurisdictions.

The World Trade Organisation (WTO) has observed that 'protectionism is not the first best choice to deal with fiscal challenges arising from trade liberalisation and globalisation'. In fact, governments are already responding to these challenges in more appropriate ways. High marginal income tax rates and corporate tax rates are falling, while consumption taxes rise. The WTO's Annual Report for 1998 observed that tax harmonisation was being discussed in the European Union (EU) and the OECD to deal with harmful tax competition, but noted: 'This option, however, should be treated with considerable caution, as the fight against a "race to the bottom" in tax rates may be used as a pretext for introducing a tax cartel.'

The Future Outlook

The OECD Initiative against non-OECD jurisdictions which it deemed to be 'harmful' commenced as an aggressive co-ordinated action by 28 of the largest developed economies against a wide range of jurisdictions, predominantly small, developing countries. Since late 2000, there have been signs of a more constructive approach, with Commonwealth ministers having played an important role in encouraging greater multilateral dialogue between OECD and non-OECD jurisdictions. However, the most significant step was the US announcement in May 2001 that it did not wish to support elements of the OECD Initiative that were viewed as anti-competitive. In particular, the USA withdrew its support for the OECD Initiative's objective of removing ring-fencing regimes.

However, the 15 EU members, who make up half of the OECD's 30 members, have an ambitious programme of reforms that parallels the OECD Initiative. The EU has been implementing removal of ring-fencing regimes and has already achieved political agreement on removal of harmful tax competition, not only in business services, but also in manufacturing. Importantly, all new EU aspirant countries will need to be compliant with the EU codes and laws prior to entry, creating a strong momentum for these countries to adopt taxation regimes that will be regarded by the EU as acceptable for regional integration.

The EU Directive on Savings Taxation has also pressed ahead with a tight timetable for exchange of information amongst EU member countries of savings interest for residents of other EU countries. As the success of this initiative is dependent on the EU's ability to secure commitments from the USA and Switzerland to undertake similar measures, the EU has now entered into negotiations with these other key financial centres in order to try to achieve its objectives.

This convergence between the EU and OECD Initiatives implies that even if the OECD membership cannot advance as ambitiously with the OECD Harmful Tax Competition Initiative, the EU will continue to press for similar outcomes via its own Directive on Savings Taxation. For non-OECD countries, this therefore poses considerable risks that they will be further driven towards greater regulation by a handful of powerful countries.

The broader context within which the OECD Initiative and the EU actions have taken place includes a number of other initiatives by the rich countries of the OECD to try to set the rules for the world economic system in a manner that is not inclusive of developing countries. These included the failed OECD Multilateral Investment Initiative (MAI), which was close to being finalised by OECD governments until it became publicly known, and provoked massive protests from civil society within the OECD as well as in developing countries.

Even within the WTO, IMF and World Bank, developing countries express considerable concerns about being excluded from the decision-making structures, with the IMF and World Bank voting rights and constituency systems dominated by OECD member countries. Within the WTO, OECD nationals exercise a large and disproportionate influence within the Secretariat, with the French grossly exceeding any fair staffing level, while the Seattle negotiations for a new round of trade talks were destroyed by the Green Room negotiating tactics of the OECD countries, whereby a group of the largest nations attempted to control the detailed negotiations, but eventually provoked a massive wave of resentment amongst developing countries, leading to the collapse of the Seattle talks.

If principles of democracy and good governance are to have any credibility, it will be crucial for OECD nations to move away from their efforts to establish a cabal or cartel arrangement for global economic decision-making. A world order governed by a handful of the richest nations may have worked in the seventeenth, eighteenth and nineteenth centuries, but the end of raw colonialism in the latter half of the twentieth century is unlikely to be able to be converted during the twenty-first century into an adapted form of neo-colonialism where the USA, EU and Japan try to run the world economy. The emergence of new industrial giants such as China, India and Brazil requires a new form of global governance architecture to be created that will be more inclusive of developing countries, and hence the broader aspirations and concerns of the world's population.

As the President of the World Bank, James Wolfensohn, said in November 2001, the developed countries must co-operate with developing countries to create new global governance structures and to redesign the global architecture to create a more inclusive global order.

The notion of two worlds of rich and poor or developed and developing collapsed at the time of the World Trade Center.

As we enter a world that is becoming more integrated, and where all the growth is going to come in the developing countries, we better have a better balance in the world.

James Wolfensohn, November 2001, in *IMF Survey*, 26 November 2001

Structure and Outline

This book comprises a collection of papers written by experts who have, for the most part, been closely involved during the period since the publication of the 1998 OECD Report in the matter of international tax competition, particularly from the small states and developing country perspective.

The papers are organised under five main headings, which consider the broad themes of globalisation, international tax competition, WTO issues, regulatory issues, and legal and constitutional issues.

The first section, on *globalisation and international taxation*, contains several papers by the political leaders of small Commonwealth jurisdictions affected by the OECD Initiative, as well as papers by academic experts on related international economic and legal issues. The papers consider the broad issues of globalisation, with the leaders of some of the affected jurisdictions providing varying perspectives on the issue.

The first paper, by Professor B. Persaud, Director of the Commonwealth Partnership for Technology Management, provides an overview of the OECD Initiative on Harmful Tax Competition and its implications for small states. It provides constructive advice on building a more co-operative framework for international co-operation on tax matters, while respecting the sovereignty of developing countries. Professor Persaud questions whether the OECD, as a narrow grouping of the most powerful rich countries, is the suitable institution to take forward such a global initiative, which might be more properly handled by a globally inclusive international institution such as the IMF or World Bank where developing countries are more widely represented (albeit still with only a fraction of the voting rights).

This is followed by a paper by the Financial Secretary of the Cayman Islands, George McCarthy, based on his speech at the High Level Consultations between the OECD and affected jurisdictions held in January 2001 in Barbados. The Cayman Islands was one of the six jurisdictions which gave the OECD advance commitment letters prior to the release of the OECD indicative list of potentially 'non-co-operative' jurisdictions in June 2000. George McCarthy's paper, on 'Promoting A More Inclusive Dialogue', is therefore particularly insightful, as it is based on the Cayman Islands' experience of working with the OECD after the letter of commitment was entered into.

In contrast, the perspective of the Governor of the Central Bank of Samoa, Papali'i T. Scanlan, expresses the concerns of a small island nation that has been targeted by the OECD. He considers the economic and legal concerns of Samoa in regard to the OECD Initiative, calling on the OECD to respect the sovereign rights of the Pacific island nations, which have already been buffeted by a wide range of international initiatives with only limited opportunities for consultation.

The paper by Sir Ronald Sanders, the Chief Foreign Affairs Representative of Antigua and Barbuda, is based on a speech to the PriceWaterhouseCoopers Conference on Financial Services Investment Practice in Nassau, Bahamas in September 2001. It provides a summary of recent developments in the process of negotiations with the OECD, as well as views on potential future steps to build co-operation.

Sir Neville Nicholls, as President of the Caribbean Development Bank, addressed the Barbados High Level Consultations on the subject of the 'Administrative and Resource Implications for Small States' of the requirements from the OECD. His paper, based on his speech at the Consultations, discusses the detailed resource implications and capacity development issues.

Dale Pinto, Senior Lecturer in Business Law at Curtin University in Western Australia, provides a detailed discussion of the implications of globalisation for fiscal sovereignty and considers the future role of the nation state faced by the forces of globalisation. He considers the impact of the internet and e-commerce on international tax revenues.

Section Two considers the role of *international tax competition in business services*. The paper on the OECD Harmful Tax Competition Initiative by Professor Michael Deveraux, Professor of Economics and Finance at Warwick University, was originally written for the Commonwealth Finance Ministers Meeting held in Malta in 2000. The paper discusses some of the international tax policy issues based on the OECD Initiative as specified by mid-2000. A key finding is that corporate revenues in OECD countries have remained steady as a share of GDP over the last two to three decades, despite significant declines in corporate tax rates, suggesting that governments have been effective in sustaining their revenue inflows despite their fears that globalisation is eroding their revenue base.

My contribution, 'International Trade in Offshore Business Services: Can Developing Countries Compete?', looks at international business services exports, finding that the OECD controls around 80 per cent of exports of these services. With developing countries increasingly turning to exports of finance, e-commerce and other IT services to build their knowledge industries, they are increasingly challenging the OECD countries for market share in key global growth industries. This has the potential to be one of the key economic battlegrounds between the OECD and developing countries over the next two decades, as developing countries try to expand their market share in these industries.

Dr Trevor Carmichael, QC, Chancery Chambers, provides a valuable contribution on the captive insurance industry and its emergence as a significant financial sector product during the last 50 years, with a number of small jurisdictions such as Bermuda and the Cayman Islands having become major international providers of captive insurance services.

Section 3 focuses on the **World Trade Organisation and fiscal competition**. A paper by Dr Roman Grynberg and Bridget Chilala of the Commonwealth Secretariat considers the WTO compatibility of the OECD proposals to take defensive measures. Their paper is complemented by a paper by Steve Orava of the Baker & McKenzie Global WTO Practice which provides another viewpoint on this issue.

The WTO has also undertaken far-reaching negotiations on investment incentives and under WTO agreements that have already been reached significant changes to international use of fiscal incentives are being made. An article by David Robertson, of Baker & McKenzie, looks at 'Export Processing Zones and the WTO Agreement on Subsidies and Countervailing Measures', discussing the impact on developing countries of the WTO Subsidies and Countervailing Measures (SCM) Agreement.

Section 4 considers **regulatory issues for financial centres**. The paper by Winston Cox, Deputy Secretary-General of the Commonwealth Secretariat discusses the crucial importance of 'getting the domestic financial architecture right'. The attention given to the financial architecture is intended to make the system more robust and less prone to crisis and to ensure that financial intermediation supports steady growth and development. The initial concern with financial architecture has been with the international financial system, but since the international system includes a linked network of domestic financial systems, it was inevitable that the architecture of domestic financial systems would also come under scrutiny. In his paper Winston Cox examines the reforms of the domestic financial system in developing countries. He argues that developing countries must continue to strengthen their prudential regulation and supervision of the financial system or face endemic crises that will wipe out gains in poverty reduction.

The paper by Colin Powell, Chairman of the Jersey Financial Services Commission, provides a practical view of the key challenges facing offshore financial centres from one of the leading experts in financial supervision and regulation. The article is based on a speech he gave to a financial services conference in 2001.

Richard Hay, a lawyer from Stikeman Elliott, discusses the implications of the OECD Initiative for international financial centres. At the least, this means that standards should be set by bodies with universal membership, so that offshore centres know that the same rules will apply to all. Importantly, he calls for offshore centres to be given a genuine and substantial part to play in the design of future regulatory changes.

The book's fifth and final section considers the **international legal and constitutional issues** arising from the OECD Initiative. A paper by David Simmons, QC is based on his speech to the Barbados High Level Consultations as the Attorney-General of Barbados.

Finally, a paper by Professor William Gilmore of the Edinburgh Law School, Edinburgh University provides a detailed technical assessment of the OECD Initiative from an international legal perspective. His long-standing reputation in international law and in strengthening Commonwealth legislation to combat serious crime make his article an important contribution to the international legal perspective on this issue.

Globalisation and International Taxation

The OECD Harmful Tax Competition Policy: A Major Issue for Small States[1]

Bishnodat Persaud[2]

Evolution of OECD Policy

On 26 June 2000, the OECD released its report, *Towards Global Tax Cooperation: Progress in Identifying and Eliminating Harmful Tax Practices*. The report listed 35 jurisdictions (nearly all small states) which are deemed to be 'tax havens' using criteria developed in the OECD's 1998 report, *Harmful Tax Competition: An Emerging Global Issue*. Following the 1998 Report, the OECD set up the Forum on Harmful Tax Practices. The June 2000 Report was the outcome of the work of the Forum, which was agreed by the OECD Council.

The term 'tax haven', recognised in the past as a neutral description for countries offering low-tax regimes to attract financial services and other economic activities, has been reinterpreted by these two reports to connote indulgence in harmful tax practices. This narrow and pejorative definition of the term by the influential OECD will restrict its future use.

The 1998 Report set out criteria for determining 'tax havens' and guidelines for dealing with harmful tax practices. The key factors used in identifying 'tax havens' were:

♦ No taxes or only nominal ones;

♦ Lack of effective exchange of information;

♦ Lack of transparency;

♦ No substantial activities – investment or transactions are mobile and purely tax driven.

It was on the basis of these criteria that 35 jurisdictions were identified in the June 2000 Report. They are all very small states with populations of

---

1 This paper is a revised version of a paper prepared for the Commonwealth Finance Ministers Meeting held in Malta, 19–21 September 2000.

2 Professor Persaud is an Honorary Professor and former Professor of the University of the West Indies, and a former Director of the Economic Affairs Division of the Commonwealth Secretariat. He is currently Director of the Commonwealth Partnership for Technology Management.

less than half a million, with the exception of Bahrain, which is just over that level, and Liberia which has a population of just under three million.

The list excluded jurisdictions which are regarded as 'tax havens' but which gave written advance commitments that they will abolish tax policies that are deemed harmful. Six jurisdictions gave such commitments, just before the list was announced.

Listed jurisdictions were given a year – until July 2001 – to provide commitments, in the absence of which defensive actions against them will be taken by OECD members on a co-ordinated basis. They would at that time be deemed 'unco-operative tax havens'. Consultations with the 35 jurisdictions have continued and three of the 35 provided letters of commitment before the July deadline. The July deadline has now been postponed because of continuing opposition on the part of the Offshore Financial Centres (OFCs) but substantially also because the Bush Administration in the USA has reservations about some aspects of the OECD policy, especially as it relates to the issue of sovereignty over tax rates, the extent of the erosion of bank secrecy and ring-fencing.

A significant development has been the formation early in 2001 of the International Tax and Investment Organization (ITIO) comprising many of the affected OFCs, including some that have provided letters of commitment. The organisation, prompted by the perception of heavy-handed pressures against small OFCs by the OECD, addresses wider tax, trade and investment concerns of developing states. The forum provided by the ITIO has helped to articulate the case of the small OFCs and to develop a common approach, and thus to alleviate the pressure on individual states to sign up to OECD policy.

However the 11 September tragic incident in New York, which has changed the world in many ways, has had a major impact on OECD policy. The new heightened concern about the international financial activities of terrorist organisations is leading to a spate of legislation on money laundering requiring cross-border co-operation which has advanced considerably, already eroding the right to privacy in the bank/client relationship.

This international shift in policy, with the USA playing a leading role, will revive talk of sanctions for non-compliance with the newly expanded anti-money-laundering legislation that countries worldwide are introducing to combat terrorism. It should be noted that most Commonwealth countries have vigorously supported the new US, UN and Commonwealth initiatives to improve co-operation against terrorism. (The Commonwealth issued a Statement on Terrorism on 25 October

2001 strongly supporting UN Security Council Resolution 1373, with a range of other measures and actions to be undertaken to strengthen co-operation against terrorism.)

The OECD has recognised that even before such defensive actions are implemented, the 'naming and shaming' involved in such a list of 'unco-operative tax havens' would begin to have negative effects on the invest-ment and trade of the jurisdictions concerned. It should be noted that this action will add to other listings and assessments being undertaken by the major countries. Standards regarding money laundering are being assessed by the Financial Action Task Force (FATF), an intergovern-mental body linked to the OECD, and on bank supervision by the Financial Stability Forum (FSF) which was set up by the G7. The FATF has issued its own list of non-complying countries, which has confused and compounded the problem.

According to the OECD stance, a state which provides an advance com-mitment would agree to a standstill, that is not to enhance such harmful practices. An advance commitment jurisdiction will develop an accept-able plan with the OECD, describing the manner in which it intends to achieve its commitment, the time-table for doing so and milestones to ensure steady progress, including the completion of a concrete and sig-nificant action during the first year of the commitment. All commitments must be fulfilled by December 2005.

Defensive measures against offending 'tax havens' are a polite usage for sanctions, and the list of possible measures is long. Severe measures include not entering into tax conventions and abrogating existing ones; imposing withholding taxes on payments to residents of the havens con-cerned; requiring comprehensive information and reporting rules on transactions involving these jurisdictions; enhancing audit and enforce-ment activities; disallowing deductions, exemptions, credits or other allowances; imposing charges and levies on transactions with the juris-dictions; adoption of controlled foreign corporation rules; and possible denial of non-essential economic assistance.

Beyond the threat of sanctions, member countries with particular politi-cal, economic and other links to 'tax havens' will ensure that these links do not contribute to harmful tax competition. They are also expected to use these links to put pressure on 'tax havens' to eliminate harmful tax policies.

Defensive actions against non-compliance will not be imposed by OECD members alone. Other countries have an interest in thwarting tax com-petition from low-tax regimes and the OECD has sought to use this converging interest to obtain wider support for pressures against 'tax havens' and for sanctions. Thus, soon after the release of the June 2000 Report, the French Minister of Finance launched a global dialogue on harmful tax practices by bringing together the 30 members of the OECD with 30 other countries to discuss how to develop a global response to harmful tax practices.

The OECD's plan to blacklist 35 OFCs is meeting stiff opposition, especially from within the Commonwealth, to which 26 of the jurisdictions named are connected, either as members or through other forms of association.

The ongoing debate came to a head at the Commonwealth Finance Ministers' Meeting in Malta on 19–21 September 2000, at which the affected Commonwealth OFCs and other developing countries mounted a concerted attack on OECD policy. Pressure was put on the OECD to relax the July 2001 deadline for declaring its list of 'unco-operative tax havens' and wider multilateral discussions of the issues were called for.

This stand, supported by continuing strong dissatisfaction expressed by non-Commonwealth OFCs, could not be ignored by the OECD. In response to the call for wider international discussions, and as a follow-up to the Malta Commonwealth Meeting, a High Level Consultation organised by the Commonwealth Secretariat in co-operation with the OECD was held on 8–9 January 2001 in Barbados, involving the OFCs, other Commonwealth members, the Caribbean Community, the Pacific Islands Forum, the Inter-American Development Bank, the World Bank and the IMF.

The Barbados Consultation set up a 13-member Working Group on Global Co-operation against Harmful Tax Practices, comprising six representatives from OECD countries and seven from developing countries, six of whom were from OFCs. The focus of the work was to be on the criteria for classifying countries as 'unco-operative tax havens'. Three principles embodied in the OECD criteria – transparency, non-discrimination and effective information exchange were to be given major attention.

However, the hope that the Barbados Consultation would lead to the adoption of a wider multilateral approach has been dashed. The OECD is maintaining bilateral pressure on the listed OFCs to secure their compliance. Many of them, although deeply dissatisfied with the whole process, are anxious to avoid the severe economic consequences of being classified as unco-operative. Already OECD action is having an adverse impact on the establishment of banks and other international companies in the OFCs.

A major challenge for the OFCs is the need for an agreed interpretation of these OECD principles before they are forced into making a commitment. As matters stand, the OECD has made a submission of what it means by these principles. These remain as uncompromising as when the whole process started. The OFCs have not been able to dilute this interpretation. This poses the great problem for the OFCs that the whole process is proceeding on the basis of the extreme OECD position.

There is still a long way to go in solving some of the more basic issues, such as the extra-territorial and unilateral threat of OECD rule-making and the OECD requirement for erosion of strongly held traditional principles of bank secrecy and bank/client confidentiality. Rule-making by the OECD for non-OECD states is of questionable international legality, especially when it involves co-ordinated sanctions, even though the sanctions regime is dressed up as a voluntary one.

A worrying question is the technical justification and legitimacy of the whole notion of tax competition as harmful, which was the original prompt for OECD action against OFCs. Even though there have been subsequent endeavours by the OECD to shift the emphasis from tax competition to harmful tax practices, assisted recently by the Bush Administration's concerns about the notion of tax competition as harmful, low or no taxes remain the first of the four classifying criteria of harmfulness in the tax regimes of the OFCs.

The main motivation for OECD action against small OFCs is the competition provided by these low-tax regimes in attracting international savings and investment. Seiichi Kondo, the Deputy Secretary-General of the OECD, in his article supporting the OECD initiative in the *Guardian*, 8 January 2001, left no doubt that tax-driven flows, seen by him wholly as tax evasion, were the main concern. Of great significance is the tendency in his article to end the long accepted distinction between evasion and avoidance.

There are other troubling features in the OECD action, not least of which is the element of dictation, coercion and excessive demands on a group of small and powerless states. The OECD action is discriminatory in that although tax regimes in OECD states themselves fall within the OECD criteria of harmfulness, these have been categorised less pejoratively as 'preferential tax regimes' and deemed only 'potentially' harmful.

Harmful Practices in OECD Countries

Concerned as the two reports were with harmful tax practices, their remit was wider than identifying 'tax havens'. They sought to take on harmful practices when they are carried out by member countries and non-member states other than OFCs. The OECD, in other words, is developing a global approach and a global framework of rules and sanctions. Through its influence the UN is now considering the adoption of a global model tax regime. However, any initiative that encourages the harmonisation of tax rates internationally is economically unjustified and will be inimical to economic growth and development in developing countries.

The preferential tax regimes of OECD countries generally have the same features as those of the 'tax havens', although they tend not to feature so importantly in overall fiscal and investment policies. Thus while the term 'tax haven' describes whole jurisdictions, in the case of OECD members and other countries, parts of the fiscal system deemed potentially harmful are identified as preferential tax regimes and targeted for remedy.

The June 2000 Report listed 47 preferential tax regimes in member countries. Members have committed themselves to removing practices which are practically harmful by April 2003, although four OECD countries have now abstained from the OECD 2001 Progress Report on the latest version of the OECD Initiative. In practice, the administrative process for dealing with preferential tax regimes, in terms of determining harmfulness and adopting sanctions, is much less stringent and much more consultative. Unlike the 'tax havens', the regimes listed are regarded as potentially harmful rather than actually harmful.

The process will involve the development of a 'generic basis of guidance' on applying the preferential regime criteria, i.e. the generic nature of harmful practices rather than the specific practice. The OECD will develop guidelines which will assist member countries in determining which potentially harmful regimes are actually harmful and how to remove the undesirable features.

Unlike 'tax havens', member countries with preferential tax regimes will have a larger involvement in determining whether a practice is actually harmful and in developing the guidelines for such determination and for the timetable of removal.

Of great significance is the fact that the whole question of defensive measures is given softer application. The June 2000 Report merely states that 'if harmful features are not eliminated by the prescribed deadlines, other countries may wish to take defensive measures'. And according to the 1998 Report, 'counteracting measures will focus both on nullifying the benefits of such regimes for tax-payers and encouraging the countries which operate such regimes, particularly those in the OECD area, to modify or eliminate them'.

In the case of preferential tax regimes in non-member countries, the June

2000 Report recognises their existence. Action envisaged, however, emphasises encouragement and assistance to remove harmful practices.

The report states that it is important to take forward the work of the Forum with regard to eliminating harmful tax practices on a global basis. To this end, the OECD's Committee on Fiscal Affairs will encourage non-member states to associate themselves with the 1998 Report and to agree to its principles. It will hold regional seminars that will encourage and assist these economies to remove harmful features of their preferential regimes. The work programme will endeavour to facilitate the removal of harmful tax practices in non-member economies by 31 December 2005.

For the future, the Forum will continue to explore ways in which non-member countries that share the concerns of the OECD and that are prepared to accept the same obligations, can be more closely associated with its work.

The OECD as an Appropriate Institution

A basic issue is whether the OECD is the appropriate institution for developing an international regime for dealing with harmful tax practices. The OECD recognises that its own members are engaged in such harmful practices, but the differential ways in which these practices are regarded, in which the consultative process takes place, and in which sanctions are emphasised and imposed demonstrate a basic weakness and inequity in the approach which justifies serious concerns. Many of the 'tax havens' have complained bitterly, not only of the nature of the process, but also of inadequate consultation and inequality of treatment.

While more consultation has now taken place, the 'naming and shaming' involved in listing jurisdictions, and the background threats of co-ordinated sanctions against small and weak states with limited economic opportunities, must raise worrying international legal and ethical questions. Issues arise not only about the consultation and the determination process, but also about the fact that the international regime being developed is driven and controlled by a group of countries which are themselves major perpetrators of the 'offending' actions.

It is clear that the global issue of tax competition and harmful tax practices require a more inclusive international approach. Relevant representative international institutions are already engaged. Hence the OECD's aggressive involvement seems unwarranted. Directly related issues of fiscal policy, and bank regulation and supervision, are already covered by institutions such as the IMF and the Bank for International Settlements (BIS). The IMF has developed a Special Data Transmission Standard, a

Code of Good Practices on Fiscal Transparency and a Code of Good Practices on Transparency in Monetary and Fiscal Policies. The Basle Committee on Banking Supervision has agreed Core Principles for Effective Banking Supervision and the International Organisation of Securities Commissions (IOSC) has developed a set of Objectives and Principles of Securities Regulation. The assessment methodology of the latter, which is to be used for self-assessments, has been proposed in co-operation with the World Bank, the IMF and regional development banks.

The WTO is concerned in a major way, through the establishment of the General Agreement on Trade in Services (GATS) which is developing an international regime for regulating trade in services. Although issues such as taxes, transparency and bank secrecy have only featured in a marginal way in its discussions, there is no doubt that they will become more substantial with time. The GATS is new in the WTO but its coverage is deepening and becoming more comprehensive.

These related international developments in representative and relevant international organisations raise the question of whether the issue of harmful practices, originated by the OECD, should not now be pursued more substantially and practically in these other institutions. They also raise the question of effective international co-ordination. However, some of the states classified as 'tax havens' are not members of international organisations such as the IMF and the WTO. This provides scope for an organisation like the Commonwealth, comprising many of the small states affected, to be given a more substantial role in the discussion of harmful tax practices. Some of the Commonwealth small states concerned are closely linked to major Commonwealth members such as the UK, Australia and New Zealand, which have encouraged and facilitated the development of financial services in these states. Their finance companies, including those from Canada, are often major players. They therefore have a strong interest in the outcome of these discussions.

Conceptual Problems and Other Issues

The many complex conceptual issues involved in notions such as harmful tax competition, harmful tax practices, the dilution of bank secrecy and client confidentiality, and 'tax havens' support the case for further analysis and a more cautious, evolutionary and consultative approach to action.

The provenance of the issue and the early OECD stress on 'competition' and on targeting low-tax regimes, raise the issue of the extent to which competition offered by low taxes and the revenue loss involved were not a major motivation for action. But such action implies interference in the sovereign right of nations to determine their own tax regimes. It is a right normally strictly guarded by states and even in regional economic arrangements it is usually conceded only reluctantly and in the advanced stages of integration.

While sovereignty is becoming diluted in a globalised world, it is important that this is not carried too far, especially as it affects the capacity for free action by small and powerless states. It must remain the case that when tax evasion by residents is involved through offshore investments, the first line of action must be the many ways open to a home country to close loopholes and adopt policies which discourage evasion.

Similarly, tax avoidance must be reduced through closing tax loopholes at home rather than by harassing nationals who find scope for avoidance abroad or by abolishing the distinction between evasion and avoidance. Co-operation is essential in cases of serious crime and terrorism. In the light of the events of 11 September, efforts must be stepped up to improve information exchange and transparency without abuse of the continuing justifiable case for bank secrecy, bank/client confidentiality and human rights. There is scope also for improving transparency in offshore business by restricting or abolishing the use of bearer shares and requiring fuller financial reporting. Great advances are being made in these areas and these efforts must continue in a determined way. However, dangers of overkill in some aspects are emerging and such overstepping could be particularly harmful to OFCs.

Beyond the sensitive issue of the impairment of sovereignty, OECD arguments and demands involve a substantial distortion of the very nature of low-tax regimes in OFCs.

Firstly, in many of these states the option of a low-tax regime is only possible because of their low public expenditure as a percentage of GDP – in some cases 20 per cent instead of the 40 per cent or so usual in the OECD countries.

The factor of size also encourages the possibility of using low taxes as a means of facilitating economic enterprises and attracting foreign investment. All states use tax policies for revenue as well as a means of creating a climate conducive to investors in a global competitive market. The wider scope allowed to small states for making effective use of tax policies as an economic investment inducement should not be seen as harmful tax competition, especially when account is taken of the dearth of economic opportunities available to such states arising from size constraints.

A misperception of low-tax regimes is that they thrive on tax evasion. Often, however, what they encourage is tax avoidance or postponed tax payments – these are legitimate activities. They may allow tax-free payments of dividends and interest, but when such earnings are repatriated, the investors are liable for taxes in home countries.

What is also not sufficiently recognised is that low-tax regimes encourage genuine economic activities, for example in manufacturing as well as in financial services. By allowing a more footloose location of service activities, the internet and the spread of e-commerce make for a greater mobility in international business. This is adding to the opportunities available to OFCs. Perhaps it is the increase in the genuine location attractiveness of OFCs that is worrying the OECD and is spurring action at this time.

Examples of genuine economic activities located in OFCs are the pharmaceutical and chemical industries as well as container port facilities in the Bahamas. A variety of financial services, such as insurance and reinsurance, captive insurance, fund management and trust services are offered in the Bermudas, Malta, Mauritius, Barbados and the Bahamas.

By focusing on tax evasion, the OECD is attempting to denigrate the economic structure of the OFCs in order to facilitate its application of pressure on them, so bringing about a change in their economies that would be to their detriment.

To curb the savings and investment activities of their nationals in the OFCs, the OECD is demanding through the criterion of information exchange that OFCs abolish traditional and revered principles of bank secrecy and client confidentiality. Banks operating in OFCs would be required to provide information on the investment and banking activities of their clients to the tax authorities of their home countries. This would be carried out routinely by an administrative order rather than through the judicial process now in use, or when criminal investigations are clearly being pursued.

Such a demand represents a revolutionary change in banking principles. It requires OFCs to comply with a requirement that would benefit the tax authorities in OECD countries at the expense of the financial service sector of the OFCs. It would be administratively costly for all concerned, and especially for small economies. It goes beyond anything the OECD countries have so far been able to achieve among themselves in tax co-operation and in fact they may never be able to achieve it. Powerful constraints are the human rights implications and their citizens' right to privacy in their personal financial affairs.

The consequences for the OFCs of compliance could be severe. Legitimate activities of tax avoidance and the investors' incentive to locate in low-tax regimes would be greatly compromised.

It took years of discussion within the EU to agree on information exchange among members for tax purposes. This was only achieved in June 2000 in Feira. There was widespread concern about this at the time and countries with offshore financial regimes, such as Luxembourg and Austria, were unhappy about the change of policy. In the final result, Austria agreed that it would comply only when countries outside Europe also co-operate. This will remain a difficult issue for a country such as Switzerland. It will be recalled that Switzerland and Luxembourg did not endorse the 1998 OECD report. In the EU, in lieu of information exchange, a few countries have been allowed the option of adopting withholding taxes on non-resident investment earnings. The OFCs believe that exchange of bank information and its extent must remain a matter for bilateral tax treaties, and should not be part of an international regime, which should only provide a framework for bilateral co-operation.

It is pertinent to note that liberal low-tax regimes were encouraged by high levels of economic, financial and monetary regulation and high taxes in other countries, and the competition provided by these regimes helped to spur international liberalisation which has generally been beneficial. They also encouraged the lowering of taxes, which may have been good for enterprise and growth, although tax competition carried too far can result in excessive income inequality. It is worth noting that countries like Ireland and Hong Kong, and some states in the USA have deliberately used very low taxes as an investment incentive.

The OECD is now de-emphasising competition as a motivation for its policy and is stating that the issue is not the level of taxes. However the starting point in delineating 'tax havens' has been low taxes, and even now low or no taxes is a presumption of harmful practice, regardless of the overall performance of low-tax regimes in terms of regulation, transparency, determination to make improvements and the extent of their international co-operation in tax and legal matters. If it is the case that the level of taxes is not now an issue, and since issues of information exchange and bank secrecy remain very controversial, then the main remaining concerns become prudential financial regulation and co-operation in handling cases of criminality.

Adequate regulation and transparency are requirements for a competitive financial centre and the need for them is not controversial. In fact many offshore financial centres are taking action to improve regulation and transparency and to prevent money laundering. Defensive action, including 'naming and shaming' for infractions in these areas, cannot be disputed if handled responsibly. But current problems in tax policies do not justify the extensive action proposed by the OECD, which can destroy the very rationale for offshore financial centres. Such action can also set back progress in co-operation in handling issues of regulation, transparency, accounting standards and criminal behaviour.

Some of the other characteristics used in defining harmful practices are also controversial. Discriminatory behaviour or 'ring-fencing' as between resident and non-resident investors has been cited. But this is not practised by some 'tax havens'. In states such as the Bahamas and Bermuda, income taxes are waived for both residents and non-residents, and local and foreign corporations. On the other hand, discrimination and incentives are used on a wide scale in OECD member countries and others, not only through their own offshore regimes in finance and shipping, but also in policies regarding withholding taxes and in tax and subsidy policies to assist deprived regions and agriculture. Singapore, for instance, has provided special incentives to attract the headquarters of multinational corporations and mutual funds. IMF figures show that the non-OECD share of the total offshore financial services industry is less than 20 per cent.

Other conceptual difficulties arise from the emphasis given to the encouragement of 'geographically mobile' activities in defining undesirability, and in consequence the large size of the offshore sectors concerned, relative to other economic activities.

It is claimed that by deflecting income from capital to offshore centres, tax burdens are being shifted to labour and consumption activities in OECD countries, and that an indication of the distortion is the size of financial sectors in 'tax havens' relative to other activities. Activities in offshore centres are seen as tax-driven and therefore undesirable.

However, tax considerations are important globally in all investment decisions. And the small tax variations among states not regarded as 'tax havens' may be more important in international investment decisions than the wider variation between 'tax havens' and other states. Capital is not easily attracted to very small states and a resort to low taxes should be seen as an attempt to overcome this problem.

Tax competition to attract savings and investments would not go away if these 'havens' are disbanded. As already pointed out, many OFCs encourage not only 'mobile' but also production activities. It should be noted, however, that most mobile activities are genuine production or service activities. In fact a weakness of the OECD reports is that it fails to recognise the substantial production and service industries that are also being attracted to OFCs.

In relation to distortions in tax structures, there is no evidence of any significant loss of revenue in home states from companies incorporating in 'tax havens.' In fact, the present situation in many major countries is revenue buoyancy leading to lower taxes, thus reducing competitiveness and harm from 'tax havens'.

A further factor is that while small offshore centres attract capital inflows, the ultimate destination of these investments is actually the major countries, thus nullifying or reducing the real effects on economic activities in industrial countries and in their revenue collection.

With development of the internet and virtual companies, and e-trading and e-commerce, and with easier sale of products and sale and transfer of services electronically, this criterion is being rendered problematic. It will, therefore, need to be reconsidered. An implication of imposing constraints on the movement of capital to 'tax havens' is that people themselves may relocate to 'tax havens', so involving a loss of the activity, and of citizens and residents with scarce skills.

Pressure on Small States

The fact that a large proportion of small states has turned to offshore financial services is an indication not only of the opportunity provided to them by higher taxes and restrictive financial and monetary policies in larger countries, but also of their needs arising from the limited range of economic opportunities available to them. The difficulties posed in attempting to diversify these economies and provide a more stable economic environment are indicated by their low levels of diversification and resulting higher levels of income volatility, even when per capita incomes reach middle and higher middle-income levels.

Another pertinent development feature of these small states is their inevitably high level of dependence on their external sectors for development. Service exports are proving particularly attractive. Tourism is a major industry in many of these economies and offshore financial activities have proved a welcome addition in order to achieve much-needed diversification.

Because of small size and special need for openness, success in these areas usually means relatively large sectors in relation to the total size of the economy. It is not helpful, therefore, to view a large offshore financial sector as a sign of artificial and distorted development.

There is little recognition of the major economic disruption that could be caused in some small states by the extent and speed of a change in OECD policies.

Offshore financial services have become a significant part of the economies of many small states. These activities generate a substantial amount of licence fees which belie the notion of a no tax situation. They also generate employment involving secretarial, administrative, accounting, information technology and professional skills. They encourage business and leisure visits. The skills developed have wider favourable economic impact. Much rental income is also generated by the sector.

In the Bahamas in 1998, employment in financing, insurance, real estate and other business services was 11 per cent of total employment. This figure relates only to direct employment and a large part – more than half – was in offshore financial services. Considering the higher average income earned in the sector, the direct GDP contribution is higher still – about 15 per cent. Similarly large percentage contributions to employment and income occur in other major offshore financial centres in the Caribbean, for example the Cayman Islands, Bermuda, the British Virgin Islands and the Turks and Caicos.

While offshore activities would not be eliminated by OECD action, there could be a considerable decline. The OECD report offers little in the way of practical relief or adjustment assistance to 'tax havens'. The June 2000 Report recognises that removal of harmful tax practices 'may adversely affect the economies of some of these jurisdictions'. It states that the OECD 'will work with other interested international and national organisations to examine how best to assist co-operative jurisdictions in restructuring their economies'.

Of particular concern is the extent to which these states are being isolated and pressured to adopt the OECD recommendations. Isolation is also caused by the fact that these low-tax jurisdictions are largely confined to small states and other states have an interest in action along the lines pursued by the OECD regardless of the technical and policy merits of the small states' case. In this matter, small states cannot even look for support from development NGOs, since the use of low-tax regimes by investors and the rich is not an issue with which NGOs tend to sympathise. Further isolation is caused by the fact that the OECD members to which the OFCs are linked, for example as dependencies and Crown Dependencies, have agreed to use their influence to secure compliance by 'tax havens' with OECD demands. This situation has even been secured by a trade-off of interests between the member countries, and a sacrifice of the interests of their own dependencies and Crown Dependencies. As part of the compromise, EU member states, and primarily the UK, have committed themselves to promoting the EU's tax information exchange system in the Channel Islands, the Isle of Man and the dependent and associated territories in the Caribbean. The ITIO would be very important in helping to co-ordinate the position of small states in international tax and investment matters.

Summary

Small states with offshore financial centres are under considerable pressure from the OECD. They have been deemed 'tax havens', i.e. undesirable tax jurisdictions which make extensive use of harmful tax practices. Unless these 'tax havens' commit themselves to removing these practices, they will be listed as 'unco-operative tax havens' and subject to co-ordinated sanctions which could also involve OECD non-member states.

The OECD is endeavouring to develop a global approach and framework for dealing with harmful tax practices and it is bringing to bear wide international pressure against OFCs. The 'tax havens' concerned are further isolated by lack of support from the OECD members with whom they are closely linked and by the lack of sympathy shown by development NGOs. The OECD represents the interests of a relatively small number of nations, and its attempts to prescribe international rules in matters which are already the concern of more broadly representative international organisations and to advocate sanctions is a policy of doubtful international legality.

The OECD recognises that its members and other states also indulge in harmful tax practices. It is endeavouring to remove these, but its whole administrative approach towards its own members, involving assessment and the use of sanctions, is softer and more consultative.

The OECD does not have a strong technical or moral case against 'tax havens'. Many conceptual problems are involved in the classification criteria used and the demands being made. Several of the basic OECD approaches are controversial, for example the notion of tax competition as harmful. Efforts to abolish bank secrecy and client confidentiality, which have advanced after the September event, pose very serious problems in relation to deeply respected principles involving the traditional right to privacy in personal finance – foundation stones of stability, progress and bank development. Curtailment of such rights and traditional practices has already been put in place by recent anti-money-laundering legislation. OFCs and those concerned with protecting liberal values must guard against the imminent danger that this can go too far. The OFC countries recognise the importance of the non-controversial areas, for example regulation, transparency and mutual legal assistance, and are co-operating to improve their regimes.

OFCs recognise their own interests in regulatory reform and are making efforts to achieve this. There is recognition that improved practices could help to make OFCs more reputable and durable. In the case of money laundering, numerous international organisations are involved – BIS, the UN, the G7's Financial Stability Forum and the OECD's own Financial Action Task Force. Model legislation and other forms of co-operation, such as mutual legal assistance to curb criminal activities, are increasingly being adopted. The Caribbean Community, for instance, has set up its own financial action task force with requirements that exceed those of the OECD's.

The OECD, prompted largely by worries over tax competition and the emerging difficulties for high tax states from the increasing mobility of economic activities through the use of the internet, is setting a dangerous precedent by usurping roles appropriate to more widely representative international organisations. The EU and OECD have themselves adopted plans for greater access to bank information, but progress in implementation is slow because of the continuing unhappiness of countries such as Austria, Luxembourg and Switzerland. Thus the demands the OECD is making on the OFCs are in excess of what it is able to achieve internally. This is clearly discriminatory.

Small states need to work together closely to resist the unwarranted pressures being put upon them. The setting up of the ITIO is a major step in this direction but it needs wider support from OFCs and wide recognition internationally of its crucial role in filling the gap in the international system. Even though some OFCs have already succumbed to the pressures and have agreed to comply, they remain unhappy and could co-operate with others through the ITIO to ameliorate pressure and achieve a more balanced and responsible approach. Small states also need to work closely with others who share their interests in low-tax regimes, such as the finance and business corporations which operate in 'tax havens' as well as with other commercial and political organisations with an interest in lowering taxes globally. They also need to maintain pressure on organisations in which they are strongly represented, such as the Commonwealth, to be more substantially involved in the international discussions and to assist them in articulating their case. Importantly, they also need to take a cue from the more developed OFCs such as the Channel Islands and Bermuda to secure greater diversification of their financial services sector and to thus become more economically resilient.

OFCs offer a useful means of extending the very limited range of opportunities available to very small states to promote diversified, durable and skill-intensive development. Tax competition is one of the few areas in which small size confers an economic advantage. Where OFCs are well established, their GDP contributions often range between 20 and 30 per cent and employment contributions, although lower, tend to be of a high-income and skill-intensive type. Removing the legitimate attractions of the OFCs could greatly set back the economic development of the countries in which they are based.

Greater consideration needs to be given to the economic impact on the affected jurisdictions of the change required by the OECD and to the requirement for appropriate adjustment assistance where mutually agreed changes are to be made. The Commonwealth Secretariat, the OECD and the World Bank should co-operate to undertake studies on the economic implications for OFCs of OECD policy.

What the OFCs should endeavour to secure is not only less stringent criteria for being classified as 'tax havens' but more radical changes in the criteria especially in such areas as 'low or no taxes' and the exchange of bank information. They must continue to resist any prescription on the level of taxes or the form of taxes. Exchange of bank information must not go beyond what is necessary to assist criminal proceedings and investigations and must discourage the use of 'fishing expeditions'.

The Working Group set up in Barbados should now be followed by a more permanent joint forum that would deal with issues involving OFCs on an equal decision-making basis rather than just having an advisory role to the OECD. The whole thrust towards OECD imposition and the threat of sanctions must be changed, and any rules developed must be jointly agreed.

In areas such as non-discrimination in tax policy and the exchange of information, OECD demands on OFCs exceed those on its own members, and one gets the clear impression that the OECD is using the OFCs as a soft target to leverage their own internal and wider objectives.

The OFCs will have the challenging task of avoiding an interpretation of the three principles of transparency, effective information exchange and non-discrimination and a political commitment on them, which in detail will strike at the very heart of their economic structure which they have carefully built up, in creative attempts to exploit their very limited economic opportunities. They are presently being lured to sign up on principles without a careful negotiation of their interpretation, and are being encouraged to do so with the promise of their involvement in a new multilateral arrangement. However their influence in such a widely inclusive arrangement would be negligible, and to wait on such a forum to interpret the principles after signing up, would mean their sure defeat.

Bibliography

Biswas, R. (2001). *Global Competition for Offshore Business Services: Prospects for Developing Countries*. Commonwealth Heads of Government Reference Book.

Devereux, M. The OECD 'Harmful Tax Competition' Initiative. Paper prepared for the Commonwealth Secretariat, July 2000.

Financial Times, 'Storm over the Tax Havens'. Six-part series, 24–29 July 2000.

OECD. *Harmful Tax Competition: An Emerging Global Issue*. April 1998.

OECD. *Towards Global Tax Co-operation: Progress in Identifying and Eliminating Harmful Tax Practices*. June, 2000.

Promoting a More Inclusive Dialogue[1]

George A. McCarthy OBE

An eighteenth-century French political advisor, writing during the ascendancy of imperialism and colonialism, is reputed to have described taxation as an art rather than a science. The analogy which he chose for his description, loosely translated, was that the art of taxation is the art of extracting from the goose the maximum number of feathers with the minimum amount of hissing. Of course in those times, claims about the legitimacy of taxation were largely circumscribed by geography, and no-one (except the goose) expected the goose either to choose which farmyard to inhabit or whether to partake in any dialogue before being deprived of her feathers.

In those times, expanding one's tax base generally meant expanding one's empire through colonialism or other more overt aggression, and the view expressed subsequently by the German tactician Clausewitz to the effect that war was merely the continuation of diplomacy by other means, prevailed.

We are now at the beginning of the twentieth-first century. The goose has become sentient and acquired the ability to analyse which farm yard offers the best value for feathers plucked. Furthermore, the goose has new abilities to move from one farmyard to the next in order to minimise the extent of plucking. The operators of the modern farmyards have realised that if they can send the goose to someone else's yard to feed, and then later demand the return of the goose, or at least the goose's feathers, they can effectively expand their own farms at little or no cost.

International relations have also evolved to the point where there is a legitimate expectation in the international arena that differences in perspective can be discussed and common ground found in order to resolve disputes and competing claims.

The Cayman Islands recognises that globalisation and the global competition among public sectors that is part of it present both potential oppor-

---

1 George McCarthy is the Financial Secretary of the Cayman Islands Government. This paper is based on a speech given by George McCarthy at the High Level Consultations on the OECD Harmful Tax Competition Initiative, Barbados, 8–9 January 2001.

tunities and potential threats for all jurisdictions. All jurisdictions are moving to optimise the opportunities and minimise the threats.

Recent trends toward globalisation have accentuated a number of concerns about the viability of nineteenth and twentieth-century taxation regimes, and in particular concern over whether current expectations of future transnational tax bases and future government tax revenues can be fulfilled in the globally competitive environment of the twenty-first century.

Many of the concerns over tax-related economic competition are not new. Jurisdictions have long competed in the international arena for investment and economic activity in order to provide employment and wealth for their peoples, as well as for tax revenues for governments. Tax-related economic competition among governments is documented as far back as the third century BC when the Romans created a special economic zone in Delos to promote the relocation of trade from Rhodes (which Rome did not rule), to Roman-controlled Delos.

The academic literature on modern tax-related economic competition similarly goes back almost 100 years. Such competition has taken many forms over time. In some cases it has involved the active creation of various types of reduced-rate direct-tax regimes for potential investors. In other cases it has involved various tax expenditure regimes and the direct payment of subsidies for specific types of investment. In still other cases, jurisdictions have been essentially passive, as is the case where multinational enterprises have sought out existing fiscal regimes based on indirect taxation rather than direct taxation.

The focus of the Barbados High Level Consultations and a great deal of other international activity is on the perceived need for the creation of a new set of universally applicable rules for international tax-related economic competition. This will probably be a process of constructive and vigorous negotiation. It is natural for jurisdictions, whether acting singly or collectively, to attempt to set the rules of economic competition, including those involving international tax, so as to achieve the greatest level of benefit for themselves. In the area of tax-related economic competition, as in all others in which nations compete, there is a need for all jurisdictions to behave responsibly in accordance with accepted international law and standards. Engaging in meaningful dialogue is a vital element in this process, as is creating a non-confrontational environment in which dialogue can occur.

The Cayman Islands has long recognised that it is better to be part of any meaningful dialogue than to be excluded from it. In this regard, the

Cayman Islands welcomes the opportunities that have arisen to engage in such meaningful dialogue in regard to tax-related economic competition. We applaud those who have created such opportunities, through the OECD Global Forum on International Taxation and through the good offices of the Commonwealth Secretariat, to mention just two. We welcome any bilateral or multilateral contact with any jurisdiction willing to join in the process of meaningful dialogue on this subject.

Creating an Environment for Dialogue

The Cayman Islands would like to suggest that the way forward in the search for a greater degree of consensus in matters of international tax-related economic competition involves a number of components, of which three key components are:

- The facilitation of more inclusive dialogue;

- Enhancing transparency through the articulation of a broad set of shared assumptions;

- Enhancing transparency through the promulgation of a broad set of guiding principles for the process as it moves forward.

The achievement of these three components will go a very long way to creating the international understanding necessary for the process to achieve its optimal outcome. It will also go a long way towards eliminating any existing misunderstandings and preventing new ones from arising. Finally, it will refute any perception that 'might makes right' and confirm the legitimacy of the process in which we are now engaged. It will also confirm to the international community that it is the rule of international law rather than 'the rule of the big stick' that determines the outcome of the process.

The Facilitation of More Inclusive Dialogue

A clear invitation to participate in meaningful dialogue is critical to the process. The Cayman Islands is pleased to have received such an invitation and to have taken it up. The facilitation of more inclusive dialogue will also involve:

- Mutual education and a shift in focus toward a broader recognition of the concerns of individual jurisdictions, the legitimacy of the various types of fiscal regimes that exist within the international community and the legitimacy of economic competition within defined boundaries;

- The use by all participants of inclusive rather than exclusive language and an avoidance of the use of pejorative and discriminatory emotive language;

- The use of many means and many fora, both new and established.

Addressing the last of these three points first, the multilateral conference hosted by the Government of Barbados in January 2001 in association with the Commonwealth and the OECD is one example of a new forum that provides a very valuable opportunity to facilitate more inclusive dialogue. I would like to commend all of those who have given of their time and effort in the organisation of this conference.

Recent dialogue among the non-OECD jurisdictions that have joined the international process commenced by the OECD is another example of a new forum in which all such jurisdictions that have joined the process, and those who are contemplating joining the process, are welcome. The Cayman Islands would be happy to share information on this emerging process with any delegation wishing further information.

Mutual Education

Mutual education is vital. There has been a great deal of misunderstanding, seemingly fuelled by narrow self-interest and rhetoric, both in regard to what are the legitimate expectations of individual nation states in regard to transnational taxation, and in regard to what each state may reasonably expect of other states in the international arena. Much of this misunderstanding will be eliminated once there is a common understanding of the political economics and jurisprudence of each participant and their legitimate expectations.

I would just like to give a simple example from our experience of the type of misunderstanding that can inhibit dialogue. As is well known, the fiscal regime that has evolved in the Cayman Islands employs indirect rather than direct taxes. The Cayman Islands has never had direct taxes on income, capital gains, wealth or any of the other direct taxes that have appeared for various reasons in the industrialised states over the past hundred years or so.

Our culture has always favoured taxes based on consumption, as such taxes are more consistent with the fundamental beliefs of our people and our desire to protect our fragile environment. It has also been the experience of the Cayman Islands that the academic models are quite correct in their prediction that consumption taxes have a very low compliance cost for business and individuals. It is also well established that if properly implemented, consumption based taxes are as equitable and broad-based as any other model, and can be efficiently administered by a relatively small and inexpensive public sector agency.

Despite the fact that our fiscal regime is both simple and transparent, there are some we have encountered in the international arena who have the completely muddled and misguided impression that the Cayman Islands somehow recently created a fiscal regime specifically to attract international business, whereas in reality the Cayman Islands simply never adopted direct taxation measures that international business finds somewhat less than appealing at times.

The Use of Inclusive Language
Language is very powerful. *The Book of Proverbs* (12 and 18) teaches that words can play a decisive role, whether for good or evil. They can be as destructive as sword thrusts or the means of healing.

Temperate language is essential in the process we are now engaged in, if there is to be progress. Intemperate language is rarely constructive. Vilification and demonisation are well known techniques which may seem to be expedient in regard to the mobilisation and shaping of domestic public opinion or some other narrow political objective when simple facts are not helpful or sufficient. However, these methods do not contribute to international harmony and they are rarely effective in the long term, as history has ably shown.

The Articulation of Assumptions
There may be much yet to be established in terms of achieving a fair playing field that is accessible to all in the international arena of tax-related economic competition. However, there are things that we all share such as adherence to the rule of international law. We can choose to build upon these shared beliefs.

Articulation of our respective assumptions can also help to identify areas for discussion and consensus building. The generation of, and response to, various position papers and other public documents over the past few years has been very useful in bringing to the fore subjects which require international debate and consensus building.

Some of the academic, and in some cases pragmatic, questions that have emerged and re-emerged in regard to these subjects include:

◆ *What assumptions define certain forms of tax-related economic competition as 'harmful' and other forms as acceptable?* The perception of some on the outside of the current processes is that the focus and scope of recent initiatives indicates that these initiatives are merely a means for large rich countries to preserve and project forward the existing global economic order at the expense of smaller less developed countries.

♦ *What are the legitimate limits of state sovereignty in regard to international taxation in general and the extra-territorial application of fiscal regimes in particular?* The perception of some on the outside of the process has been that the limits proposed by the large developed states are just another case of might attempting to define right.

♦ *What is 'fair' in terms of allowing for economic diversification in smaller states?* The perception of some on the outside of the process has been that no economic diversification is to be tolerated if it potentially competes with the interests of large developed states.

♦ *To what extent is it appropriate for the rich and developed nations to restrict the movement of investment capital to small less developed states which offer investors the potential for diversification and a higher after-tax rate of return on their investments?* This question is often coupled with the parallel question regarding investment incentives offered by large states that have distorting effects on international investment activities.

♦ *To what extent are historical events and current aspirations for the future relevant?* The perception of some on the outside of the process appears to be that the historical removal of people and wealth from what are now the developing regions for the benefit of the now rich and developed regions is relevant. The question that is asked is that if wealth started out, for example, in the West Indies and went to Europe, when did it stop being wealth to which the now developing nations have a claim? Similarly, when does money leaving the now developed world cease to be money on which the developed world has an ongoing claim?

♦ *To what extent is there a relevant question of proportionality in regard to international taxation?* The extra-territorial application of fiscal regimes, for example through Controlled Foreign Companies regimes, results in the potential for arguably disproportionate taxation of non-monetary inputs, that is the taxation of inputs arising from the natural and human resources of another jurisdiction. Some may ask whether an international convention could be developed which would define the scope in respect of which the jurisdiction which was the most recent source of the money only has a tax claim in respect of a portion of any income or gain in wealth proportionate to that jurisdiction's relative contribution to the creation of new wealth.

It is highly unlikely that consensus in respect of the answers to even these few semi-rhetorical questions can be achieved during the course of this conference. However, if we can openly identify what the questions and assumptions are, then we will be able to establish working groups or other forms of communication to enable us to build consensus and work towards an acceptable outcome.

Developing a Set of Guiding Principles to Take the Process Forward

Achieving transparency in regard to the principles which are to be followed in the process, as well as in the mechanisms of the process itself, will go a long way to encouraging dialogue and achieving a workable outcome. The Cayman Islands would like to suggest by way of illustration, that the guiding principles that participants in the dialogue may wish to consider and adopt could include the following concepts in one form of words or another:

♦ Acceptance of the general principles of public international law, including the defined sovereign rights of states;

♦ Acceptance of the general presumption against the validity of the extra-territorial application of laws of individual states;

♦ Acceptance of the legitimate expectation of consistency and equitable treatment;

♦ Acceptance of the right of individual jurisdictions to negotiate the terms of international tax arrangements and to determine whether that particular state wishes to enter into bilateral or multilateral arrangements, or similarly whether any arrangements should take the form of double taxation agreements or otherwise;

♦ Acceptance of the general proposition in favour of the right to privacy of the individual in respect of personal information including financial information;

♦ Acceptance of the right of all individuals to due process before the law;

♦ Acknowledgement of a general presumption in favour of following the format of existing international conventions and practice to the extent applicable and practical, except where there is a clear international consensus for change to a specific new format which is consistent with the other principles listed above.

It may be that for one reason or another, one or more of the concepts set out here are not acceptable to one or more participants in the dialogue.

If so, even that information would assist in the dialogue. Similarly, there are likely to be suggestions for modifications to those general principles listed here, or additions which one or more jurisdiction might wish. The Cayman Islands welcomes any suggestions in this regard and would be glad to participate in any forum in which these principles can be further developed and articulated.

Conclusions

Having begun with one agrarian analogy in regard to farmyards and geese, I would like to end with another, this time having to do with water.

On our planet water in its liquid form often defines our borders. It moves internationally in rivers and oceans. It leaves its liquid form in evaporation, travels the winds across international boundaries in clouds, returns to liquid form in condensation and falls as rain, whether close to where it originated or in distant lands. Having fallen as rain, it again begins the life-giving process of flow, nourishment and evaporation. In all of these forms and with all this movement it is what gives us life. If we stop its movement it becomes stagnant and fetid. If we conserve its natural cycle and use it wisely, it will sustain us all.

Perhaps in regard to the international economic flows that are the focus of the discussions here, there are analogies that will give us perspective. The potential wealth of this planet is a resource we all share. We would hopefully all agree that no upstream nation would be justified in unreasonably depriving its downstream neighbours of life sustaining water by virtue of the geographic or historical accident that put them upstream.

Similarly, no nation should pollute waters that move internationally making them unhealthy or unproductive for their neighbours. Further, there are internationally accepted limits to which a nation may go in causing water to deviate as it flows internationally. Finally, conservation is to be applauded in all jurisdictions.

The approach of the Cayman Islands is to participate fully and constructively in the international process of establishing new international law and norms in regard to tax-related economic competition. The Cayman Islands encourages all jurisdictions to participate in this process and would be pleased to engage in dialogue with any jurisdiction in this regard. The Cayman Islands commitment to the OECD is part of our involvement in the process. The terms of our commitment to the OECD is a matter of public record and we would be happy to share the full text of this commitment with other delegations.

Globalisation and Tax-related Issues: What are the Concerns?[1]

Papali'i T. Scanlan

On behalf of a small independent Pacific State, Samoa, I would like to highlight our concerns about the OECD's Harmful Tax Competition Initiative on globalisation and tax-related issues.

The history of the people in the Pacific Forum island countries has for centuries been shaped by various processes through which concepts and ideals were imposed from afar. Pacific people have confronted and struggled with the processes of colonisation, decolonisation and independence, and most recently globalisation.

Small Pacific Forum island states like Samoa have economies which are fragile, being typically based on agriculture. Because of its vulnerability to natural disasters, dependence on foreign aid and difficulty in becoming competitive in the manufacturing sector, owing mainly to smallness in size, Samoa made a critical economic assessment and decided, after much deliberation, to establish its Offshore Finance Centre in 1988 as an alternative source of government revenue. Such revenue is vital for the development of our economy to meet the increasing expectations and demands of our growing population. We need to continuously improve our education system and health services. We need to provide the necessary infrastructure to assist our private sector to grow. We need to provide employment for an increasing number of school leavers. Our export sector needs to be made more competitive in order for us to earn the much-needed foreign exchange to meet our rising import costs and other overseas payments.

So, just as countries in the developed world (for example, Ireland) and the developing world (for example, Malaysia and Singapore) provided incentives to specific sectors to encourage economic growth, the same was done in Samoa to encourage the growth of our Offshore Finance Centre. As one of the jurisdictions which offers offshore financial facilities, Samoa in a relatively short period of time has had to confront various international initiatives, including the Financial Stability Forum, the

---

1 This paper is based on a speech given by Papali'i T. Scanlan, Governor of the Central Bank of Samoa, to the OECD-Pacific Island Forum Countries Consultations on the OECD Harmful Tax Competition Initiative in Tokyo in February 2001.

Financial Action Task Force on Money Laundering and the OECD Harmful Taxation Report. Such initiatives bring with them many complex challenges which seem insurmountable, given the fact that they place exceptional demands on already scarce and limited human and other resources available to small economies. Samoa acknowledges the laudable objectives of the Financial Action Task Force on Money Laundering and the general principles sought to be achieved by the various initiatives, such as protecting financial centres from illicit activity, strengthening supervisory skills and the gathering of information on volatile assets. We are, however, deeply concerned about the OECD Initiative on Harmful Tax Competition for the following reasons.

Limited Consultation

Firstly, the OECD has, without much consultation with non-OECD member countries, gone to great lengths to identify criteria as to what constitutes a 'tax haven'. Yet there appears to be little economic theory to support the idea that tax competition is harmful. And it is notable that the OECD Report on Harmful Tax Competition did not take into account a substantial body of literature which supports the notion that such competition is essentially beneficial. Nonetheless, the OECD has directed an internationally identified list of such countries to move away from being 'tax havens'. Whilst we acknowledge the principles being promoted, we are seriously concerned about the manner in which the OECD and other member organisations have sought to achieve their proposed objectives. The lack of, or inadequate, consultation undertaken by the Harmful Tax Practices Group with the non-OECD countries affected is a classic example. In Samoa's case, the bilateral consultative process consisted of a request to respond to questionnaires and a one-day country visit in June 1999. To date, as a listed jurisdiction, we have not been offered any coherent vision of how the OECD views our jurisdiction and how our obligations and relationship should evolve, if we were to commit to OECD's requirements. We believe there are many issues inextricably linked to the OECD Initiative which require careful examination and definition. To date, Samoa has not participated in any multilateral discussions, and we would welcome the opportunity to become involved at all levels in an open and transparent consultative process which should reflect the interests of all stakeholders, including academic experts, taxpayers and the international business community. As with other initiatives spearheaded by the Financial Stability Forum and the Financial Action Task Force, we urge the OECD, for the sake of fairness and transparency, to pursue a global process in which economically and legally sound international standards on taxation are established by which all jurisdictions are assessed.

Sovereignty

Secondly, we firmly believe that the power to tax is a sovereign right. The 1998 OECD report appears to concede that a jurisdiction should be free to devise its own tax system as a matter of sovereignty. However, the OECD went on to qualify such right of sovereignty, by placing a condition on such freedom, stating that it existed only 'as long as they abide by international standards'. Several questions come to mind about this condition. These include questions such as:

◆ What are internationally acceptable standards?

◆ Who determines these standards?

◆ Will they apply equally to all jurisdictions, non-OECD and OECD?

◆ What is an optimal global tax system anyway?

Samoa is an independent constitutional democracy which cherishes the common law rights of its citizens. It considers its Parliament to be supreme, its laws effective and the choices it makes for its citizens to be determinative. With the OECD process which has been promoted to date, we feel that sometimes this fact may be overlooked or, if not overlooked, then certainly discounted. Indeed, we wonder whether the work of the OECD Harmful Tax Practices Group has had sufficient regard to the sovereignty of the Parliaments of affected countries.

What Standards are being Applied?

It can be argued that the idea that tax competition is 'harmful' is empty of logical content and totally contradictory to the generally accepted conclusion of most economists and organisations (including the OECD) that competition is a means to maximise world economic welfare. It contradicts the modern trend advocated by many developed countries to encourage competition and allow capital to move globally without national restrictions. Indeed, small island states in the Pacific (like Samoa) are presently striving to comply with initiatives to encourage financial liberalisation. In the case of Samoa, we are in the process of seeking accession to the WTO, despite the impact on local tariffs, levies and taxes which this implies. Moreover, the criticism of tax havens being harmful or carrying on harmful tax practices, in our view lacks the benefit of dialogue, co-operation and peer review by academic and other experts. Yet it remains an allegation which has had, and will continue to have, a negative impact on our international reputation in some quarters, though those who know us are aware that Samoa is a responsible and reputable member of the family of nations. In this context, countries which find themselves in the position that we face with such a body as the OECD, must seek a return to basics and ask the following questions:

♦ What specifically are the tax laws of our country which are harmful?

♦ To whom are these laws harmful?

♦ According to what measure and to what extent does our tax regime provide tax havens?

♦ To whom and to what are we, as a sovereign country, accountable?

♦ Are there solutions to any alleged harm which do not involve loss of any country's sovereignty?

In this context, we would like to learn of the evidence, if any, of the harm that we are causing as a 'tax haven', and to whom?

Samoa as Part of the International Community

My fourth point is that Samoa is, and wishes to remain, a responsible and respected member of the international community. Being mindful of the responsibilities which come with that reputation, Samoa has made considerable efforts to comply with international standards on offshore supervision. As a consequence, we recently enacted comprehensive anti-money-laundering legislation which is based on a model originally prepared by the Commonwealth Secretariat. As a result of its efforts to combat money laundering, Samoa did not feature on the list of unco-operative countries compiled by the Financial Action Task Force.

On this initiative, it is implied from the text of the OECD report that 'tax havens' are failing to take sufficient responsibility and to consider the effect of their legal and fiscal regimes on other countries. We would suggest that this is not so in Samoa's case.

Being a prominent organisation, charged with promoting economic co-operation and development, we ask the OECD to acknowledge the hardships of the less privileged small island states already disadvantaged by other economic and geographical factors. Yet, we are now faced with a threat to our international reputation and status in a process which appears to us to be the case of the strong dictating to the weak, the rich to the poor and the big to the small. As with the English Civil War and the American Revolution, history shows that attempts to impose coercive taxation measures may be misguided.

I would hazard a guess that many of the OECD member countries have felt this way in some dealings with other more powerful economies, perhaps in areas such as lamb, bananas and leather to use some current examples, and felt a threat to their sovereign status in those cases as we do to ours now.

Our Offshore Financial Centre, like those operated by other Pacific Forum island countries, not only provides an alternative to earning foreign revenue, but constitutes an important component of the Samoan economy, by promoting economic diversification and a highly-skilled industry. Revenue earned directly by our government from the fees paid by offshore companies has continued to increase over the years. There are other economic spin-offs such as telecommunication revenues, value added tax and income tax which also benefit our domestic fiscal position. The loss of such revenue will be highly detrimental to our Government's present focus on improving the health, education and overall welfare of our people.

Last, but not least, if the OECD wishes these discussions to be regarded as advancing efforts to achieve global understanding of international taxation issues, then the threats of defensive measures that are being suggested should be removed as a sign of its good faith and a reflection of its willingness to encourage review by outside experts. At the same time, we ask the OECD to consult with and respond to the concerns expressed by other parties, be they governments, businesses, taxpayer organisations or legislators from member and non-member countries.

Like most Pacific Forum island countries represented around this table, Samoa's Offshore Financial Centre was not set up to facilitate the laundering of proceeds of crime. Nor was it set up to deprive OECD countries of tax revenue. Rather, our Offshore Financial Centre was established to provide our Government with much needed revenue for the development of our country, in order to improve the living standards of our people.

In concluding, I would like to point out that most of the tax and legal practices adapted in offshore financial centres are based on British and European precedents. Among those guiding precedents is a respect for the rule of law and a rejection of despotism.

Governments are instituted to protect the property and liberties of their citizens, and not to destroy them. In the event, we urge that the OECD recognise and respect the rights of individuals as well as those of sovereign nations, even those of small Pacific Forum island countries.

The Future of Financial Services in the Caribbean[1]

H.E. Sir Ronald Sanders KCN, CMG

Were it not for the threat to the Caribbean's financial services sector posed by the OECD, I believe that the Caribbean would now be in a far more competitive position in the provision of global financial services than it was before.

Few can argue with any credibility that the anti-money-laundering regimes in all but a small number of Caribbean countries are not now entirely consistent with the highest international standards. Most of our jurisdictions are in full compliance with the criteria set by the Financial Action Task Force established by the G7 countries as a sister to the OECD.

The criteria for judging the compliance of jurisdictions were tough. They required a comprehensive review of laws, regulations and practices to ensure adherence to international best practices including rules for reporting and investigating suspicious activities, the requirement to know beneficial owners of bank accounts and international business corporations, and to share information on criminal matters.

In the case of my own country, Antigua and Barbuda, the Prime Minister, Lester Bird, established a Working Group, under my chairmanship, to study our arrangements against the FATF criteria and to recommend any changes required to our legal, supervisory and enforcement regime that might be necessary to ensure compliance. As a consequence of that work, Antigua and Barbuda overhauled many of its laws, strengthened its supervisory capacity and enhanced its investigative facilities. Subsequently, we were found by the FATF to be a fully co-operative jurisdiction in the fight against money laundering and we were never 'named and shamed' on its list. Other countries that were listed undertook the tough task of similarly overhauling their systems.

Undoubtedly, compliance with the FATF criteria has cost every Caribbean country dearly. Many financial institutions and international business corporations have left our jurisdictions because they did not like our new regimes, or we struck them from our registers for non-compliance

---

1 This paper is based on a speech given by His Excellency Sir Ronald Sanders, Chief Foreign Affairs Representative of Antigua and Barbuda, to the PriceWaterhouseCoopers Conference on Financial Services Investment Practice held in Nassau, Bahamas, 7 September 2001.

with our new rules and regulations. Governments lost much-needed revenue from licence fees, and our economies also lost much-wanted jobs for our people. In addition, governments have faced increased costs by strengthening supervisory, regulatory and investigative mechanisms. But at the end of the day the countries that have complied with the FATF criteria have made themselves more reputable and reliable, and therefore more attractive to legitimate business. In the long run, it is legitimate business that will sustain our economies, provide jobs and increase revenue.

However, like the sword of Damocles, a threat still hangs over the financial services sector of the Caribbean, because of the so-called 'Harmful Tax Competition Initiative' of the OECD. But the Caribbean region is in a far better position today to resist that threat than we were a year ago.

Two principal factors have led to our strengthened situation.

The first is the universal recognition and acknowledgement of the considerable strides that several of our jurisdictions have made in establishing regimes to effectively combat money laundering and other financial crime. Today, the Caribbean cannot be described by any objective standard as a 'haven for crooks and money launderers'. Indeed, most of our jurisdictions are now in the forefront of the battle against money laundering with some of the most stringent legislation in the world on our books.

The second is the significant work done by representatives of our governments to sensitise the international community, including the new government in the USA, to the wrongness of the OECD's original initiative. That included much work to inform members of the US Congress and Senate and the new US Government of the serious flaws in the OECD initiative.

I believe it is true to say that the intervention of the US Secretary of the Treasury, Paul O'Neill, caused the OECD to amend its Initiative. While there were other countries, such as Canada, that earlier saw the wisdom of change, they lacked the strength to resist the domination of the OECD by the 15 EU countries who have been the driving force behind this scheme. These factors have led to a significant modification within the OECD of the so-called 'Harmful Tax Competition Initiative'.

We have now entered the final phase of an unfortunate confrontation between the OECD and over 30 jurisdictions around the world that they have targeted as so-called 'tax havens'. In less than three months time, on 30 November,[2] the OECD plans to 'name and shame' these jurisdictions

---

2 *Editorial note*: The OECD deadline was extended to 28 February 2002 in November 2001.

as practising 'harmful tax competition' unless they publicly state their agreement to eliminate aspects of their fiscal arrangements that the OECD alone has determined to be harmful. If, by 30 April 2003 at the earliest, they have still not complied with the OECD's demands for changes in their fiscal systems, the 30 OECD member countries will apply sanctions against them as they see fit.

Originally, this 'naming and shaming' exercise was due to take place in 2000. But, in the wake of strong resistance from the targeted jurisdictions and an international campaign in which the matter was raised in almost every global forum, the OECD agreed to delay 'naming and shaming' until 31 July 2001.

In the interim, a Joint Working Group of OECD and non-OECD countries was established in January 2001 under the co-Chairmanship of the Prime Minister of Barbados, Owen Arthur, and the Australian Ambassador to the OECD, Tony Hinton. That Joint Working Group, of which I was a member, met twice, first in London in January 2001 and then in Paris in March 2001.

The point of the Joint Working Group was to try to seek ways in which confrontation could be avoided and the concerns of the OECD about what it called 'harmful tax competition' could be met in a mutually satisfactory manner. As a starting point, both sides in the Working Group agreed on the need to address three broad principles. These were: non-discrimination, transparency and effective exchange of information. However, that was as far as agreement went.

The OECD members of the Working Group expected the targeted jurisdictions to simply accept the OECD definition of these principles and, therefore, the manner in which they would be applied, while the non-OECD members anticipated that the three principles would be defined by agreement.

Further, the non-OECD members expected that the two sides would discuss the establishment of a truly international forum, in which all interested countries and institutions would be represented, to determine, in a democratic manner, how these three broad principles would be applied equally and universally with representative machinery for monitoring implementation and deciding on measures to address non-compliance by all countries, large and small.

The OECD countries, however, were adamant that its own ironically named Global Forum on Taxation would be the only forum in which the matter would be discussed. The only concession that they made to membership of the forum was that targeted jurisdictions would be allowed to participate, but only after they had blindly accepted the OECD's definition of the three broad principles and publicly declared their acceptance. I need hardly say that the discussions were stalemated and the members of the Joint Working Group left Paris no nearer to resolving the impasse than when we started.

Amazingly to us, 17 questions which we posed to the OECD in written form, and which they promised to answer while we were in Paris, were still unanswered five months later when Ambassador Hinton, as co-Chair of the Joint Working Group, wrote to Prime Minister Arthur, the other co-Chair, to forward a set of responses. These 17 questions were designed to ascertain from the OECD whether or not its own member states would be bound by the same rules that were being applied to the targeted jurisdictions. The answers, none of which was plain and explicit, clouded the issues even more and gave rise to deeper suspicion about the motives behind the OECD's 'harmful tax competition' scheme.

In any event, the OECD decided to extend the deadline for 'naming and shaming' from 31 July to 30 November 2001 and to delay the imposition of sanctions until 30 April 2003 at the earliest when they would also be applied against their own defaulting members. In addition, according to the letter written by Ambassador Hinton to Prime Minister Arthur and circulated to the members of the Joint Working Group, the OECD has also decided to remove one of their criteria in naming a jurisdiction as a 'tax haven'.

One of the OECD criteria for deciding whether or not a jurisdiction is a 'tax haven' was whether or not it has a regime that facilitates the establishment of entities with 'no substantial activities' in the country. Such entities were regarded as 'ring-fenced' if the tax regime it enjoyed was available only to non-resident investors or if its activities were limited to international transactions. That criterion has now been eliminated.

Essentially what the OECD is now seeking from us is a commitment to two things. The first is effective exchange of information in both civil and criminal tax matters when it is relevant to a *specific* tax investigation or examination. According to the OECD, appropriate safeguards will be implemented to ensure that information is used only for the purpose for which it is sought.

The second is adherence to standards of transparency which the OECD has not attempted to define in their communications with our jurisdictions, but which has been detailed by US Treasury Secretary Paul O'Neill in a statement to a US Senate Committee.

The US Treasury Secretary says 'transparency means two things: (1) the absence of non-public tax practices, such as secret negotiation, or waiver, of public tax laws and tax administration rules; and (2) the absence of obstacles, such as strict bank secrecy or the use of bearer shares, to obtaining financial or beneficial ownership information within a jurisdiction'.

Jurisdictions that make commitments to the OECD on these two matters will have a year in which to develop plans to implement them. The OECD would like commitments to these two matters to be made before 30 November 2001 when it plans to 'name and shame' jurisdictions by publishing a list of what it calls 'unco-operative jurisdictions'.

The OECD's communications have also indicated that OECD countries will not apply sanctions against non-OECD countries any earlier than they would apply such sanctions against their own members. No date has been given for the application of such sanctions, but in his statement to the Senate Committee, the US Treasury Secretary indicated that this would not be 'until April 2003 at the earliest'. On the face of it, the two matters on which the OECD is now seeking commitments may not appear contentious. Indeed, on the basis of the definition of transparency given by the US Treasury Secretary, none of our jurisdictions in the Caribbean should have any difficulty.

Certainly, none of our jurisdictions make secret tax deals with investors, nor is any government authorised to waive public tax laws and tax administration rules. With respect to strict bank secrecy or the use of bearer shares as obstacles to obtaining financial or beneficial ownership information, the new legislation and regulation established by most, if not all, our jurisdictions under our anti-money-laundering regimes ensure that there are no such obstacles.

With regard to effective exchange of information, under Tax Information Exchange Agreements or Mutual Legal Assistance Treaties, many of our jurisdictions already co-operate with some OECD countries, particularly the USA and Canada. Therefore, the principle of information exchange in specific cases where it is relevant to a tax investigation or examination is not a problem by itself. The real problem is that there is no clear or accepted international definition of what 'civil' means, and no explicit description of how the information would be exchanged. As usual, the devil may be in the detail, and jurisdictions will want to size up that demon before deciding to live with it.

The OECD also states that the two principles, exchange of information and transparency, will be focused on geographically mobile services, including financial services, shipping, distribution services, service industries and company headquartering.

In its communications, the OECD has indicated that jurisdictions that make a commitment will be invited to participate in the OECD's Global Forum Working Group which is addressing these two principles. As far as it goes, this appears a more reasonable proposition than the original 'Harmful Tax Competition Initiative' which attempted to dictate the tax economic systems and structures of other nations for the benefit of the OECD's member states. The original scheme sought to limit the authority of non-OECD governments and legislatures over their own countries' tax economic systems and structures through the constraints of a framework set by the OECD.

But a fundamental difficulty still remains. It is one that has far-reaching implications and it is by no means limited to this particular initiative of the OECD. The difficulty simply put is this. Should 41 jurisdictions around the world accept that the OECD has the right or authority to set itself up to make tax rulings which they expect non-members to follow? By doing this, would these 41 jurisdictions, targeted by the OECD as 'tax havens', not be opening the floodgates to a raft of other demands by an organisation with no authority except the coercive power of its member states?

We must recall that the OECD is a multinational grouping of 30 countries. It is not an international organisation and it has no legal authority to speak for the world or to establish rules, norms or standards for any state except its own members. Nonetheless, it is now dictating terms on what, in short, could be described as cross-border tax matters. Even with the helpful intervention of the new US Government, and the subsequent modification of the original initiative, the threat of sanctions has not been removed. In other words, the OECD is still determined to invoke economic power to force surrender wherever it meets resistance.

Recently, the OECD launched a wide range of papers on e-commerce to develop global approaches to a number of e-commerce issues including fiscal matters. One of the initiatives is to develop a new fiscal approach to indirect taxation of e-commerce. This will require non-OECD suppliers to register in each OECD country for indirect tax payments and to pay indirect taxation in each of the OECD countries to which they export goods and services through e-commerce. It is envisaged that this will create substantial hurdles for small developing country entrepreneurs seeking to use e-commerce to overcome market access barriers of distance and cost into major OECD markets. The EU countries would not be subject to such taxes within the EU boundaries due to harmonisation of indirect taxes. Hence this would mainly affect developing country e-commerce exporters.

In addition, the 1998 OECD report flagged that manufacturing industries in developing countries would be addressed later. Many of our countries give fiscal incentives and have special legal and fiscal regimes to attract investment to particular sectors such as hotels, export processing zones and manufacturing. The extension of the scope of the OECD initiative beyond geographically mobile services would affect most, if not all, our countries.

It is significant that in the summary of modifications to the tax haven work which the OECD has circulated to our jurisdictions, it continues to assert that the modifications do not 'affect the application of the 1998 Report' whose criteria for identifying tax havens 'remain unchanged'. This assertion emphasises that while the OECD has made a tactical withdrawal on one front, it has not abandoned the battlefield altogether and may be merely postponing a further onslaught until after it has secured an opening into our camp and weakened our capacity for resistance.

Our governments cannot disregard this important dimension of the problem. They will have to take serious account of it in reaching a decision about whether or not to make a commitment to the OECD on the two remaining aspects of the so-called 'Harmful Tax Competition Initiative'. By the same token, they will also have to carefully consider the consequences to their economies of the application of sanctions by the members of the OECD who are more important partners to us in financial services. The key players in this regard are the USA, Canada and the UK.

What Sanctions Would be Applied?

The US Treasury Secretary told the US Senate Committee that the work in the OECD to refine the identification of appropriate sanctions is still at an early stage, but that some of the measures already identified have been part of the international tax policy of the USA and other OECD countries for many years. They include enhanced audit and enforcement activities with respect to transactions and jurisdictions which may be used by their taxpayers to evade tax, and no tax treaties, such as double taxation agreements. This probably means that the recent financial advisories, applied to and then lifted from several of our jurisdictions after the FATF exercise on money laundering, would be reinstated. Mr O'Neill also pointed out that the sanctions envisaged by the OECD would require legislation in the USA and therefore would have to be approved by Congress.

The OECD currently has a team in the Caribbean which will be visiting several jurisdictions in an attempt to persuade them to make a commitment to the 'harmful tax' project based on the modifications that have been made.

It should be noted that these modifications have not yet been approved by the OECD Council which does not meet until later this month. Indeed, the modified proposals that I have outlined have not yet been de-restricted by the Council. I suspect, therefore, that this is the first time that any Caribbean government representative is discussing the modified proposals with any section of the private sector. Yet, in less than two months, the OECD expects governments to make commitments which they have not had the opportunity to fully discuss in their countries with their social partners.

Representatives of OECD governments and the OECD Secretariat have assured me in several fora over the last few weeks that there will be no change to the modified proposals.

So, the question is – where do we go from here?

Let me say at the outset that my own jurisdiction, Antigua and Barbuda, is not a non-cooperative jurisdiction. Based on the consultations within the non-OECD members of the Joint Working Group, I feel I can say beyond fear of contradiction that all the targeted jurisdictions are ready and willing to co-operate with the OECD in trying to find a mutually acceptable way of dealing with the issues of exchange of information and transparency.

On 30 August, I met Ambassador Hinton of Australia, the co-Chair of the Joint Working Group of OECD and non-OECD countries, and representatives of the OECD Secretariat headed by Jeffrey Owens, the Head of the Centre for Tax Policy and Administration, specifically because I wanted to explore any avenues that might exist for taking this project forward in a co-operative manner.

They were anxious to point out to me not only the modifications that have been made to the Harmful Tax Competition Initiative, but also the fact that they were offering technical and capacity-building assistance to jurisdictions that made a commitment. I had to respond to them that technical and capacity-building assistance, while helpful, was more for their purposes than for ours. Of far greater importance to us would be measures that would encourage our jurisdictions to look more favourably on giving a commitment to the world's 30 richest nations. Essentially, from their standpoint, this project is about pursuing their taxpayers who, they believe, may be evading the payment of their taxes.

We do not know that their premise is correct. And, indeed, neither do they. For instance, US Treasury Secretary Paul O'Neill himself told the

US Senate Committee that 'it is impossible to quantify precisely the extent to which US taxpayers are using offshore entities to evade their US tax obligations'. The information, he said, is 'anecdotal', but he believes that the 'potential' is significant.

The OECD is expecting our jurisdictions to institute measures and practices to facilitate a hunch that some of their taxpayers may be evading taxes. However, these measures may have the effect of causing perfectly legitimate activities to leave – or not come – to our jurisdictions simply because they want to maintain the privacy of their business. In other words, our financial services sector and our economies could suffer real hardship because of the desire by OECD countries to seek out possible tax evaders, rather than known tax evaders.

In my view the OECD project would have a better chance of success if the OECD countries were to demonstrate a readiness to deal effectively with the problems they create for our jurisdictions. For instance, the OECD could implement a number of confidence-building measures. Among these would be:

- A clear declaration that the OECD will shelve its 1998 Report which details arbitrary factors for identifying 'tax havens';

- A plain statement that the OECD will not extend the scope of the Initiative beyond geographically mobile services to include legal and fiscal regimes which attract investment;

- An invitation to all interested countries to join its Global Forum Working Group whether or not they make a commitment to transparency and effective exchange of information. In this way, the non-OECD countries would be able to see at first hand the nature and scope of the discussion and might be encouraged to join voluntarily and not by coercion. They could also make a constructive contribution to the elaboration of the two principles and their application;

- The unequivocal withdrawal of any list intended to name jurisdictions as 'unco-operative'.

Such confidence building measures would demonstrate good faith by the OECD countries and would show that it has departed from its previously flawed process of forcing other countries to accept standards and practices unilaterally devised by the OECD.

The second measure that the OECD countries should consider is the establishment of double taxation treaties with jurisdictions that commit to transparency and effective exchange of information. Such treaties would help to attract investment and improve the economies of the targeted jurisdictions. Again, this would show good faith by the OECD countries.

Whether or not the OECD would be willing to consider and implement these measures is anybody's guess. But we in the Caribbean should put it to them strongly as a condition of any commitment we might make now or later.

The OECD has a team touring the Caribbean trying to secure commitments in advance of the 30 November 2001 deadline for publishing its list of unco-operative jurisdictions. These conditions should be put to the OECD firmly, and governments should carefully consider whether to give any commitments before the OECD Council gives an undertaking to satisfy them.

It may be that the OECD will proceed to publish their list on 30 November on which the 35 jurisdictions will appear as non-co-operative in their harmful tax competition scheme. If they do so, they will be naming jurisdictions that have been recognised and acknowledged to be fully co-operative in the frontline of the battle against money laundering. We can hold our heads high on that score. Our collective transgression – if transgression it is – would be that we simply do not accept that the OECD has any legal right to unilaterally devise schemes that they seek to impose upon others in order to deal with their own taxpayers who, on anecdotal information only, they believe to be evading taxes.

The truth is that 80 per cent of the total offshore financial services industry is located in the OECD countries, excluding their colonies. The remaining 20 per cent is in the non-OECD countries with even this segment dominated by a few large centres such as Hong Kong and Singapore which, conveniently, the OECD has not named as 'tax havens'.

This means that less than approximately 10 per cent of offshore business in the world is done in our jurisdictions. The law of averages suggests, therefore, that very little tax evasion money is in the Caribbean. Much of it may well be in the OECD countries themselves.

It is noteworthy that on the money laundering side, while much publicity surrounds illegal activity uncovered in the Caribbean, the actual incidents and sums involved are a tiny fraction of the numerous incidents and vast sums of money discovered in the OECD countries.

I have no crystal ball that can foretell the future. But I do know that we in the Caribbean have the same right as every other country to compete in the financial services sector globally. Our well-educated populations, their high propensity for computer literacy, the relatively lower costs of business in our jurisdictions, our first-class telecommunications and our low tax levels give us the chance to compete efficiently.

In the last 18 months, we have moved rapidly to a well-supervised financial system onshore and offshore. Most, or all, of our countries now meet the highest international standards. With the transparent accounting practices that meet international best practice and global standards, such as those which PriceWaterhouseCoopers and other reputable auditors provide in our region, we should not hesitate or waiver in our resolve to continue to grow this important sector in the interest of our people, the OECD notwithstanding. We should proceed to do so.

Administrative and Resource Implications for Small States[1]

Sir Neville Nicholls

Significant conceptual and technical issues have been raised on the appropriateness or otherwise of the OECD Initiative on Harmful Tax Competition. This paper considers administrative and resource implications from the point of view of the economic development and related fiscal management challenges facing small states, with a focus on those in the Caribbean region.

As has been demonstrated in the Commonwealth Secretariat-World Bank *Report on Small States* (2000) and in the consultations which were intended to guide the production of that report, there are a number of characteristics associated with small size which impose a range of restrictions on the kinds of traditional economic activities in which small countries can expect to become involved on a sustainable basis. The characteristics also affect the nature and functioning of the private and public sectors in the economies and, through effects on their individual capacities, influence their relative roles. Finally, the characteristics affect the extent and nature of the interaction between small economies, both jointly and separately, and the rest of the world.

In our small countries, these characteristics need to be placed in a context in which incomes are mostly low, infrastructure and services are relatively underdeveloped, the level and extent of educational attainment and skills are generally not broad and deep, and in which poverty continues to be a major issue. The situation is further complicated by increasingly strong demonstration effects of lifestyles in developed countries, with the social strains resulting from the mismatch between aspirations and the capacity to meet them manifesting themselves in a number of dysfunctional ways, some of which are quite serious. Not surprisingly, the major focus of governments and administrations in these countries is on economic development: to design, encourage and support activities which appear likely to contribute to sustained growth in incomes, both to facilitate private income growth in order to expand the potential for indi-

---

1 This paper is based on a speech given by Sir Neville Nicholls as President of the Caribbean Development Bank at the High Level Consultations on the OECD Harmful Tax Competitive Initiative, Barbados, 8–9 January 2001.

vidual freedom (to follow Amartya Sen's usage), and to enable public sector delivery of appropriate general social services, regulatory services, and targeted and other support services which are thought to be necessary for the attainment of the country's objectives and which are in accordance with accepted cultural practices.

Key development challenges these characteristics pose for many of our countries include:

♦ A high degree of openness to trade in order to satisfy domestic consumption and investment requirements, given the nature of domestic production capacity, which reflects constraints on the range and volume of physical goods production as a result of limitations on natural resource endowments, including population, and consequential competitiveness issues related to scale economies;

♦ Production flexibility issues in the private sector, related both to the physical goods capacity constraints identified above and to similar constraints on the human resources side. The two sets of constraints here compound the normal difficulty in switching products and product lines in response to changes in market demand induced by changes in tastes, competitiveness, and in production and consumption technologies. A related issue here is the extent to which, in many of our countries, the term 'private sector' means the same thing as it does in large economies, both in an objective sense, and subjectively from the point of view of the private sector itself;

♦ Public sector capacity limitations, in both human and financial resources, which affect, on the domestic side, the provision of physical and institutional infrastructure to support private sector production, provide social services, and to maintain security and effective system regulation; and on the external side, the capacity to participate effectively in the ever-expanding range of international consultations and negotiations which have become a feature of modern times;

♦ Constraints on the capacity for the development of broad, deep and competitive market structures, with consequential implications for the development of attitudes, practices and systems associated with competitive market conditions, for the nature of approaches to, and the effectiveness of, regulation, and for the nature of state intervention in the economy.

These characteristics have given rise to a number of behavioural practices which have had all sorts of consequences for the functioning of our economies. Firstly, the high degree of openness coupled with the narrow range of product items have contributed to considerable market concentration in our trading patterns. The specific markets of concentration have tended to reflect historical circumstances, with the situation being further complicated by a practice of providing external assistance via export price subsidies. This has had the effect of further limiting production flexibility.

Secondly, partly for historical reasons, domestic production linkages are not nearly as developed as international ones, with domestic production remaining near the lower value-added end of the scale. This factor, together with the narrow range of product items, have historically had significant implications for the education and skills requirements of many Caribbean societies. It has only been with the post-war development of mining and tourism activities, and much more recently with broader services industry emergence and development, that some demand for a broader range of skills has led to increased focus on tertiary education domestically and on the attraction of skills from abroad. Nevertheless, domestic market demand for particular types of skills remains thin, and the number of persons whose movement results in a shift from excess supply to complete shortage remains very small in many of our countries. For those skills which are in demand in the developed countries, Caribbean countries have discovered that, notwithstanding immigration restrictions which might exist, domestic and external labour markets are fully integrated, with consequential Dutch disease effects emerging across the board.

Thirdly, private sector activity has in the past been focused on serving the export sector, and on import activities to meet the consumption and investment needs of the societies. The emergence of domestic production to meet domestic requirements (small-scale foodcrop farming aside) has been relatively recent, initially involving assembly-type operations under protected market conditions. The emergence of a growing entrepreneurial focus outside the traditional export areas appears to have reflected a perception of domestic and external opportunities facilitated by the growth of tourism and associated service activities. The effort, beginning in the 1950s, to develop a domestic manufacturing sector, with substantial support from governments and based on an import-substitution approach, has not been particularly successful, partly because the protection arrangements did not promote efficiency and partly because of the characteristics of the industries (producing mainly household durables and low-value consumption items) which attracted investors to the sector, although some operations continue. (As an aside I should like to express the view that the heavy involvement of the public sector in directly productive activity in the region, and the extent and nature of public sector support for private sector activity, is largely justifiable on the basis of the nature of the private sector which mirrored the historical evolution of the broader society.) Service activity development in the private sector has been considerably more successful, and more recent, with many of the operations being directly or indirectly associated with tourism.

Production flexibility, in the sense of the ability of economies in our region to change products and product lines in response to changes in market demand, and to identify new product opportunities and to take advantage of them, has been severely constrained both by physical area issues and by issues relating to population characteristics. On the natural resources side, small size has resulted in such a large proportion of domestic resources being allocated to the production of the traditional export goods that not many resources have been available for new activities, particularly during the pre-services industry period. In many cases, shifting to other activities would have required the closing of some existing operations, a circumstance which would be contemplated only in a *force majeure* situation, because of the income loss and social and economic dislocation which would result from such an approach in poor countries. This is in contrast to what normally obtains in large economies, where production shifts occur as new enterprises utilising new resources introduce new products alongside the old operations, displacing them over time, or as divisions within technologically and managerially progressive firms maintain their information and product contacts with the markets. In both cases, the income losses and economic dislocation is absorbed, at least in the first round, by institutions rather than by individuals, by a combination of public sector safety nets and by labour reallocation schemes within individual firms. Safety net arrangements in the English-speaking Caribbean are in many cases rudimentary.

The contribution that external assistance through subsidising export prices has made, and continues to make, to production inflexibility has been mentioned briefly above. This is despite the very real contribution to national income that the assistance provides. Even with the announced termination of the preferential marketing arrangements, shifting production has continued to prove a major challenge for some countries. The situation should be read as an example of production-switching difficulties arising from human and natural resource constraints.

On the human resources side, these societies have not developed in ways that would make them responsive to perceived economic opportunities in the manner that current conventional wisdom would expect of 'modern' economies. Private sector capacity has tended to have a stronger focus on trade rather than on enterprise, and for a long time (and even today in some of our countries) the private sector has tended not to see itself as a self-conscious entity. This situation has posed difficulties for attempts to develop a national consensus and approach to development. Unlike in large economies, such an approach is required if the process of development is not to take a very long time, or even perhaps if development is to take place at all.

Similarly, the public sector has developed with a 'regulatory and control' focus, rather than one that is supportive of individual and social development and facilitates a proactive, expansionary approach to economic activity. In many countries, the public sector has been slow in recognising and institutionalising the critical proactive role it needs to play in small societies where capacity is otherwise limited. There is, however, increasing recognition of this role across the region, even though there has been a parallel recognition of the financial and other constraints to its institutionalisation.

A fourth behavioural practice has been the reliance on trade-based taxes on the movement of goods, and to a lesser extent on income taxes, to finance public sector operations. With exports constituting a high proportion of GDP, and with consumption and investment needs met largely from imports, governments have found it convenient to raise revenue from border taxes on goods, and to supplement these collections with excise taxes on selected locally produced items (for example alcohol, tobacco and fuel). This has been a source of significant fiscal pressure, and a number of Caribbean countries have experienced major fiscal and balance of payments problems as a result of expenditure growth outstripping sustainable financing capacity. As incomes have risen over time, both personal and business income recipients at the higher end of the scale, as well as the self-employed, have refined their tax-planning activities to avoid paying in excess of their legal liabilities, with the result that middle-income employees have tended to account for a substantial share of income tax collection. With a rise in the domestic production of non-traded items, particularly in the area of services, and with services featuring much more heavily in trade, a number of countries have been shifting their tax system focus to a more transactions-based approach. Only a small number of countries in the region have significantly advanced their tax-system focus in this direction so far. This is partly because of the significant administrative burden involved, given public sector staffing levels and skills. The introduction process has required a considerable amount of consultation, persuasion and sensitivity in those countries where it has been successful. Significant issues remain to be addressed in many countries in the region. Among them are:

♦ How to deal with the regressiveness of transactions-based systems in the context of significant poverty;

♦ How to treat transfer pricing issues in intra-Group transactions;

♦ How to encourage the appropriate degree of record-keeping and accounts verification in the business sector;

♦ In the context of e-commerce, establishing and verifying liability where cross-border activities are increasingly commonplace.

A fifth aspect of small state behaviour is the extent to which they are affected by external shocks, whether these shocks result from natural disasters or from adverse external economic events. Caribbean countries have been badly affected by hurricanes during the last five years in particular, and those familiar with the small states in our region will readily appreciate that hurricane damage is almost always country-wide in scope. The pace of capital accumulation, especially in infrastructure development, has been slower than it might otherwise have been because of the ongoing need to repair and rehabilitate. The actual costs of construction are higher than would otherwise be the case because of the need to build strong structures. On the economic side, output product concentration results in significant exposure to adverse factors affecting one or two industries, given difficulties in diversification.

This vulnerability has led to significant income volatility, with consequent effects for private sector calculations of minimum acceptable returns to risk, and with similar effects for the ability of the public sector to plan future activities. To the extent that financial institutions adopt conservative lending strategies in this environment, such an approach contributes to an overall pattern which tends to slow the overall rate of investment and the expected rate of economic growth.

The situation is further complicated by developments in the free trade enterprise in which we are all now engaged. Under the current regime, we can expect fairly rapid declines in the allowable rates of tariffs on the movement of goods and services, and strong pressure for the effective removal of any remaining restrictions on the movement of capital, management, skilled labour and entrepreneurial talent. Falls in tariffs will subject Caribbean producers to levels of competitiveness with which many of them will not be able to cope, and many of them may go out of business. It is not clear how our societies and fiscal systems will cope with the increase in unemployment which will result, given our rudimentary safety net systems and the fact that nowhere in the globalisation process and negotiations has explicit attention been paid to its effects on labour in small countries. The present globalisation debate, as reflected in the statements coming from the developed countries and their agencies, does not refer to the movement of labour as part of the liberalisation process. This flies in the face of economic logic.

While people in Caribbean societies have always, like others around the world, sought to improve their living levels, the rate of expansion of their aspirations has grown tremendously as a result of the development of tourism as an important industry, and particularly with the more recent enhanced penetration of our region, and by the demonstration effects of developed country lifestyles resulting from the information and telecommunications revolution. Physical constraints associated with small size have prevented countries in the region from expanding the production of goods for export in a sustainable way, and they have accordingly been relying increasingly on service sector activity in their quest for sustained growth over the long term. Incentives for investment in real sector enterprises, as opposed to service sector enterprises, have not (with the exception of mining), yielded the expected results, largely because of the physical resources production constraints discussed above.

In these circumstances, Caribbean societies have had to make a realistic assessment of the economic opportunities open to them, and have sought, in full compliance with their international obligations, and in accordance with the advice and assistance provided to them by their bilateral and multilateral development partners, to encourage perfectly legal longer-term business activities in their jurisdictions. These activities are expected to contribute to the income growth which will help Caribbean citizens to achieve their development objectives with the same dignity and sense of self-reliance as other countries. Income growth is also required in order to finance the public sector activities necessary for the discharge of international obligations and maintenance of self-respect.

Attention needs to be drawn forcefully to the fact that all countries are not the same, and that they should not, therefore, be expected to behave in exactly the same ways. Differences in resource endowments, resource accessibility, patterns of utilisation and, critically, culture and outlook, will significantly influence behaviour and practice. The spirit of international co-operation and the principles of multilateralism and self-determination to which we all profess to subscribe, require that countries do not seek to impose their domestic cultural practices on others. Instead they should assist others to eliminate poverty and to enhance the personal development and personal freedom of all individuals in our world.

Governance in a Globalised World: Is it the End of the Nation State?

Dale Pinto[1]

Introduction

Every era is characterised by vogue words that suddenly become ubiquitous. For the 1990s, this word is undoubtedly 'globalisation'. Like other vogue words, globalisation has wandered in and out of journalism and has almost become an instant cliché. Perhaps as the result of it being used by many writers on every possible occasion, globalisation has come to mean different things to different people. At the same time, it has caused apprehension, excitement, expectation and widespread confusion among citizens and governments alike.

Different theories are advanced to explain the meaning of globalisation: some of them appear simple and logical, while others seem merely to add to the confusion. At the extreme optimistic end of the spectrum are those who see globalisation as the technologically inevitable product of the internet.[2] These 'techno-globalists'[3] argue that the shift from a manufacturing-dominated industrial economy to a service economy represents a 'Third Wave' comparable to the earlier replacement of agricultural civilisation (the First Wave) by industrial civilisation (the Second Wave).[4]

At the other end are those who argue that globalisation is an unmitigated disaster, replacing the social-democratic prosperity of post-war Europe with a plutocratic nightmare.[5] According to this argument, globalisation will produce a '20/80 society', in which the benefits of change will be experienced by transnational corporations and the highly skilled 20 per cent of the workforce they need.[6] The other 80 per cent face a bleak outlook, bouncing between unemployment and insecure jobs.

---

1 Dale Pinto is Senior Lecturer, School of Business Law, Curtin University, Western Australia

2 John Quiggin, 'Globalisation: Brave New World or Techno Trap?', *The Australian Financial Review*, Sydney, 1 October 1999, Review Section 5.

3 An excellent guide to the theory of techno-globalism is provided by Alvin Toffler and Heidi Toffler in their book, *Creating a New Civilisation: The Politics of the Third Wave* (1994).

4 Quiggin, above, n 2, Review Section 5.

5 Ibid. Also see generally Hans-Peter Martin and Harald Schumann, *The Global Trap: Globalisation and the Assault on Democracy* (1997).

6 Ibid.

Between these two extreme views is to be the moderate explanation that globalisation has resulted from a combination of factors. One important factor has been the deregulation of the international financial system that has produced a more integrated world economy. In addition, revolutions in technology have seen costs of transport and communication fall dramatically. According to this view, it is the combination of these factors, together with market forces, that has led to the increasingly globalised world in which we live today. Whatever one's view of globalisation, debate about it has raised some serious questions about the viability of fiscal sovereignty and, therefore, the nation state. Proponents of the view that globalisation will see the decline of the nation state would have us believe that globalisation will be the most significant economic factor to shape our future, and the 'death of distance'[7] that results from it will see nations drift off into the twilight of sovereignty, thereby diminishing the role and significance of the state.

Others have taken the contrary view that globalisation has changed nothing and that the world economy was just as integrated in the nineteenth century as it is today. For instance, it can be argued that technologies like the telephone and telegraph unleashed the greatest revolutions in communications since the development of the printing press, annihilating distances between people and shrinking the world further and faster than ever before. While this is certainly true, it can also be argued that the globalisation of today is very different to that of the nineteenth century.[8] Thus, while the transatlantic telegraph allowed rapid communications between major financiers, governments and the like, cheap telecommunications now offer everyone (or at least, everyone with a telephone and a computer) instant access to the world.[9] Indeed, people today use technologies such as the internet to play card games with people on the other side of the world, something which would have been inconceivable in the nineteenth century.

Given these polarised views, it is timely to question whether globalisation will see the decline of fiscal sovereignty and the nation state. The first part of this article will examine the meaning of globalisation, including the rise of the internet and related technologies. The concepts of 'sovereignty' and 'jurisdiction' are central to any study of globalisation and nation states, and the meanings and bounds of these terms in the context of a traditional and integrated (globalised) economy will be explored in

---

7 The phrase used in the book by Frances Cairncross, *The Death of Distance*, 1997.

8 See generally Thomas Friedman, *The Lexus and the Olive Tree*, 1998.

9 Quiggin, above n 2, Review Section 5.

the second part of this paper. The challenges that globalisation presents to sovereignty and jurisdiction will be discussed in relation to various areas of law in the next section of the paper. Particular emphasis will be placed on the challenges presented to taxation laws. Possible policy responses to deal with identified challenges will also be discussed. The final part of the paper examines the central question that this paper seeks to answer – whether globalisation will spell the end to the nation state.

The Meaning of Globalisation and the Rise of the Internet
Globalisation

The process of globalisation can be described as the evolution from a situation of 'economic nationalism' to one of 'international economic integration'.[10] The essential characteristic of such a change is that economic activity occurs on an international, rather than national, level.

In the period of economic nationalism, international trade took place between various economic units that were organised within the boundaries of states:

For some three hundred years, from its emergence in the mid-seventeenth century, the nation state was regarded, rightly, as the dominant actor in international economic relationships. Historically, the state was the primary regulator of its national economic system. The world economy, quite legitimately, could be conceptualised as a set of interlocking national economies. Trade and investment in the world economy were literally 'inter-national'.[11]

Moreover, it has been asserted that the idea of 'borders' or 'boundaries' corresponds with a State's jurisdiction, that is, its right of regulation, which does not necessarily correlate with its actual physical boundaries, although it is often the case because, *inter alia*, of the territorial basis on which jurisdiction can be asserted.[12]

With international economic integration, various economic units have transcended national boundaries and trade occurs in, and is defined by, an international sphere. Rapid advances in telecommunications and associated technologies (especially the internet) have accelerated this trend and

---

10 See generally Ramon J Jeffery, *The Impact of State Sovereignty on Global Trade and International Taxation*, 1999, p. 15.

11 Peter Dicken, *Global Shift: The Internationalisation of Economic Activity*, 1992, p. 148.

12 Jeffery, op. cit., n 10, 16 (footnote 60).

have increasingly rendered insignificant the national boundaries that defined the period of economic nationalism.

The notion of a 'global web', of which the internet is a prime example, is a good analogue of international economic integration. A global web entails the idea of the various actors in the economic process, whether individuals, groups or conglomerations such as transnational corporations, entering into a myriad of different relationships with other actors around the world.[13] These relationships can be broadly characterised either as 'formal' (such as a parent/subsidiary relationship) or 'informal' (such as loose collaborations between people and entities in different parts of the world for a common outcome).

In times of international economic integration, entrepreneurs are building what Negroponte terms 'global cottage industries'.[14] This phrase sounds like an oxymoron, but according to Negroponte, it is not:

To be a multinational company in the past, you had to be huge, with offices around the world capable not only of handling your corporate atoms but dealing with local laws, customs (in both senses of the word) and the physical distribution of products. Today, three people in three different cities can form a company and access a global marketplace.[15]

With appropriate use of technologies (such as intranets[16]), collaborations can lead to the development of software, the designing of a car and the provision of consulting services taking place between different people in several countries. Therefore, an engineer who works in one country can e-mail a colleague in another country (and time zone) and can receive a reply to his request when he comes to work the next day. Virtual corporations and informal joint venture arrangements, which will be able to bring together experience and expertise for particular tasks and outcomes, will become more common as we move to a '24 x 7' environment, where entities are open for business 24 hours per day, 7 days a week.

In sum, the evolution of the transnational corporation and associated developments in transportation and communications technologies are integral threads of this vast global web.[17]

---

13 Ibid, p. 17.

14 Negroponte, p. 237.

15 Ibid.

16 An 'intranet' may be defined as a private network inside a company or organisation that uses the same kinds of software that you would find on the public internet, but that is only for internal use.

17 Robert B Reich, *The Work of Nations: A Blueprint for the Future* (1991) pp. 110–11.

The Rise of the Internet

In many ways, the internet is the epitome of globalisation, with its decentralised and interconnected series of networks that span the globe and render distance and geographical boundaries irrelevant. It is, therefore, instructive to examine some of the salient features of the internet as it relates to globalisation and sovereignty. The transition from an industrial age to a post-industrial or information age has been discussed so much and for so long that we may not have noticed that we are passing into a post-information age.[18] The rise of the internet has been described as the revolutionary transformation in world trade from 'atoms' to 'bits',[19] that is, a move from an industrial world to an information world – a world in which intangibles will increasingly dominate over tangibles.[20]

The industrial age, very much an age of atoms, gave us the concept of mass production, with the economies that come from manufacturing with uniform and repetitious methods in any one given space and time.[21] The information age, commonly associated with the era of computers, displayed the same economies of scale, but with less regard for space and time. The manufacturing of bits could happen anywhere, at any time, and, for example, move among the stock markets on New York, London, and Tokyo as if they were three adjacent machine tools.[22] The information superhighway that we hear so much about is really concerned with the global movement of these weightless bits at the speed of light.[23] It has also given rise to the now often heard phrase 'anything, anytime, anywhere'.

At the same time, and perhaps somewhat paradoxically, the information age is characterised by mass media that is bigger and smaller at the same time, as are governments. For example, Europe finds itself dividing itself into smaller ethnic entities while at the same time trying to unite economically under the auspices of the European Union. In the post-information age, we often have an audience the size of one.[24] It is the period of customisation, with everything being made to order, and information becoming extremely personalised. Many believe that this individualisa-

---

18 Negroponte, p. 163.

19 Ibid., p. 14: 'A bit has no colour, size or weight, and it can travel at the speed of light. It is the smallest atomic element in the DNA of information'.

20 Ibid., p. 4.

21 Ibid., p. 163.

22 Ibid., p. 164.

23 Ibid., p. 12.

24 Ibid., p. 164.

tion is an extrapolation of narrowcasting – you go from a large to a small to a smaller group, ultimately to the individual.[25] The post-information age will increasingly become a 'place without space' where the limitations of geography will be removed. This will mean that there will be less dependence on being in a specific place at a specific time to carry out particular tasks.

Already, teleworking (or telecommuting) is being undertaken by Australian workers; instead of going to work in the city, workers are logging into their computers and carrying out their work from home. As at May 1999, there were 587,000 adults in Australia (7 per cent of all employed adults) who were able to access an employer's computer from home through a modem.[26] An estimated 412,000 of these (70 per cent) have an agreement with their employer to work from home.[27]

Knowledge workers (doctors, lawyers, consultants) who are not dependent on time and place will be able to take advantage of new technologies such as the internet and decouple themselves from geography. Already remote diagnosis and telemedicine are emerging as examples of these possibilities. This is planned to extend to the provision of advice via teleconferencing facilities, to web-based communication between doctors, hospitals and pharmacies, and to the use of e-mail by GPs to keep up with developments in the profession.[28] In the future, writers and money managers may find it more appealing to be in the Caribbean or South Pacific while preparing their manuscripts or managing their funds.[29]

This paradox of distance has led Negroponte to conclude that time zones will probably play a bigger role in our digital future than trade zones.[30] This view is supported by Cairncross, who asserts that it will not be long before people across the globe will organise their work on the basis of language and three time shifts – one for the Americas, one for Europe and one for East Asia and Australia.[31]

---

25 Ibid.

26 Australian Bureau of Statistics, 3 Million Internet Purchases and 1.5 Million Households Online – ABS, Media Release 106/99 (6 September 1999). Available at <http://wwww. abs. gov.au> (copy on file with author).

27 Ibid.

28 John Breusch, 'The Bare Facts of E-Health', The Australian Financial Review, Sydney, 1 October 1999.

29 Negroponte, p. 166.

30 Ibid., p. 228.

31 Cairncross, op. cit., n 7.

In summary, the internet represents the quintessential example of global-isation. Because of its unique characteristics, it presents many challenges to the sovereignty of nations. Several of these challenges arise from the fact that most laws were conceived in and for a world of atoms, not bits, and these laws tended to be local and physical. The difficulty of isolating where activities take place on the internet, combined with the intangible nature of goods and services provided over the internet and the anonymity that the internet provides, presents formidable challenges for any legal system. These challenges will be examined in more detail once the con-cepts of sovereignty and jurisdiction are explained in the next section.

Sovereignty and Jurisdiction

The concepts of 'sovereignty' and 'jurisdiction' are central to any study of globalisation and nation states, and the implications of these concepts in the context of a traditional and integrated (globalised) economy will be explored in this part of the paper.

Sovereignty

Sovereignty refers to the bundle of rights and competencies which go to make up the nation state.[32] It is therefore analogous to statehood. Con-sistent with rights normally attributable to statehood, a nation state should possess the following qualifications: (a) a permanent population; (b) a defined territory; (c) government; and (d) the capacity to enter into relations with other states.

Sovereignty is determined by two factors as observed by Franck: 'The power of the sovereign state can be bound by its own constitution ... and by international law'.[33] This reflects the dual dimension of sovereignty – that is, the power of a sovereign state is bound by its own constitution (the internal dimension of sovereignty) and by international law (the external dimension of sovereignty).

Jurisdiction

Jurisdiction refers to a state's right of regulation manifested in its judicial, administrative and, perhaps most importantly, legislative competence.[34]

---

32 Jeffery, op. cit., n 10, p. 26.

33 Thomas M Franck, *Fairness in International Law and Institutions*, 1995, p. 446.

34 Jeffery, op. cit., note 10, p. 26. Also, as noted by Beale, 'The power of a sovereign to affect the rights of persons, whether by legislation, by executive decree, or by the judgment of a court, is called jurisdiction': J. H. Beale, 'The Jurisdiction of a Sovereign State' (1922–23) 36 *Harvard Law Review* 241.

In other words, jurisdiction refers to particular rights of the total bundle of rights that comprise statehood.[35] As it is a subset of sovereignty, it follows that jurisdiction cannot extend further than sovereignty. Traditionally, jurisdiction is established by reference to either the territorial or personal bases of jurisdiction.[36] The personal base of jurisdiction is founded on the nationality or domicile of a person as a connecting factor.

The territorial basis of jurisdiction is the most commonly referred to approach in establishing jurisdictional connections under the traditional approach. Territorial jurisdiction refers to regulation over persons and things within the geographical boundaries of a state. For example, in relation to taxation laws (fiscal jurisdiction), income that has its source or is derived by a person within a territory, is subject to taxation in that territory, as the requisite territorial (geographical) nexus is satisfied.

The territorial theory of jurisdiction has been summarised by Mann in the following terms:

(1) As every nation possesses an exclusive sovereignty and jurisdiction within its own territory, the laws of every State affect and bind directly all property, whether real or personal, within its territory; and all persons who are resident within it, whether natural-born subjects or aliens; and also all contracts made and acts done within it.

(2) No State can, by its laws, directly affect or bind property out of its own territory or bind its own subjects by its own laws in every other place.[37]

Used in this context, the concept of territory is defined in the sense of a geographical area – that is, as a physical concept. Brownlie notes that the word territory in 'a legal context denotes a particular sphere of legal competence and not a geographical concept'.[38] Despite this, territory has very much been interpreted in a physical, geographical, bricks and mortar sense.

Evaluation of the Territorial Basis of Jurisdiction in a Traditional and Integrated (Globalised) Economy

Having explained the meaning of sovereignty and jurisdiction, it is instructive to compare how these concepts apply to the period of econ-

---

35 Ibid.

36 There are three other bases of establishing jurisdiction under the traditional approach: (a) the Protective Principle, (b) the Passive Personality Principle; and (c) Universal Jurisdiction. A detailed consideration of these principles is beyond the scope of this article, but a discussion of these principles may be found in R. Higgins, 'The Legal Bases of Jurisdiction' in Cecil J Olmstead (ed.), *The Extraterritorial Application of Laws and Responses Thereto*, 1984, p. 3.

37 Fritz A. Mann, *Studies in International Law*, 1973, p. 20.

38 Ian Brownlie, *Principles of Public International Law*, 1990, p. 116.

omic nationalism (traditional economy) and the period of international economic integration (globalised economy).

When one considers the period of economic nationalism, economic activity mainly took place within the physical (territorial) boundaries of a state. It therefore was sensible, and reflected reality, that jurisdiction during this period was established by looking at matters that took place within the territory. However, when one moves forward to a globalised world and the period of international economic integration, frontier-based regulatory regimes that rely on physical concepts and geographical boundaries to determine jurisdiction are called into question. There is also the problem of how the territorial basis of jurisdiction can cope with the fleeting presence of individuals within a territory.[39]

In short, in the period of international economic integration, greater mobility of capital, people and trade is experienced, with a consequent rise in cross-border activities. This will mean that states will be left trying to assert jurisdiction over transactions and events that have links with the asserting state that are much more tenuous and difficult to establish than was the case before these developments, in the period of economic nationalism. It will be the purpose of the next section of this paper to articulate more particularly these challenges, looking at various areas of law, particularly the challenges presented to taxation laws. The paper will then seek to answer the central question addressed – whether the nation state can survive the challenges presented by a globalised world.

Challenges Presented by Globalisation

With the advent of globalisation and the rise of new technologies, we increasingly find ourselves as participants in global markets, and also in cybermarkets. Laws have been traditionally designed through democratic political processes that have given rise to laws that are essentially national. These laws are normally enforced within national frameworks. In other words, we have developed a system of frontier-based legal and regulatory systems.

In a globalised economy, and indeed in the cybermarket, frontiers or national boundaries mean very little, and the validity of nation-based laws are therefore called into question. This sentiment is echoed in Negroponte's words: 'Laws were conceived in and for a world of atoms, not bits'.[40] This section of the paper examines the challenges presented to

---

39 Jeffery, op. cit., n 10, p. 48.

40 Negroponte, p. 8.

traditional laws by new technologies and the globalisation of the economy. If it is shown that traditional laws are of no practical use in a globalised world, people may indeed question the utility of nation states. In other words, if a nation state cannot protect the interests of the groups that comprise its political community, then its purpose is in doubt.[41] This issue will be addressed in the last part of this paper.

Consumer Protection Laws

A good starting point for examining the challenges presented by globalisation and new technologies is to examine the operation of consumer protection laws in an integrated economy. Consumer protection laws represent a prototypical example of laws that have been predicated on the existence and operation of nation states. In the context of a globalised economy, there is uncertainty about the existence of reliable mechanisms to redress a number of situations, including:

♦ What would occur if a product ordered through the internet never arrives?

♦ What would happen if goods ordered over the internet turn out to be defective?

♦ How would unfair market practices apply (such as misleading and deceptive conduct)?[42]

♦ How would infringements on privacy be controlled? For example, using appropriate technologies, including 'electronic footprints'[43] and 'cookies',[44] it is now possible for merchants to collate and 'mine' data on the internet, revealing people's browsing and consumption patterns.

♦ How would the unauthorised use of data be controlled?

A final illustration of the uncertainties and the challenges in this area is

---

41 John Goldring, 'Consumer Protection, the Nation-State, Law, Globalization and Democracy', 1996, 2(2) *Journal of Computer-Mediated Communication* <http:wwww.ascjsc.org/jcmc/vol2/issue2/goldring.html> (Copy on file with author).

42 In Australia, the Australian Competition and Consumer Commission (ACCC) has teamed up with the US Federal Trade Commission (FTC) to crack down on a global internet scam which takes unsuspecting users to pornographic web sites then takes control of the user's browser, repeatedly bringing up more pornographic pages. Commonly referred to as a 'mousetrapping' or 'pagejacking', the ACCC believes the conduct breaches the Trade Practices Act 1974 (Cth) as it is misleading or deceptive conduct: The Online Australia Update, 27 September 1999 <http://www.onlineaustralia.net.au> (Copy on file with author).

43 These are essentially the traces someone leaves behind when moving (surfing) from one web site to another.

44 Information stored in the consumer's hard drive which can show which sites have been visited.

the story of how in 1995 Virgin Atlantic Airways was fined $14,000 by the US Department of Transportation for placing misleading advertising on the Internet.[45] A statement was made on its Web page that a certain fare for a designated sector was available when, in reality, the lowest fare for that sector was much higher. While the outcome of this case seems encouraging to consumers, it leaves other questions unanswered, such as problems in identifying where misleading advertising occurs in an internet environment. Determining who is the proper defendant(s) could also prove difficult. In this case, Virgin Atlantic was the defendant, but what about the host of the web site, the Internet Service Provider and others? In other words, where should the line of liability be drawn? In all the above cases, it is easy to appreciate that the application of existing laws is at best tenuous and consumers might find themselves left without a suitable legal remedy in cross-border electronic transactions. Globalised economies and new technologies afford new opportunities for transnational marketing practices that may simply ignore the restrictions created by national consumer protection laws.

US Anti-trust Laws

US anti-trust laws challenge concepts of sovereignty and jurisdiction by trying to proscribe activities occurring outside its geographical boundaries by persons who are neither residents nor citizens of the USA.[46] In so doing, US policy-makers do not wish to concede that their laws can be thwarted simply because the forbidden acts occur outside the USA and the actors are not US citizens.[47]

This 'long-arm' approach is in contrast to the traditional 'waters-edge' stance taken by most countries, which confine the operation of such laws to the territory of the legislating state and to individuals over whom the state exerts effective control. Attempts by countries to apply such laws either to non-citizens or to activities outside its territorial borders is seen as an encroachment of national sovereignty. The validity of the purported exercise of jurisdiction in this situation would also have to be questioned in the light of public international law. Despite this, the USA continues to assert its sovereignty in these situations so long as the activities in question impact on businesses in the USA – a very weak basis upon

---

45 Jim Carroll, 'Lawsuit Sends a Wake Up Call to Senior Management', 1995, 21(26)
    Computing Canada 28. Also Paul Taylor, 'Virgin Air Fined for False Ad on the Internet',
    National Post, Canada, 24 November 1996, p. 7.

46 Goldring, op. cit., n 41, p. 4.

47 Ibid, p. 5.

which to justify the exercise of legislative jurisdiction. This scepticism is shared by a leading international lawyer.[48]

Copyright Law

It is widely accepted that many challenges are presented to traditional copyright laws by new technologies such as the internet. Some have already branded the laws relating to copyright as being totally out-of-date, a 'Guttenberg artefact'.[49] Concerns about copyright infringement normally relate to the ease of making copies. In a digital world, there are issues beyond the easy ways in which copies can be made. In a digital world, a bigger concern is that copies can be exact, and with appropriate computing technologies (such as error correction technology) can in fact be better than the original. In addition, the marginal cost of producing an extra copy is minimal or close to zero. For example, once a piece of software is created and uploaded onto an internet site, the cost of delivering to one person or 100 people is the same – a point and a click and it is simply downloaded. Reading a newspaper article and sending it to either one person or 100 people takes only a few keystrokes and costs nothing.

Recent and protracted legal proceedings in relation to downloading music over the internet illustrate the escalating problems in this area. This has led some commentators to observe that in a digital world, the medium is no longer the message, but merely represents the embodiment of it.[50]

Defamation, Obscenity and Censorship Laws

Existing laws governing defamation and obscenity should apply equally in a globalised world, though determining where an offence has been committed, and so under whose jurisdiction it comes, is problematical given the nebulous nature of the internet. Censorship laws are easily circumvented by technologies such as the internet.

Retail Trade Regulation and Other Licensing Laws

In the face of a globalised world, one has to also question the applicability of retail trade regulations designed, like other laws, for a bricks and

---

48 Higgins, op. cit., n 36, pp. 7–13.

49 Negroponte, p. 58.

50 Ibid., pp. 61, 71.

mortar world. These laws include regulation restrictions on matters such as the size of stores and opening hours, limitations on pricing and promotion, granting of monopolies for the sale of certain products (such as liquor) and permit and other licensing requirements.

Similar concerns arise in other occupations and professions that have licensing rules, as they tend to be nation-based. For example, if a doctor who is registered in Brazil provides telemedicine services over the internet to someone in Australia, the question arises as to whether the doctor would need to be registered in Australia and other countries to which he provides his services over the internet. If so, questions as to how this would be facilitated, co-ordinated and controlled would arise.

Taxation Laws

The power to tax has traditionally been regarded as an exercise of sovereign power. Sovereignty in this context has been interpreted to mean that in the absence of an agreement or treaty arrangements, the courts of another country will not recognise or enforce revenue judgments or orders made by courts of other countries.[51]

The best explanation of the theoretical basis of the rule is that given by Lord Keith of Avonholm in *Government of India v Taylor*.[52] His view was that the enforcement of the taxation laws of one country by another country would be an extension of the sovereign power that imposes the taxes, and to assert sovereign authority by one state within the territory of another would be contrary to all concepts of independent sovereignties.

The exercise of this sovereign power to tax has been questioned in the light of an increasingly globalised economy and also new technologies, such as the internet. So what has changed so radically that calls into question the operation of existing laws? The challenges presented by globalised economies and new technologies to taxation laws will first be examined, followed by possible policy responses to address these challenges.

The Challenges

While many would argue that globalisation is not new, the pace of integration of national economies has quickened. As seen above, this trend

51 In the UK, Australia, Canada and most Commonwealth countries the decisions by the Privy Council in *Sirdar Gurdyal Singh v Rajah of Faridkote* [1894] AC 679 and *Attorney-General (New Zealand) v Ortiz* [1984] AC 1 and the House of Lords in *Government of India v Taylor* [1955] AC 491 still represent the law.

52 [1955] AC 491, 511.

has been accentuated by the removal of restrictions on investment flows and improved communications technologies, as well as the development of regional trading blocs. This has led to greater mobility of capital and also savings. The benefits to the world economy of these changes are clear enough – liberalisation of financial markets improves the international allocation of savings and capital, thereby reducing the cost of capital to firms. The concern is that tax systems, particularly international tax systems, have not always kept pace with these developments.

It is widely feared that the gradual liberalisation of financial markets and globalisation will make international capital flows more sensitive to differences in the tax regimes as between countries and will therefore lead to tax competition. The concern here is that intensified tax competition will lead to an erosion of the worldwide tax base and a 'race to the bottom' as countries adjust their tax rates to align with other competitors.

The recent Review of Business Taxation in Australia (the Ralph Review) recognised these concerns and had as one of its prime objectives to improve the competitiveness and efficiency of Australian business while providing a secure source of revenue for government.[53] In the words of John Ralph, the Chairman of the review:

We are living in a time of unparalleled change. Australia must have a taxation system which equips it for the coming decades, not for those that have passed.[54]

Responding to intensified tax competition, Ralph observed:

Increasing globalisation will translate into an increasingly competitive environment for Australian business. The impact of the telecommunications revolution and associated technologies, in diminishing the significance of national boundaries, will make more businesses feel the chill wind of much stiffer competition. We may remain an island geographically [isolated] but we will not be able to hide from the forces generated by globalisation.[55]

Apart from an announced proposal to reduce the company tax rate to 30 per cent to bring Australia's rate more into line with the rates of other countries in the Asia-Pacific region, Ralph announced proposed changes to the capital gains tax regime, again with tax competition considerations in mind:

---

53 John Ralph, 'A Tax System by Design Rather Than Accident', *Business Review Weekly*, Melbourne, 24 September 1999, 34.

54 John Ralph, Chairman's Introduction to *Review of Business Taxation: A Tax System Redesigned* (1999) <http://www.rbt.treasury.gov.au> (Copy on file with author).

55 Ibid.

A more competitive capital gains regime to encourage investment, particularly to attract highly mobile international capital for which there is strong and increasing competition, to encourage entrepreneurs to start new businesses in Australia, and to achieve a better functioning capital market.[56]

In summary, the Ralph Review announced its proposed changes to the company tax rate and capital gains tax in response to the considerations of intensified competition for highly mobile capital and the need it perceived for a better functioning capital market in an increasingly globalised world.

Leaving considerations of intensified tax competition aside, the sheer speed and borderless mobility of transactions in the globalised economy has called into question the ability to apply traditional transactional analysis inherent in transfer pricing laws. Transfer pricing laws allow revenue authorities to adjust the income of parties to international transactions (for example, multinational enterprises) to prevent the diversion of income from high-tax jurisdictions to low-tax jurisdictions (for example, tax havens). With no national borders, work on the same project can be undertaken in several countries, with intranets allowing the sharing of information. These new collaborative opportunities produce many challenges in applying traditional methods underlying transfer pricing rules. While globalisation and electronic commerce may not necessarily present any unique problems for transfer pricing, the growth of electronic commerce will be likely to make some of the transfer pricing problems more common.

Tax treaty concepts (such as permanent establishment) are also challenged by globalisation and new technologies. The combination of the internet and globalisation has allowed taxpayers to operate internationally for low cost, 24 hours a day, 7 days a week. Global communication systems will see an increase in cross-border activities and may dispense with the need for businesses to maintain a physical presence (for example, a sales force or distribution network) to do business in a country. In a business sense, this means that simple and cheap access to global markets will be available and that barriers of distance and location have disappeared. In a legal sense, it puts pressure on concepts such as 'permanent establishment' contained in most double tax agreements, as it relies on the existence of a physical presence (for example, an office or factory).

In relation to the jurisdiction to tax, jurisdiction has traditionally been based on geographical territorial connections. Generally, therefore, entities or individuals need to be geographically located (resident) or the

---

56 Ibid 2.

source of income needs to be located in a country for jurisdiction to be asserted. Practical jurisdiction depends on an identified taxpayer (and also assets) being located in a jurisdiction. While it may be argued that jurisdictional rules have always been a problem for revenue authorities, they have been relatively contained, but now even smaller organisations can trade and bank globally, and location and identity become more difficult to determine.

A simple example illustrates the problems of attempting to apply traditional jurisdictional rules is trying to determine a company's central management and control, and thereby its residence, in a globalised world. This determination may become problematical where a board of directors can meet electronically from a number of different locations via videoconferencing facilities. It is not inconceivable that in this situation it may be difficult to isolate the location of central management and control to one specific location. Also, virtual corporations can be created to carry out a particular task or venture, thereby putting further pressure on rules created for an established physical presences, rather than transient presences.

Similarly, new technologies can weaken the relationship between services provided and their location. For example, physicians can now remotely diagnose patients via the internet, and an ever-increasing number of workers can now telecommute with their employers, thereby reducing the need for a physical presence at their workplace.

In sum, the absence of borders and the lack of border controls undermines the jurisdictional rules of source and residency as they are currently formulated and applied. This is because transactions on the internet occur everywhere, but nowhere in particular, or as one writer has put it 'the trouble with cyberspace ... is that there's no "there" there'.[57] A related problem posed by globalisation and the internet is the anonymity it offers and the difficulty of isolating where a transaction occurs.

More pressure is brought to bear on tax laws by the intangible nature of many goods and services that can be delivered via the internet. This challenges traditional rules relating to the characterisation of income as it blurs distinctions between the sale of goods, provision of services and royalties. This in turn impacts on source rules underlying various taxation regimes. For example, if one looks at the simple example of the sale of an encyclopaedia, in a traditional sale (such as books), the income would be classified as sales income. Likewise, if the encyclopaedia is provided on a

---

57 R. Resnick, 'Cybertort: The New Era', 1994, *National Law Journal*, A1.

CD-ROM, a similar result would probably ensue. But if the encyclopaedia is provided via online access, the classification becomes more difficult – is it sales income or services income?

Up to now, the ability to move capital across national borders and access offshore financial centres has been limited to an elite of high-wealth individuals. In many ways, the problem was contained because it required a great deal of international mobility and expensive advice to exploit it and so at most it led to a fraying at the edges of the tax base. Now, the pace of globalisation, combined with new technologies, has made capital more mobile and therefore increased the accessibility of offshore centres, which have become easier to locate and cheaper to access. And while it may be argued that no major changes to laws were needed in the past (as any activity was marginal), when this activity becomes mainstream, more attention needs to be given to it and tax rules need to take account of it.

Already the effect of a more mobile capital base has exerted pressure on other taxes (such as gambling and funds transfers), where the impacts of globalisation have already been felt. Apart from differences between tax rates and tax bases that may produce distortions in the patters of production and trade, the integration of the world economy gives rise to other problems. One is that it becomes more difficult to determine which country is entitled to tax a particular transaction and a related difficulty is that practical enforcement can also be problematic, especially if an entity has no physical presence or assets in a jurisdiction in which it transacts its business. These problems are exacerbated by the fact that investigative and enforcement powers typically stop at the border of a country and rely on co-operation with other nations to have any force.

In conclusion, it may be stated that the current tax systems of many countries reflect a period (before, during and immediately after the Second World War) when economies were closed and capital movements were much more limited. Today, the assumption of a closed economy has become increasingly anachronistic. The internet's capacity to transform the world into global communities may see the displacement of some national law, as technology reduces the significance of sovereignty. Electronic commerce is difficult to contain within geographically defined trade areas and frontier-based regulatory regimes. In a period of economic nationalism, laws were *prima facie* territorial and this reflected the general correspondence between physical space and law space. That is, geographical borders make sense in a physical world. In an integrated economy, however, territorial-based laws come under pressure, as geographical borders have little significance.

Responses to the Challenges

In trying to develop solutions for the challenges presented to taxation laws by an integrated economy, one can consider the applicability of four basic competing models for the governance of the internet as put forward by Johnson and Post.[58]

First, Johnson and Post suggest that existing sovereigns can simply seek to extend their jurisdiction and amend their laws as necessary in an attempt to govern all actions on the internet that have substantial impacts on their own citizens. In other words, under this approach, countries could simply seek to unilaterally modify their rules to try to preserve their revenue bases. This policy stance is, however, fraught with danger – as John Donne once cautioned, 'No man is an island, entire of itself; every man is a piece of the Continent, a part of the main'. Donne's aphorism, suitably adapted, may be that no national tax system is separate from the main and therefore unilateral measures which do not have regard for other countries' systems will cause more problems than they solve, including the possibility of double taxation.

Under the second model, sovereigns could seek out bilateral or multilateral agreements to establish new and uniform rules specifically applicable to conduct on the internet. Again, this model has specific problems, including the considerable competition between countries, how to deal with countries that remain outside the treaty system, the unequal international playing field that exists in treaty negotiations, not to mention the expense and time involved in trying to negotiate such treaties.

The third model seeks to create a new international organisation to establish new rules for governance and also a new means of enforcing those rules and of holding those who make the rules accountable to its stakeholders. This may be described as a centralised model and seeks to overcome the chief problem with regulating a medium like the internet – the lack of a central locus of control or leverage point that one can seek to regulate.

And it is true that at present there is no World Tax Organisation – a GATT for Taxes – charged with the responsibility of establishing desirable rules for taxation and with enough power to induce countries to obey them. Some would suggest that it is time to establish such an institution. However, one should not be too sanguine about the possibility of such an

---

58 David R. Johnson and David G. Post, 'And How Shall the Net be Governed?', 1996,
Cyberspace Law Institute <http://www.cli.org/emdraft.html> (Copy on file with author) [1].
The ensuing discussion on this point is adapted from this source.

institution emerging easily or quickly. Political difficulties aside, there would be problems in obtaining agreement on the set of rules; it would also be difficult to reach consensus on the constitution and powers of such an institution.

Also, the desirability of adopting this model has been called into question by some as:

[t]he bottleneck characteristic of any centralized law-making machinery, and the natural frailties of law-making processes based on writing authoritative texts make centralized systems unsuitable for tackling a diverse, rapidly changing, large scale set of problems like those posed by the net.[59]

The first three models put forward may be described as 'top-down' centralised models, while the fourth model seeks to adopt a decentralised solution to attack a decentralised medium, like the internet. Essentially, this model would involve the voluntary acceptance of codes or standards on a decentralised, emergent basis. The argument here is that:

the same decentralized decision-making that created the net at a technical level may be able to create a workable and, indeed, empowering and just form of order even at the highest level of the protocol stack – the realm of rules applica ble to the collective social evaluation and governance of human behavior.[60]

This last model therefore argues for a self-regulatory structure, by means of decentralised emergent law-making. In support of this proposal are those who favour minimalist regulation and interference with a medium that should be allowed to develop without undue regulatory interference. It is also argued that this approach would save considerable resources that might otherwise have been spent on trying, perhaps without greater success, to adopt other means of regulation. Opponents of this regime would, however, argue that less formal mechanisms will not work and will ultimately lead to complete chaos and unmitigated disasters in the international tax arena.

While all these models have a theoretical attractiveness, they may be impractical utopian hopes as existing sovereigns are not about to give up their law-making powers, especially when revenue is at stake. As alternatives to adopting models in the area of taxation, perhaps countries will seek out new taxes. In recent times, a carbon tax, the Tobin tax and bit taxes have been discussed. It is worth briefly examining these proposals.

The carbon tax proposal, commonly dubbed an 'energy tax' or 'green tax',

---

59 Ibid [25].

60 Ibid [18].

has gained currency in recent times on the basis of an increased public awareness of environmental issues (including the greenhouse effect), even ignoring the benefits of such a tax from a public-finance point of view. At the same time, there are considerable political sensitivities about such a proposal. Big companies such as Alcoa, Western Mining Corporation and BHP are all very nervous about such proposals and the effects it could have on their cost structures. If the tax is introduced, these companies have threatened to close down their Australian-based operations, as they would no longer be viable in terms of rising costs.[61]

External pressures for the implementation of a carbon tax have arisen from an agreement reached at a conference in the Japanese city of Kyoto in 1997 (the 'Kyoto Protocol'). Under this agreement, most of the world's industrialised countries agreed to a formula aimed at limiting the production of problem gases produced by each country (mainly carbon dioxide, methane and nitrous oxide). The dilemma now is how to apply the protocol in Australia, and whether Australia should attempt to lead the world in cutting gas emissions where other industrialised countries, notably the USA, are not rushing to embrace the protocol.[62]

So while a carbon tax may become a self-fulfilling prophecy, the real issue for Australia may be how green can it afford to be? The Tobin tax initiative[63] is a proposal to tax currency transactions on foreign exchange markets through multilateral co-operation. Essentially a transaction tax on currency speculation, the purpose of the tax is to discourage volatile short-term or speculative trading. On that basis, non-speculative transactions would be exempt. Notwithstanding the simple attractiveness of applying a low rate of tax on a wide base that would generate considerable revenue, there are difficulties with such a proposal. These include definitional problems (such as what a 'speculative transaction' is) and the raft of problems associated with trying to achieve multilateral agreement on any issue, especially revenue matters.

Finally, a bit tax (essentially a tax on the flow of information) has been suggested in recent times as a measure that would be suitable to reflect changes in the economy at large. That is, as the economy has changed from an industrial economy to an information economy, proponents of a bit tax would argue that consideration should be given to adjust the tax system to reflect this shift. Despite the strength of economic arguments

---

61 Tim Treadgold, 'Industries Threaten to Flee a Costly Carbon-Tax Regime', *Business Review Weekly*, Melbourne, 24 September 1999, 44.

62 Ibid., 45.

63 The name 'Tobin tax' derives from James Tobin, a Nobel-laureate economist at Yale University.

that would support such a tax, and also the simplicity of it, the bit tax has been almost universally rejected.

In the end, the short-term policy response in the taxation area may be for countries to take the path of least resistance, and simply shift their tax base from footloose factors, such as profits and savings, toward consumption and labour.[64] But in a world of mobile capital, it may be difficult to tax goods and services sold over the internet. A disturbing consequence, therefore, is that labour is likely to bear a growing share of the tax burden – especially unskilled workers who are least mobile.[65] If this happens, it may lead to the plutocratic society referred to above.

Another target for taxation may be property. In years gone by, property taxes, such as land taxes, were major sources of revenue. Dependence on property taxes has steadily reduced over time. It may be that in a globalised society, where mobility is greatly increased, governments may have to seek to tax more heavily immovable physical presences, such as property.

Conclusions: Is it the End of the Nation State?

The central question that this paper seeks to answer is whether globalisation will spell the end of the nation state. The process of globalisation was explained in the first part of the paper, followed by a discussion of the concepts of sovereignty and jurisdiction. In the third part of the paper, the challenges that globalisation and new technologies present to sovereignty and jurisdiction were examined, with a particular focus on the challenges presented to taxation laws. In light of those challenges, a compelling case can be made to support the argument that globalisation may spell the end of the nation state.

It was observed that laws have evolved through essentially national frameworks, and represent the outcome of democratic political processes within nation states. If it is shown that these laws have little practical use in a globalised world, this raises the question of what functions may remain for democratic politics and nation states.

It is widely accepted that the role of the nation state has changed considerably as we have moved from an era of economic nationalism into a period of international economic integration. Accepting this position, and in light of the challenges that globalisation presents to sovereignty

---

64 The Economist, 'The Taxpayer Vanishes', *The Australian*, Sydney, 4 June 1997.

65 Ibid.

and jurisdiction, it is easy to conclude that the nation state is becoming increasingly irrelevant as the economy continues to globalise and new technologies dominate the commercial landscape.

However, against this conclusion the author prefers to take the view that the nation state has not become an irrelevance and that it will survive the onset of globalisation and the continued (and rapid) emergence of new technologies.

The transition from a period of economic nationalism to international economic integration has seen the emergence of a number of challenges to sovereignty and jurisdiction, largely and simply because economic activity is structured and occurs on the international, rather than national level. To respond to this evolution, nation states have two broad policy options open to them:

They can try and cling to the mirage of absolute sovereignty ... or alternatively they can regard self-interest as inextricably entwined in the mutual interest in acclimatising to the changes in the global economy which are taking place, through co-ordinated action at the national and international levels.[66]

While the choices appear clear enough, the reality is that nation states are reluctant to cede sovereignty, especially in revenue matters. This attitude manifests a fundamental assumption that sovereignty is to be equated with empowerment and conversely that cession or restriction of it is to be associated with disempowerment.[67]

However, absolute sovereignty is largely illusory and this is illustrated well by what has come to be known as Hobbes' paradox. According to Hobbes, if men were to hold on to all their rights and liberties and be able to do as they wish (i.e. exercise absolute sovereignty), this would necessarily imply the right to invade other men's rights, leading to a state of anarchy or war.[68] In reality, equilibrium or peace can only be achieved when there is a mutual laying down of rights for mutual benefit.[69] Hobbes paradoxically asserts, therefore, that in fact giving up sovereignty can lead to empowerment (by harnessing mutual benefits), while retaining it can actually lead to disempowerment.

One can extrapolate Hobbes' paradox to nation states in a globalised economy – that is, if nation states are to achieve mutual benefits and

---

66 Jeffery, op. cit., n 10, p. 23.

67 Ibid., p. 21.

68 Ibid.

69 Thomas Hobbes, *Leviathan*, 1991, p. 92.

adapt to the new global world, there can be no room for the exercise of absolute sovereignty. Rather, the mutual laying down of rights by nation states, by means of cession or restriction of sovereignty, has to be done in a manner which is tailored to the new global forces so that the harnessing of mutual benefits can be maximised.[70] Consistent with this is the assertion that nation states will give up or cede sovereign rights if they can secure mutual advantages for their citizens – that is, their decision to give up sovereignty will be guided by the benefits that accrue to the individuals making up the nation state.

While the author believes that nation states will ultimately come to the above realisation, it is accepted that this will not occur uniformly, clearly or quickly but will represent an evolutionary policy change eventually leading to the situation described above. Indeed, in the short term, it may be expected that nation states will do nothing or very little, as they cling dearly to their cherished rights of sovereignty and jurisdiction. This may be from fear or simply from a desire to retain the positive outcomes that may accrue to nation states as a result of the deregulation that is consequent upon the forces of globalisation. For example, it may be expected that countries such as the USA that currently dominate the internet environment and are net exporters of technology will do little to push for changes in regulation of the internet, as the current situation gives them substantial economic benefits.

In the medium term, one would expect fragmented approaches by countries (on either a unilateral or bilateral basis), as it becomes evident that their laws and revenues are no longer on a stable platform to deliver the economic and legal benefits expected from them. During this period, nation states will start to come to the realisation that they need to take active steps to continue to exercise their sovereign powers (especially on taxation) and their rights of jurisdiction.

Ultimately, there will be a need for co-ordinated multilateral action to overcome the inconsistencies that arise from fragmented approaches. Many see the attainment of such consensus as 'an impractical utopian hope'.[71] However, while it is easy to adopt this view, perhaps there is too much scepticism about the possibility of achieving multilateral consensus.

One only has to go back to the 1920s when the League of Nations first undertook to study ways to avoid international double tax. Much of this work is now embodied in tax treaties developed by the OECD and UN.

---

70 Jeffery, op. cit., n 10, pp. 21–2.

71 D. A. Ward, 'Abuse of Tax Treaties', *Intertax*, 1995, 181, pp. 177.

This shows that despite sovereignty, it is possible to reach international consensus.

Another example of multilateral co-operation is The Nordic Pact Multilateral Convention on Administrative Assistance in Tax Matters[72] which has been described as 'the most far-reaching form of co-operation between tax authorities at present in existence'.[73] However, this statement needs to be tempered by the fact that the success of this agreement is probably due largely to its regional nature:

This far-reaching form of co-operation seems to have been made possible by the resemblances between the participating States in various fields, in particular mutually understood languages, similar legal systems, and the fact that most participants had already been co-operating intensively for some years under bilateral assistance agreements.[74]

Two other examples of multilateral co-operation may be noted here. The first is an EU Directive covering mutual assistance, which provides for the exchange of information based on that contained in Article 26 of the OECD Model Tax Convention, but at the same time, does not provide for the enforcement of foreign revenue laws in another state.[75]

Finally, the joint Council of Europe/OECD Multilateral Convention on Mutual Administrative Assistance in Tax Matters of 1988, represents another example of a multilateral initiative. This Convention, which came into force on 1 April 1995, has not been embraced by many countries (including Australia), probably because of its perceived breadth, in that it contains provisions allowing for the exercise of enforcement by one state in the territory of another.[76] At the same time, signatory states can limit their involvement when signing such conventions, so such concerns may be overstated.

In summary, it is submitted that while globalisation and new technologies continue to exert pressure on the concepts of sovereignty and jurisdic-

---

72 Entered into in 1972 between Denmark, Finland, Iceland, Norway and Sweden.

73 W. B. Westerburgen, 'Ways and Means to Improve European and Wider International Co-Operation Against Tax Evasion and Avoidance, Including Those Proposed in Recommendation 833 (1978) of the Parliamentary Assembly', *European Taxation* 1980, 168, 172.

74 Ibid.

75 Council Directive of 19 December 1977 Concerning Mutual Assistance by the Competent Authorities of the Member States in the Field of Direct Taxation.

76 Article 11 provides that the requested state shall take steps to recover foreign claims as if it were its own. Article 17 provides for the sending of tax demands abroad.

tion, the nation state can work symbiotically with, rather than against, these forces. It must be remembered that the forces that benefit most from globalisation (large multinational enterprises) are predicated upon and constantly require support from the legal systems of nation states.[77] Businesses and consumers similarly depend on nation states to underpin commerce by providing 'last resort' mechanisms for enforcing contracts and bringing legal certainty (and trust) to the marketplace.[78] Therefore, despite the pressures created by globalisation and new technologies, it is submitted that the nation state will emerge as the enduring custodian of jurisdiction and sovereignty, both of which will have undergone necessary changes and evolutions along the way.

---

77 Goldring, op. cit., n 41, p. 12.

78 Ibid.

International
Tax Competition
in Business Services

The OECD Harmful Tax Competition Initiative[1]

Michael P. Devereux

Introduction

In April 1998, the OECD published a report, *Harmful Tax Competition: An Emerging Global Issue*. The report contained 19 recommendations to counter what it saw as the 'harmful' tax competition of capital income. Subsequently, the OECD set up the Forum on Harmful Tax Practices to oversee the implementation of the recommendations. The first main output of this work was published in June 2000, in a second OECD report, *Towards Global Tax Co-operation: Progress in Identifying and Eliminating Harmful Tax Practices*.

This paper briefly summarises these two reports. It goes on to consider a number of issues which arise. The first is the underlying rationale for the OECD's approach. This has several components. For example, is there a case for not taxing capital income? What are supposed to be the aims of the process? Does the notion that tax competition can be separated into forms which are 'harmful' and others which are, by implication, 'not harmful' have any rational basis? Clearly one factor in the OECD's approach is a concern about 'significant revenue losses'.[2] A further part of this paper therefore examines patterns of tax revenue on the income from capital in OECD countries, and explores the extent to which revenue losses have become a significant problem for OECD countries. The report goes on to consider the implications for jurisdictions which are labelled by the OECD as either 'co-operative' or 'unco-operative' 'tax havens'.

The OECD Initiative

In its 1998 Report, the OECD distinguished two forms of 'harmful' tax practice. The main distinction was in the countries involved: the first form involved OECD members and the second non-members.

---

1 This paper was prepared for the Commonwealth Secretariat by Professor Michael P. Devereux, Professor of Economics and Finance, Warwick University, UK. It was originally presented at the Commonwealth Finance Ministers Meeting held in September 2000 in Malta.

2 See the Executive Summary of the second report.

The first form concerned 'harmful preferential regimes in member countries'. According to the report, four main factors determine whether a particular regime is 'harmful'. They are:

◆ The regime imposes low or no taxes on the relevant income;

◆ The regime is ring-fenced from the domestic economy;

◆ The regime lacks transparency;

◆ There is no effective exchange of information.

Other factors were also considered including, for example, the extent of compliance with the OECD Transfer Pricing Guidelines. The OECD emphasised that the first criterion – low or no taxes – was not, in itself, considered to represent a 'harmful preferential regime'. Rather it was important that there was an element of discrimination in the regime. Lack of openness – characterised by a clear set of tax rules and the potential for exchange of information – was also considered an important element. The guidelines introduced by the report recommended that any features in member countries' tax regimes identified as 'harmful' should be removed within five years.[3]

The OECD established working groups of the Forum to identify such regimes. The 2000 Report listed 47 preferential regimes – in a number of OECD countries – which were '*potentially* harmful', since there has not yet been an overall assessment of whether the regimes are '*actually* harmful'. These included regimes such as Belgian Co-ordination Centres, and Irish International Financial Services Centres.[4] The Forum was unable to reach a conclusion about whether a number of holding company regimes were potentially harmful. These were not included in the list.

The next stage in the OECD's work on preferential regimes will be to issue guidance (application notes) on applying the criteria in the 1998 Report. This will be on a generic basis, in that no specific regime will be referred to. The Forum aims to verify by June 2003 whether member countries have eliminated 'harmful' regimes, although the deadline for removing the benefits to taxpayers from such regimes is December 2005. However, the 2000 Report does not outline any action which will be taken against countries which have not complied with eliminating such regimes. It merely states that 'other countries may wish to take defensive measures'.

---

3 The 1998 Report, and the recommendations, were approved by the OECD Council with abstentions from Luxembourg and Switzerland.

4 But *not* the Irish intention to set a low corporation tax rate of 12.5 per cent on all activity.

The second form of 'harmful' tax practice identified by the 1998 Report concerned jurisdictions outside the OECD identified as 'tax havens'. Here the focus is, therefore, on jurisdictions, rather than on specific features of their tax regimes. Again there were four main factors which would identify such a jurisdiction:

◆ No or only nominal tax on the relevant income;

◆ No effective exchange of information;

◆ The jurisdiction's regime lacks transparency;

◆ The jurisdiction facilitates the establishment of foreign-owned entities without the need for a substantive local presence.

Again, the OECD emphasised that the first of these factors – low taxation – was necessary, but not sufficient in itself, to identify a jurisdiction as a tax haven. Again, transparency and exchange of information figure prominently amongst the criteria listed by the OECD. The OECD also appeared to consider it important whether or not a jurisdiction had a significant untaxed offshore financial services sector relative to its overall economy.

Again, study groups were established by the Forum to identify such jurisdictions; the study groups invited jurisdictions under consideration to submit relevant information, and invited them to verify the factual accuracy of the reports. The OECD published a list of 34 'tax havens' meeting its criteria in the 2000 Report.[5] In doing so, the OECD did not follow the procedure which it adopted towards its own members of declaring regimes to be only *potentially* – as opposed to *actually* – harmful. It is not clear whether the OECD considered that it had more information on which to base a judgement concerning 'tax havens' than it had concerning 'preferential regimes' in member countries.[6] Just prior to the publication of the report, six further jurisdictions made a public political commitment to eliminate their 'harmful' tax practices and to comply with the principles of the 1998 Report. As a result, they were not named in the 2000 Report.

The OECD intends to put in place a two-pronged strategy to deal with these 'tax havens'. It aims to draw up a list of 'unco-operative tax havens' by 31 July 2001. Any jurisdiction regarded as such will be liable to 'defensive

---

5 The OECD's list is given on page 17 of the 2000 Report.

6 It does seem unlikely that, within a period of time, the OECD could have found out more about the overall tax regimes of the 47 potential tax havens which it considered than it could find out about specific features of the regimes of its members.

measures' outlined by the OECD in its 2000 Report. These are described below. The timescale for this process is therefore much shorter than for OECD member countries, which have an additional two years before the OECD will even declare whether their regimes are *actually* harmful.

To avoid being in this position, identified jurisdictions need to co-operate with the OECD. In effect, this means to make a public political commitment to eliminate by December 2005 any practices which the OECD considers to be 'harmful'. Further, such jurisdictions would generally be expected to develop an acceptable plan in collaboration with the Forum, and to agree not to enhance further any 'harmful' tax practices. Beyond this, the OECD intends to encourage further co-operation by, for example, developing a model vehicle for the exchange of information. As a possible 'carrot' part of a 'carrot and stick' approach, the OECD mentions possible assistance to jurisdictions in transition, involving 'examining how their bilateral assistance programmes can be re-targeted', encouraging international organisations to take into account their special needs, and offering assistance on strengthening tax administrations.

The OECD Forum recommends that jurisdictions identified as 'unco-operative tax havens' by July 2001 should be subject to a range of possible 'defensive' measures. Jurisdictions co-operating with the Forum (presumably including non-OECD members) will be invited to adopt the measures recommended by the OECD (although such measures would be at the discretion of countries).[7] The measures proposed in the 2000 Report relate partly to the enforcement of existing tax regimes. For example, they include the enhancement of auditing and enforcement activities, a requirement for comprehensive information reporting rules and a recommendation to adopt controlled foreign corporation (CFC) rules, all with respect to unco-operative tax havens. However, the measures go beyond this, effectively introducing a penalty for dealing with such jurisdictions. They include proposals to:

◆ Impose withholding taxes on certain payments to residents of 'unco-operative tax havens', and 'transactional' charges on certain transactions involving 'unco-operative tax havens';

◆ Deny the availability of the foreign tax credit or the participation exemption with regard to distributions from 'unco-operative tax havens';

◆ Disallow deductions, exemptions, credits or other allowances related to transactions with 'unco-operative tax havens'.

---

7 It is not clear whether there would be any consequences of not adopting such measures.

Governments are also invited to reconsider whether to direct non-essential economic assistance to 'unco-operative tax havens'.

A Background to Taxing Capital Income

The main focus of the OECD initiative is clearly on the spillover effects of taxation across countries – that is, how the tax regime in one country can affect the welfare of residents in another country. Before addressing this in detail it is useful to take a step back to consider the underlying rationale for taxing capital income.

An academic and policy debate has continued for decades about whether the main form of taxation should be based on income or expenditure. A tax applied to all income would be applied to all forms of income from capital and all capital gains. A pure expenditure tax would tax only that part of income which was not saved; it would also tax net reductions in saving (i.e. those which represent part of expenditure). But in effect, an expenditure tax would not tax capital income.

There have long been advocates of an expenditure tax, including for example, the Meade Committee in 1978.[8] Advocates of an expenditure tax have made a case on several grounds, including the administrative difficulty of implementing a full (or comprehensive) income tax and the avoidance of distortions to savings decisions. There is not room to summarise these arguments here. However, there is one additional reason for not taxing capital income, not often appreciated, which concerns the effective incidence of a tax on capital income in an open economy with mobile capital.

Suppose investors elsewhere in the world could earn a post-tax return of 10 per cent by investing on world markets. Then they will only invest in any particular host country if they earn the required post-tax rate of return of 10 per cent. But suppose that the host country charges a 50 per cent tax rate on capital income. Then non-resident investors will demand a pre-tax rate of return of 20 per cent – worth only 10 per cent after tax.

How could such a high rate of return be achieved? Most probably by a reduction of total inward investment – with only the better projects selected. And who then bears the effective burden of the tax? Non-residents still earn 10 per cent post-tax. It must therefore be borne by residents: there is less investment in the country, and this will be reflected

---

8 *The Structure and Reform of Direct Taxation*, Institute for Fiscal Studies, 1978, the report of a committee chaired by Nobel Laureate James Meade.

either in higher unemployment or lower wages, or both. A more efficient tax regime would be one in which (immobile) residents were taxed directly – through a tax on labour instead of a tax on capital. Such a tax would not distort inward investment decisions. So inward investment would be higher and overall welfare would be higher. Local residents bear the tax burden in any case.

However, the argument against taxing capital income is not merely an academic one. Many countries in practice do not tax such income to any great extent. An example is the UK, which has numerous forms of savings vehicles which are effectively untaxed, including pension funds and individual savings accounts (ISAs). Of course, the UK Government, like most other OECD countries, still attempts to tax capital income in the hands of companies active in, and resident in, the UK. The rationale for doing so is undoubtedly that it raises considerable revenue. But the burden of that taxation is probably borne by the immobile labour force in the UK (and UK consumers), rather than by the owners of capital. And there is a good argument that distortions to the UK economy would be lower with other forms of tax. The same would be true for other countries.

Issues in Tax Competition

In evaluating the OECD's initiative it is useful to consider whether it is reasonable to consider some forms of tax competition as 'harmful' or 'not harmful'. A starting point is the normal competition in economic markets. The principle here is that a process of competition between different suppliers to a particular market results in lower prices to the consumers, which in turn tends to lead to more efficient production. But is there an analogy with tax competition?

There is certainly a sense in which jurisdictions may compete with each other, since the tax regime in one jurisdiction is likely to affect the welfare of other jurisdictions. There are at least two distinct ways in which this might happen.

First, a tax cut in one country which increases, say, the probability of a multinational firm locating there makes it less likely that the firm will choose some other location. In practice, most countries aim to encourage inward real investment, since this may have positive effects on domestic welfare through raising total investment and employment, or by increasing productivity. The tax cut may also induce financial flows. Since financial capital is highly mobile, differences in tax rates between jurisdictions are likely to be especially influential in the location of financial activities, and hence there is more likely to be competition over taxes on financial capital.

Second, introducing a new low-tax regime is likely to attract mobile taxable income (through a variety of devices) from other jurisdictions. This may have little or no impact on real economic activity, but serves to reduce the taxpayers' overall tax liability in higher-taxed jurisdictions, and possibly increase the tax revenue of the host jurisdiction.

The OECD does not clearly distinguish between these two possible ways in which the tax policy of one country can affect the welfare of other countries. In places, the OECD reports refer to the misallocation of resources between countries, which seems to reflect a concern with the first effect. However, in its concentration on revenue, it indicates more concern with the second effect.[9]

The OECD also does not distinguish between tax avoidance (reducing tax liabilities by arranging one's affairs in a legally acceptable way) and tax evasion (illegally failing to declare taxable income). While the distinction between these two may sometimes be blurred, the policy implications for combating them are rather different. If OECD countries are concerned only about tax avoidance, they should in principle be able to collect any information required from their resident taxpayers. The focus of the OECD on exchange of information therefore seems more relevant to the problem of tax evasion. Unlike the main thrust of the OECD initiative, this ties in more closely with international concerns over money-laundering.

If there is tax competition between jurisdictions, then the analogy with economic competition would suggest that this would improve welfare. In economic markets, dominant firms with market power seek to restrict competition by a number of means, in order to maintain higher prices and to create higher profit. By this analogy, the OECD plays the role of a cartel of dominant firms: it seeks to pressure jurisdictions which undermine its ability to charge high taxes and raise high revenue from capital income. Low-tax jurisdictions are threatened with sanctions in order to prevent them from reducing the high-tax jurisdictions' ability to raise tax

Of course, as with most such analogies, this one can only be taken so far. The main reason is that it is far from clear that a process of tax competition is beneficial overall. The 'prices' involved in tax competition are tax rates on mobile tax bases – which can apply to the location of real or financial investment, or the location of taxable income. Reducing the

---

9 In fact, the OECD sends conflicting signals as to its chief concerns. The Executive Summary of the 2000 Report states: 'It is important to note at the outset that the project is not primarily about collecting taxes ...'. Later in the same paragraph, however, it claims that 'The project is focused on the concerns of OECD and non-OECD countries, which are exposed to significant revenue losses as a result of harmful tax competition'.

'price' of locating activity in one country makes that country more attractive relative to other countries. In the long run, other countries are likely to respond by reducing their tax rates as well. Many economic models suggest that the long-run outcome of this process must be 'prices' – i.e. tax rates – of zero.

But there are costs of reducing tax rates: the opportunity costs of raising the same tax revenue from other sources, or going without the expenditure made possible by the tax. These costs may vary from country to country. But high costs do not necessarily imply 'inefficiency'; they will reflect the alternative means available to different governments of raising the same revenue, or the benefits of the foregone government expenditure. The fact that most OECD countries continue to have high corporation tax rates – relative to the theoretical prediction of zero – is consistent with them having relatively high opportunity costs.

So the fact that competition in the economic market place may be beneficial is no reason to suppose that a general process of tax competition – whether competition over the location of real economic activity or over taxable income – is beneficial. But attempts by the OECD to define 'harmful' tax competition imply that there is such a thing as tax competition which is not harmful – or even positively beneficial. Instead, differences in tax regimes across jurisdictions, possibly – although not necessarily – as a result of a competitive process, may well leave some individuals or jurisdictions better off and some worse off.[10]

As a final point, the OECD's position is that simply setting a low (or zero) tax rate is not enough to be considered as a tax haven; rather the criteria listed above must be met. But this reflects a lack of economic logic behind its position. Suppose a jurisdiction has a zero tax rate, but exchanges information and meets all the other criteria necessary to be considered not to be a tax haven. That country is still likely to attract capital and taxable profit away from its high-tax neighbour. This may well be considered an outcome of tax competition and it may well leave the high-tax neighbour worse off. But it does not fall foul of the OECD's definition of harmful tax competition.

Tax Revenues in the OECD

The main motivation for the OECD's initiative is apparently concern about the erosion of tax revenues in OECD countries. It is therefore use-

---

10 This can be seen even within OECD countries: Ireland has benefited from very high investment arising at least in part from its low corporate tax rates.

ful to consider the recent pattern of these revenues. The obvious form of taxation to consider is corporation tax revenue, which is the main (although not the only) type of tax on capital income. If there was reason for increasing concern about the erosion of corporation tax revenue, one would expect to see such revenues declining both as a share of GDP and as a share of total tax revenue.

Figures 1 and 2 present evidence between 1975 and 1997 on the pattern on corporation tax revenues in a number of major economies as well as an average for the EU. Figure 1 presents these as a proportion of GDP in each country. Figure 2 presents them as a proportion total tax revenue in each country.

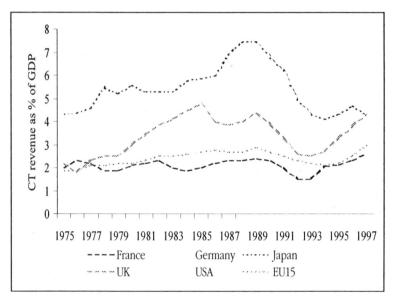

Figure 1. Corporate Tax Revenues as a Share of GDP

Note: EU15 is an average of the 15 EU member states, 1989–1997, and 14, excluding Portugal, prior to 1989. The average is weighted by GDP.

Source: OECD, *Revenue Statistics*, various years.

Both figures demonstrate that the importance of corporation tax revenues varies considerably across countries. Revenues are also quite volatile, tending to move in line with the economic cycle. Although revenues declined in the first half of the 1990s, they recovered up to 1997. Overall, however, there is no clear discernible trend. On average, corporation tax revenues are at roughly the same level as they were 20 years ago.

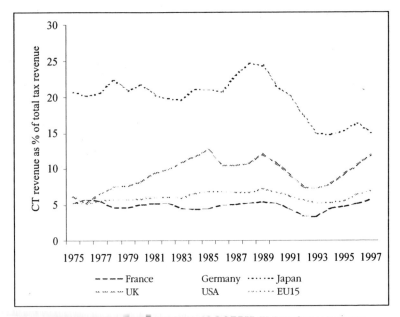

Figure 2. Corporate Tax Revenues as a Share of Total Tax Revenue

Note: EU15 is an average of the 15 EU member states, 1989–1997, and 14, excluding Portugal, prior to 1989. The average is weighted by total tax revenues.

Source: OECD, Revenue Statistics, various years.

This is despite the fact that, on average, statutory corporation tax rates have tended to fall over the last two decades. Table 1 indicates movements in the statutory tax rates in a number of OECD countries since 1980. Statutory tax rates have fallen in all but one of these countries since 1980, in some cases by a considerable margin. Part of the explanation of why revenues have held up while statutory tax rates have fallen is that tax bases have tended to be widened over the same period, so the effective tax rate has not changed so substantially.

The evidence here can only really be consistent with the notion of a threat to corporation tax revenues if, in fact, corporate profits have been increasing over the last 20 years, but this increase has coincided with increasing opportunities for tax avoidance and evasion. In this case, the net effect might be to leave revenues unchanged. Unfortunately this hypothesis is not easy to test, because of the difficulties in adequately defining and measuring levels of profitability. However, I am not aware of any study which supports the hypothesis and, to the best of my knowledge, such evidence has not been available to, or been presented by, the OECD.

Table 1. Typical Corporate Tax Rates Over Time[a]

	1980	1990	1999
France	50.0	37.0	40.0[b]
Germany[c]	62.2	57.7	51.6[b]
Ireland[d]	45.0	10.0	10.0
Italy[e]	36.3	46.4	37.0
Japan[f]	52.6	50.9	40.9
Sweden	56.8[c]	52.0	28.0
UK	52.0	34.0	30.0
USA[c]	49.6	38.4	39.3

[a] The rate given applies to retained earnings for a manufacturing company.

[b] Includes a surcharge on corporate income tax.

[c] Includes a deductible local corporate income tax.

[d] The 10 per cent rate for certain manufacturing activities and financial services was introduced in 1981. It is being phased out, and the standard rate of corporate tax is being reduced to 12 per cent on trading income from 2003.

[e] A deductible local corporate income tax of, on average, 16.2 per cent was replaced in 1998 by a regional tax on productive activity of 4.25 per cent, calculated on the net value of production rather than taxable profits, which is not deductible from the corporate income tax.

[f] Includes two local taxes: the enterprise tax (which is deductible) and the inhabitants tax (which is not deductible).

The Impact of the OECD Initiative on 'Tax Havens'

As far as I am aware, there has been little research on the impact of the OECD initiative on those jurisdictions labelled as 'tax havens'. In any case, it is important first to consider carefully the pressure on 'tax havens' to reform the most important features of their regimes. Only then is it possible to consider the economic impact of such reforms.

Jurisdictions labelled by the OECD as 'tax havens' have a choice. First, they can publicly commit to abandoning those elements of their tax regime which the OECD considers relevant; and they will have to actually abandon them by 2005. However, according to the OECD, this specifically does *not* mean that they will be forced to abandon a low tax rate policy.

The crucial issue, therefore, is how important the other elements of the tax regime to which the OECD objects are in making a particular jurisdiction attractive to non-residents. To recap, the three other main elements identified by the OECD as important in recognising a 'tax haven' are exchange of information, the degree of transparency with regard to, for example, financial disclosure, and the extent to which foreign-owned entities are required to have a local substantive presence.

From the perspective of other countries, the first two of these are most likely to be of importance in illegal activity, for example where residents of other countries can evade taxes by holding funds in a 'tax haven' which cannot be traced by the home tax authorities. (Clearly, too, these two factors may be of importance in money laundering, although that is not the focus of this OECD initiative, or of this paper.) But these two factors may have relatively little impact on legal, even if lightly taxed, financial or real activity. A very important issue both for the response of those jurisdictions labelled as 'tax havens' and for the OECD is therefore the relative size of these two kinds of activities. If most financial activities take the form of legal activity, then the 'tax havens' may have little to lose in agreeing to engage in more transparency and in the exchange of information – since if the activity is legal there is no need for the taxpayer to hide it.[11]

The second option for such regimes is to choose not to comply with the OECD initiative. At the moment, there is considerable uncertainty as to what the implications of such a stance would be. It does seem likely that jurisdictions already listed by the OECD would be transferred to the new list of 'unco-operative tax havens', and that the OECD would then invite its members, and possibly other countries as well, to take 'defensive measures' against that jurisdiction.

What is less clear is the extent to which individual countries would enact these defensive measures. Indeed, it is puzzling that larger and richer countries which have apparently been concerned about specific jurisdictions have not unilaterally imposed at least those defensive measures aimed at collecting their own tax revenue (as opposed to attempting to penalise the other jurisdiction). For example, many OECD countries already have complex anti-avoidance regimes in place, which could be extended to attempt to deal with a perceived threat from another jurisdiction. But if there is a cost to taking such action (for example, administration costs), then it seems at least possible that such countries would not be willing to take such action in response to the prompting of the OECD.

---

11 In any case, where countries do have exchange of information agreements, very little information tends to be exchanged in practice.

But there is a more general problem for the OECD in its dealings with 'unco-operative tax havens'; that is, that financial capital and taxable profits may be so mobile that it is virtually impossible to properly implement any of the defensive measures. To take a concrete example: suppose that the UK introduced as a 'defensive' measure a 'transactional charge' on all transactions with, say, Seychelles. That is if, for example, a UK resident paid money to a resident of Seychelles, the UK Government would levy a charge. It is likely then that such a transaction would be unattractive. But would this halt business between the UK and Seychelles?

This seems unlikely. Instead it seems more likely that there will be third countries which could act as an intermediary in the transaction. Either the UK Government would also have to levy a charge on transactions with the third country, or it would have to 'look through' the initial transaction with the third country to discover if there was ultimately a transaction with Seychelles. Essentially, to have a significant effect on business between the UK and Seychelles, the defensive measures would have to be comprehensive. For example, if any one of the OECD member countries decided not to introduce such a charge, then all money paid to Seychelles could be routed through this OECD country.[12]

In sum, the threats of the OECD may be less severe than they appear at first sight. If jurisdictions choose to comply with the OECD to avoid being on an 'unco-operative' black list, they may in principle still maintain their status as low-tax jurisdictions, although they would probably have to agree to more transparency and exchange of information. If they choose not to comply with the OECD demands, they face a more uncertain future. However, given the possible reluctance of countries to undertake penalising 'defensive measures', and the expertise of tax lawyers and accountants in devising tax-minimising strategies, it may be some considerable time before any serious effects of defensive measures are felt.

If the OECD maintains its stance that it will not force 'tax havens' to raise their tax rates, then the economic impact on such jurisdictions depends on their response. In turn this may depend on the extent to which the jurisdiction depends on illegal activity. If this affects a relatively small part of the jurisdiction's economy, then that jurisdiction may have little to lose from agreeing to greater transparency and an exchange of information with the OECD.

---

12 This is a vital difference from the position of trade and the WTO. If a small country chooses not to sign up to WTO agreements that has little effect on other countries as they trade between themselves. But a small country can, in principle, have a large effect on international tax revenues.

However, it seems that some jurisdictions are likely to increase their tax rates in response to the OECD's initiative. This could have far more serious consequences. Given the great mobility of financial capital, any country which increases its tax rate on such capital is liable to drive it away.[13] Although it is impossible to identify the monetary cost of increasing tax rates, it is reasonable to assume that, for countries which depend heavily on such financial capital, the cost would be very large.

Conclusions

This paper has reviewed the recent OECD initiative on 'harmful' tax competition, primarily from the viewpoint of jurisdictions which the OECD defines as 'tax havens'. Such jurisdictions must choose whether to comply with the OECD in reforming their tax regimes or face the prospect of having 'defensive measures' taken against them.

This paper argues that:

◆ The planned OECD timescale is significantly shorter in taking action against jurisdictions defined as 'tax havens' than it is against its own member countries which have 'preferential regimes';

◆ The threats to those jurisdictions judged to be 'tax havens' seem more severe than those against 'preferential regimes' in OECD countries;

◆ The OECD has not succeeded in making a definition of 'harmful' as opposed to 'not harmful' tax competition;

◆ By analogy with economic markets, the OECD is akin to a cartel of high price firms seeking to undermine competition;

◆ There is no evidence that OECD countries are facing a reduction in corporation tax revenues as a result of tax competition – either 'harmful' or 'not harmful';

◆ 'Tax havens' could accept more transparency and exchange of information with the OECD to the extent that there is no illegality involved in the financial activity within their jurisdiction;

---

13 This is despite the claim by the Business and Advisory Committee (BIAC), an independent but official consultative body to the OECD, that 'multinational enterprises that utilise the environments offered by the tax havens ... have *not*, in general, done so primarily for tax saving reasons, but because these locations have developed an expertise in servicing such activities, which, today, are far more significant than tax benefits on attracting business', ('A business view on tax competition', *Tax Notes International*, 19.3, July 1999).

◆ The 'defensive measures' threatened by the OECD may be difficult to enforce;

◆ Jurisdictions which feel obliged to raise their tax rates may face a very significant outflow of capital and hence reduction in welfare.

The OECD's 'harmful tax competition' initiative could have a potentially very large economic impact on jurisdictions labelled as 'tax havens'. Even within the scope of the current framework, the analysis in this paper suggests two recommendations. First, that there should be multilateral discussion between the OECD and 'tax havens' to facilitate discussion of common issues. Second, that the timescale for dealing with 'tax havens' should reflect the difficulties which the OECD acknowledges that its own members will have in reforming their tax regimes; this would, for example, imply delaying the drawing up of a list of 'unco-operative tax havens' until 2003.

International Trade in Offshore Business Services: Can Developing Countries Compete?[1]

Rajiv Biswas

Introduction

For many developing countries, diversification away from traditional primary industries to international business services has been a highly successful means of achieving economic development. Governments have pursued economic development policies for diversification into industries such as financial services, shipping, commercial services, computer services and, more recently, e-commerce, in order to build comparative advantage in these industries, which are among the fastest-growing sectors of the global economy.

Many Commonwealth countries have benefited strongly from pursuing such strategies, escaping the vicious cycle of deteriorating long-term real prices for agricultural and mineral commodities, highly volatile commodity prices and vulnerability of crops to extreme weather conditions.

Table 1. Growth Rate of Global Exports by Industry Sector, 1990–98

	Annual average growth rate in world trade value (%)
Agricultural Products	4
Mining Products	1
Commercial Services	7

Source: WTO

While globalisation has often assisted such industrial diversification strategies, since many international services are relatively mobile geographically, there are increasing concerns that global competition in such industries will be subjected to regulation by a handful of the most power-

---

1 This paper was written by Rajiv Biswas as Senior Economist in the International Finance and Capital Markets Department, Commonwealth Secretariat and editor of the *Commonwealth International Capital Markets Review*.

ful developed countries, potentially locking out developing countries from competing effectively in a number of these industries.

The recent OECD Initiative on Harmful Tax Competition, as well as other OECD initiatives such as the previous OECD initiative on the Multilateral Agreement on Investment and planned new e-commerce initiatives, are raising concerns in developing countries that a small number of advanced economies are raising new barriers to competition from developing countries in the global business services industries, where the OECD countries have had a dominant position historically. The WTO is also phasing out use of investment incentives and export incentives as a tool of economic development, which will affect many developing countries.

The Growth of International Business Services

The international business services industry has shown rapid growth in the last two decades. This reflects a number of global trends, including the deregulation of domestic financial markets in many countries, rapid growth in world trade and investment and the globalisation of many segments of the services industry. Initiatives in the GATT Uruguay Round to liberalise trade in services have underpinned the growth of the international business services industry. The process of liberalisation of trade in services is likely to continue to be an important component of future WTO discussions. At present, the OECD countries control almost all world trade in commercial services, accounting for around 80 per cent of total global service sector exports.

Table 2. Share of World Trade in Commercial Services, 2000

Region	Share (%)
OECD Countries:	
North America	22.0
Western Europe	44.4
Japan	4.8
Developing Countries:	
Africa	2.2
Latin America	4.3
Non-OECD Asia	13.0

Source: WTO

Although the OECD countries continue to dominate world trade in services, developing countries have benefited from even their small share of global services trade. Diversification into offshore IT and financial services has benefited many developing economies very substantially in a number of ways. Firstly, the offshore financial services industry has been a high growth sector globally. Therefore it has provided a dynamic growth sector for national output in comparison with the existing alternatives available to many countries. For example, many Caribbean economies were heavily reliant on traditional industries, namely subsistence farming and the export of primary commodities. Moreover, from a terms of trade perspective, the price of international services has been rising far more rapidly for decades than for secondary industries, while primary product prices have actually been declining. Indeed, a major problem faced by developing nations has been the declining terms of trade for primary commodity exporting nations. Consequently, the international services industry has provided an excellent economic development driver and a strategic growth industry which has helped to lift per capita incomes and national living standards in many developing countries.

The promotion of information and communication services represents, for the Government of Grenada, a vital part of our diversification effort, and our search for alternatives to commodity agriculture. The decline of Grenada's commodity export trade has had a devastating impact on the country's capacity to earn foreign exchange, to generate employment and to pursue agricultural and rural programmes. Moreover, the liberalizing of trade and the reduction of tariffs levels in response to global requirements have seriously weakened the government's revenue-generating capacity, in some areas.

Dr Keith Mitchell, Prime Minister of Grenada, June 2001

For some jurisdictions, the offshore business services industry has transformed their economies. Barbados is a good example of how a strategy of diversification away from traditional agricultural industries to international business services has been a highly successful means of achieving economic development. In the 1950s, the economy was heavily reliant on sugar cane production, with sugar accounting for 30 per cent of GDP, a third of export earnings and 25 per cent of total employment. Moreover, the economy was subject to large volatility in global sugar prices, which given the high dependency on this single agricultural product, caused great economic vulnerability. Barbados was also subject to deteriorating terms of trade in the long term, as the price of manufactures and services imports was rising far more rapidly than export prices for its agricultural exports.

With the development of the international business services industry over the last two decades, the domestic economy has been transformed, with Barbados now having a strong economic base consisting of a wide range of international financial and other business service exports. Indeed, these new international service industries account for 30 per cent of GDP, while sugar's share has fallen to just 3 per cent of GDP. The strategy of diversifying away from sugar has been extremely judicious, as the viability of the sugar industry is increasingly uncertain, due to uneconomical field operations, ageing factories and declining world sugar prices. Barbados is now classified as an upper-middle-income country, with its workforce having employment opportunities in a wide range of highly skilled professions in many service industries, compared with the limited opportunities in agricultural employment just a generation ago.

As an industry sector requiring a skilled workforce, the financial sector has also provided a means for bringing about workforce skilling and employment opportunities for tertiary-trained local employees who may have had far more limited opportunities in the absence of such an export-driven financial sector. Graduates in areas such as management, law, accountancy, finance and social sciences have far greater scope for employment through the development of such a sector. Moreover, the relatively high incomes and associated investment in this sector generate considerable multiplier effects through corporate and household expenditure into construction, retailing, business and government services. Generally such multiplier effects could result in two or three jobs created in other sectors for every job created in the offshore financial sector directly.

Table 3. Contribution of International Financial Services Industry to GDP in Selected Commonwealth Jurisdictions

	Estimates of international financial service sector as share of GDP (%)
The Bahamas	15
Barbados	30
Bermuda	20
British Virgin Islands	36
The Cayman Islands	21
The Cook Islands	7
Grenada	5
Isle of Man	42
Guernsey	64

The financial services industry, while an important component of international business services, is only one of many industries being developed. Other important sectors include shipping services, distribution services, service centres and company headquartering. The most dynamic new growth sector is e-commerce, software and electronic data processing services.

Financial Services

The offshore financial services industry has evolved substantially during the last 30 years, in response to the globalisation of the world economy and financial markets. The size of the offshore industry is estimated at $5–6 trillion, with around 70 offshore financial centres worldwide. Offshore financial services includes the provision of financial services to overseas clients, so that major international financial centres with a high share of such business, such as the City of London, are also considered to be offshore centres. Indeed, recent IMF estimates of global offshore financial services activity indicate that around 60 per cent of total global offshore centres activity is in London, the USA and the Japanese offshore market.

After taking into account the substantial offshore centres in other OECD countries, the non-OECD share of the total offshore financial services industry is estimated to account for less than 20 per cent. With major international financial centres such as Hong Kong and Singapore included in this 20 per cent figure, there are a large number of small offshore centres which are involved in the provision of a relatively small share of the total market.

While the City of London has hundreds of years of history as an international centre for the provision of international banking, insurance and other financial services, many of the other offshore centres have emerged relatively recently. A large number of these are Commonwealth jurisdictions; the recent IMF list of offshore centres includes 29 Commonwealth countries. Of the 29, ten are British-administered, reflecting the historic role of British financial institutions in international finance. Indeed, these close linkages with Britain have been an important factor in assisting their competitiveness due to the use of well-established Commonwealth legal systems, stable government and defence security.

The evolution of many of these OFCs reflects initiatives for economic diversification into more sustainable, highly-skilled industries, so as to boost economic development and living standards in small states. For example, in many Caribbean countries, economic strategies to diversify away from agricultural dependency were encouraged by the international development community, resulting in strong efforts to move into sectors such as financial services and tourism. In many cases, colonial administrations initiated the establishment of these offshore financial centres, in order to try to create sustainable industries that would allow economies to develop and generate employment, as well as to reduce dependence on fiscal support from their European masters.

In parallel, the deregulation of global business services allowed greater geographic mobility of capital, while the value of world trade and international corporate activity has risen sharply. This has created demand for the international provision of a range of business services, including global banking, insurance, reinsurance, funds management, leasing, factoring, shipping, distribution centres and a wide range of other business services.

Table 4. Commonwealth Countries and Territories with Offshore Financial Centres

Europe	Caribbean (continued)
Cyprus	Belize
Isle of Man (UKDT)	Cayman Islands (UKOT)
Jersey (UKDT)	Dominica
Gibraltar (UKDT)	Grenada
Guernsey/Sark/Alderney (UKDT)	Montserrat (UKOT)
Malta	St Kitts and Nevis
UK (City of London)	St Lucia
	St Vincent and the Grenadines
Africa	Turks and Caicos Islands (UKOT)
Mauritius	
Seychelles	**Asia/Pacific**
	Australia
Caribbean	Cook Islands
Antigua	Labuan (Malaysia)
Anguilla (UKOT)	Nauru
Bahamas	Niue
Barbados	Samoa
British Virgin Islands (UKOT)	Singapore
Bermuda (UKOT)	Vanuatu

Source: IMF

Many of the largest financial centres have substantial hosting of global institutional investment funds. These include mutual funds, investment trusts, pension funds and hedge funds. This component of international financial services has been growing at a rapid pace as international investors or managers seek to provide for privately-funded retirement, long-term savings and international portfolio investment. Generally these funds are collected and taxed in the country of the investor's residence, but are pooled for investment purposes into a common fund. It is more advantageous to locate such investment funds in a jurisdiction where they will be taxed minimally, since generally the investment distributions are already taxed in the jurisdictions where the investments were originally generated and distributed.

Some offshore centres have specialised in certain areas. Bermuda, for example, is a major international insurance centre. This has resulted in the establishment of highly skilled expertise in Bermuda for insurance-related services, giving the jurisdiction global competitive advantage in this particular sector due to the congregation of large numbers of insurance firms and industry professionals on the island. Barbados is a major centre for foreign sales corporations, with an estimated 2,300 registered in 1997. The Bahamas offshore services industry includes the world's third largest international shipping registry, with around 1,500 ships registered. A number of Caribbean offshore centres are also major centres for highly specialised commercial products, such as specialisation in aircraft leasing for international airlines, for which Cayman Islands and British Virgin Islands are major specialist global centres with high quality professional expertise in these sophisticated products. Indeed, the vast majority (on a dollar-weighted basis) of Caymans' business is institutional business, i.e. Special Purpose Vehicles used in international trade and debt structuring, etc. Cayman Islands has also become a major centre for specialist captive insurance products, with strong professional expertise in how to structure such complex insurance products. Much of the business of offshore centres is also sourced from activities of blue-chip multinationals which comply with the highest international accounting standards.

A large part of private investments in non-OECD international financial centres relates to blue-chip investment funds which are fully transparent and fully taxed at point of distribution, with around 6,000 such funds located in OFCs. For example, the Cayman Islands has an estimated 3,200 mutual funds, with over US$200 billion in funds managed in Cayman, but the bulk of these funds are institutional funds, such as large global fund managers or the many large US tax-exempt institutions such as US university endowment programmes.

The OFCs are also playing an increasingly important role in financing multinational corporate investments in developing countries. For example, Hong Kong plays a predominant role as funding hub for business in North

Asia, particularly for the global Foreign Direct Investment (FDI) flows in and out of China. The Caribbean financial centres are also playing an important role in regional foreign direct investment flows with North Asia, with more than half of Hong Kong's FDI going to the British Virgin Islands, the Cayman Islands and Bermuda (UNCTAD World Investment Report, 2001). This investment is mainly into corporate investment vehicles, with the bulk reinvested in China or Hong Kong as FDI or equity flows. For example, a major recent deal was a cross-border mergers and acquisitions deal by China Mobile (Hong Kong) Ltd, which acquired seven mobile networks in China in 2000 in a US$33 billion deal. The deal was part financed by capital raised through new shares issued to its parent company in the British Virgin Islands, resulting in FDI inflows of US$23 billion into China Mobile (Hong Kong), or around one-third of Hong Kong's FDI inflows in 2000. India has had a similar relationship with Mauritius, which has served as a major financial centre for foreign corporate investment vehicles into India.

Banking in offshore centres constitutes an important part of the global international banking industry. Based on reporting by a number of major offshore centres to the BIS on offshore deposits, the size of international banking provided by centres such as Cayman Islands and the Bahamas is comparable to the offshore banking sectors of some of the small OECD countries, though just a fraction of major offshore banking centres such as London. However, even this comparison overstates the role of centres like Cayman Islands in global international banking, with over 80 per cent of Cayman bank deposits estimated to be held by large global financial institutions, such as large US and European banks, which sweep overnight funds in and out of wholesale overnight money accounts with their Cayman subsidiaries. Such overnight institutional deposits are fully transparent and regulated in the USA and other onshore centres by their own banking regulatory authorities, as well as by the Cayman Islands Monetary Authority, which has very strict legislation and enforcement mechanisms in place to comply with FATF guidelines. Therefore, the role of the Cayman Islands in the provision of non-institutional banking services is relatively small in comparison with the large scale of institutional banking activity, which is related to the attractiveness of the Cayman Islands as a tax neutral platform for global institutional banking and fund management.

India and China are also providing financial services to their diaspora, due to the very large emigrant communities established abroad. It has to be recognised that diaspora from countries in East Asia and India, as well as other developing countries like South Africa, do have substantial potential to become an important source of capital inflows for many developing countries, and these developing countries need to provide off-shore financial services centres if they wish to tap this market. For example, India has provided a wide range of banking and other financial services products for its non-residents globally, with special preferential taxation exemptions. This has helped to generate very large foreign exchange deposits in the Indian economy, providing a key source of capital inflows for the current account. Total non-resident bank deposits in Indian financial institutions were estimated at around US$15 billion in 1999, and are estimated to have risen to US$23 billion in 2000. While this is still relatively small compared to the size of offshore deposits in large offshore financial centres like Hong Kong or Luxembourg, the size of total non-resident deposits has tripled during the last decade, and more than doubled since 1997.

The Indian diaspora has also become an important new market for the international growth of Indian domestic financial institutions, assisting them to become more globally competitive in international financial markets by developing sophisticated international financial products. India has also used its overseas Indian community to raise sovereign debt, rather than the usual tapping of foreign bond markets utilised by most countries. Two such bond issues in 1998 and 2000 raised a total of around US$10 billion from Indians abroad. There are also very large remittances from Indian workers in the OECD and in the Middle East, which have created a significant offshore financial services sector in India. Consequently the offshore financial services sector is playing a key role in financing Indian economic development and providing critical foreign exchange inflows for India's current account position.

The Indian example may provide a useful model for other developing countries. There is probably a strong case on economic development grounds for allowing emigrants from developing countries to be given incentives to invest in their home countries and exemptions on savings taxation on any such investments back to their home countries by rich industrial countries where they work. This could take many forms, including the Indian model of retail bond raisings, special venture capital or unit trust funds for emigrant investors, and other such long-term savings vehicles. This will provide a valuable mechanism for generating foreign exchange for development in many developing countries at a time when finding sources of financing for development is one of the most pressing issues on the international development agenda. It is also one of the potential measures that developed countries can take to compensate developing countries for attracting their scarce skilled personnel, although other measures, such as aid funding for boosting training capacity, are also necessary.

E-Commerce and IT Services

E-commerce and other IT services have become a key strategic focus for many developing countries in their export diversification and industrial development strategies. Many Commonwealth developing countries are now focusing policy initiatives on building competitiveness in exporting IT services and e-commerce. This includes software services, e-commerce and data-processing services. Many Commonwealth countries, including India, Malaysia, Singapore, Malta, Mauritius and South Africa have been encouraging the development of these new growth sectors, in order to strengthen their competitiveness in the leading growth industries for the twenty-first century.

For example, Forrester Research has projected that B2B e-commerce will reach US$2.7 trillion in 2004, with 17 per cent of all business trade transacted through the internet. Jupiter Research has predicted that by 2005, the largest online B2B markets would be in computer and telecommunications, food and beverages, autos and parts, industrial equipment and supplies and real estate. Developing countries that are seeking to be at the forefront of global competitiveness are trying to develop industry strategies that position them to compete effectively worldwide in these fast-growing industry sectors for the digital age.

For example, India is benefiting from a major transformation occurring in the economy due to its offshore IT industry. This is resulting in strong positive effects on the current account balance, as IT exports are growing at a 50 per cent pace year after year. Software exports are now making a substantial contribution to overall exports, accounting for around 10 per cent of total exports. Software exports are forecast to rise by a further 60 per cent in 2000–01, to an estimated US$6.3 billion, with the very rapid growth of this sector resulting in a fundamental transformation of both the growth rate and overall composition of India's exports. Domestic sales from the industry are estimated at US$2.3 billion, giving total industry output of US$8.6 billion. The US is the dominant export market for India, taking around 65 per cent of India's software exports in 1999–2000, while the EU accounted for a further 25 per cent. However, the EU market is rapidly growing, with Indian software exports to the EU estimated at US$842 million in 1999–2000, but rising by a projected 35 per cent in 2001.

A large share of Indian software companies domestic revenue is attributable to offshore services, which is work done by a software company in India for an offshore client.

Table 5. India's Offshore IT Services, 2000

	Offshore services revenue as share of total (%)
Infosys	67
Wipro	52
Satyam	58
Mastek	33
Sonata	47
HCL Tech	63
Polaris	49
Silverline	36
Visualsoft	49

Source: Economic Times of India

Indian software and related services are expected to grow by a further 50 per cent in 2001–02, with export revenue rising to US$9.5 billion and total output of US$13 billion. This rapid pace of expansion in India's technology exports offers new scope for optimism about the medium-term external trade outlook, as well as generating new foreign direct investment flows and equity capital flows into India. McKinsey & Co has estimated that India's IT exports could rise to US$50 billion by 2008. The Indian National Association of Software and Services Companies has projected industry revenues rising to US$87 billion by 2008, and accounting for 7.5 per cent of national GDP.

In India, there are already tax exemptions for exports from Export Processing Zones, Free Trade Zones and Software Technology Parks. Tax holidays are also provided to export oriented units set up anywhere in India. The 2001–2 Budget extended special tax exemptions to profits from on site exports of services provided from software technology parks. Of India's total software exports of US$6 billion in 2000–1, an estimated 74 per cent was from its Software Technology Parks.

Developing countries are also working together to build their leading edge IT export industries. In Mauritius, the government has launched a new strategy to make Mauritius a free trade zone for the IT industry and promote the island as a leading regional e-commerce hub. IBM has recently decided to establish its regional headquarters in Mauritius. The Indian Institute of Technology in Chennai has plans to open a hi-tech hardware centre in Mauritius, with a feasibility study underway for the hardware centre, which would be set up under a US$100m line of credit facility being offered by India to the Government of Mauritius for import of Indian IT-related products for a proposed Cyber City and IT education projects. India's ISRO is also planning to establish a space research centre in Mauritius.

Table 6. Software Exports from Software Technology Parks of India
(Crore Rupees)

Centre	1999–2000	2000–01
Bangalore	4321	7475
Bhubaneswar	89	200
Calcutta	150	250
Chennai	1890	2956
Gandhinagar	27	102
Hyderabad	1059	1990
Jaipur	15	30
Noida	2450	4350
Mohali	15	40
Pune	572	960
Navi Mumbai	962	1610
Thiruvanathapuram	57	88
Total	11607	20051

Source: STPI in *Economic Times of India*

The EU proposed VAT rules in June 2000 that could have impacted seriously on developing country e-businesses. In terms of the current provisions no VAT is payable by a developing country e-business on sales of digital products and services to the EU. To protect European e-businesses, the EU proposed legislation that would have forced overseas online sellers from around the world to collect VAT on sales of digital products and services to non-business customers in Europe. E-businesses with more than 100 000 Euro in sales in the 15 EU member states would have been forced to register in one of the EU countries and file EU VAT returns. The EU's attempt to charge extraterritorial VAT was seen as overreaching and the proposals encountered many comments and complaints. According to estimates, the scope of these sales was merely 2 per cent of e-trade. International principles for taxing e-commerce were also discussed at the OECD Ministerial Conference in Ottawa in 1998. It was agreed that, for consumption taxes, the rules should result in taxation in the jurisdiction where consumption takes place.

Given the number of markets they operate in, the potential tax compliance burden this could create for multinationals is enormous.
PriceWaterhouseCoopers' E-business Tax Consulting Leader, Christina Rich

Furthermore, a developing country e-business that supplies digital products to private consumers in the EU would have been deemed to have a permanent establishment in the EU. This could have resulted in e-businesses being liable for direct taxes in EU member countries as well. In May 2001, the UK vetoed a revised proposal by the Swedish Presidency of the EU to apply VAT on e-commerce. The UK has suggested a moratorium on the taxation of e-commerce between internet suppliers and EU consumers, although all the other 14 EU members supported it, indicating that continued EU pressure on the UK to concede on this matter is likely to continue.

The OECD also agreed that an e-business that carries out an essential or material portion of its business through a website on a server that the business owns or hires in an OECD member country, will have a taxable presence wherever the server is situated, even if there are no staff where the server is situated. Further consensus was reached by the OECD member countries that internet service providers who have servers in other countries in order to provide services such as the hosting of web sites, have a taxable presence in the place where the servers are situated.

Free Trade Zones and Other Investment Incentives

The OECD Initiative extends not just to financial services, but to all geographically mobile services, including, but not limited to, shipping, distribution services, service industries and company headquartering. The OECD is already taking steps to extend its work to e-commerce and its 1998 Report flagged that manufacturing industries in developing countries would also have to be addressed later.

... it is recognised that the distinction between regimes directed at financial and other services on the one hand, and at manufacturing and similar activities on the other hand, is not always easy to apply. The Committee intends to explore this issue in the future.
OECD 1998 *Report on Harmful Tax Competition*, p. 8, para. 6

The OECD requirements for reforms in developing country jurisdictions which have agreed to make advance commitments to comply with the OECD requirements under its Harmful Tax Competition Initiative include the requirement that 'foreign-owned entities must be able to do business in the domestic economy'.

The implications of this requirement as part of the OECD programme of eliminating harmful tax competition are very significant for many developing countries. Many developing countries, including major economies such as India and South Africa, do not allow equal access to foreign-owned entities in their domestic economies.

Foreign ownership is strictly limited in many industry sectors throughout the Commonwealth, and many developing countries do not allow automatic access to foreign companies to do business in their domestic economies in all sectors. In many industries, developing countries require a phased approach to liberalisation in order to give domestic firms time to develop efficient and competitive industry sectors before being forced to compete on equal terms with international market leaders.

In relation to the OECD principles of removal of harmful tax competition in geographically mobile services, there are also implications for the tax and investment practices in place in many Commonwealth countries other than those that are listed by the OECD. Specifically, the OECD requires that 'Any preferential tax rates available to offshore regimes must also be available to domestic business of the same type'.

Many developing countries offer preferential tax regimes to foreign investors or export-related investment, which are not available to domestic companies which operate in the domestic market, or even to domestic company business sales to the domestic market. Many developing countries also utilise special export processing zones, free trade zones and other incentive regimes to encourage investment in export processing industries.

Many of the East Asian economies have had considerable success, through use of competitive taxation packages, in attracting foreign investment into infant industries. Countries like Mauritius, India and Dubai have used free trade zones and other low-tax regimes for export development very successfully.

Indeed, the Indian Budget for 2001–2 has introduced ten-year tax holidays for developers of special economic zones, with income from long-term investment for the development of special economic zones being exempt from tax. There are already tax exemptions for exports from export processing zones, free trade zones and software technology parks. Tax holidays are also provided to export-oriented units set up anywhere in India. The Budget extended special tax exemptions to profits from on site exports of services provided from software technology parks. Similar fiscal regimes are in place in many of the other developing countries in Africa and Asia, in order to encourage foreign investment.

Two of the most successful economies to attract regional headquarters are Hong Kong and Singapore … Singapore began to attract regional headquarters actively when it introduced, in 1996, various incentives under an International

Business Hub Programme. By end-2000, some 200 foreign affiliates there had regional headquarters status …

UNCTAD, World Investment Report, 2001

The importance of subsidies for economic development has been recognised by the WTO. Even though the WTO's Agreement on Subsidies and Countervailing Measures which came into effect in January 1995 requires the phasing out of most export subsidies by developed countries by 2000 and by developing countries by 2002, there are exemptions. In particular, the WTO SCM Agreement recognised the important role that subsidies can play in economic development of developing countries and exempted countries with a per capita GDP income of less than US$1,000 per year from any SCM rules on prohibited export subsidies. A key concern is the impact of having such a low level of cutoff for GDP per capita, since many relatively poor developing countries could face a large-scale shift in foreign investment in export processing industries to developing countries with GDP per capita below this cutoff level for no particularly compelling economic rationale.

The basic idea behind an export platform (such as a free trade zone) is to create an enclave in which the problems of poor trade policies, weak infrastructure, and inconsistent rule of law that plague the rest of the economy are at least partially eliminated.

Perhaps the most compelling piece of evidence in support of export platforms is that the vast majority of manufactured exports in the successful economies utilised at least one of these facilities. In Taiwan and Korea, for example, essentially all manufactured exports were either produced in a zone or a bonded warehouse. The vast majority of China's manufactured exports come through the special economic zones. Over 95 per cent of Mauritius's manufactured exports are produced in EPZs. Exports from Mexico's maquiladoras account for over 50 per cent of total manufactured exports.

Steven Radelet, Harvard Institute for International Development,
CAER Discussion Paper 43, November 1999

Strong arguments in favour of tax competition, including use of incentives, include the design of taxation on capital. In many countries, there is multiple taxation of capital, first through corporate taxes on the income stream from the investment, and then as taxes on individual income from the dividend streams and capital gains from the same capital (Mattey and Spiegel, 1996). Many have argued that this creates a tax bias against business investment, and therefore tax competition and incentives provides one means of partially offsetting this bias. Mattley and Spiegel also discuss a range of other efficiency effects from tax competition.

One of the potential consequences of tax competition is a reduction in government revenues, which could constrain government services to suboptimal levels. However, formal demonstrations of this result have relied on models where the local governments are limited to a single tax instrument. Allowing other revenue sources can overturn this result. Indeed, the limited empirical evidence suggests that revenue losses from competition over state and local corporate income and property tax receipts are at least partly offset by increased taxes from other sources, such as individual income taxes or sales taxes.

There are a number of other salient arguments that state and local government tax competition can enhance efficiency. One is that properly managed tax competition can create positive 'spillover effects' within a community by attracting or retaining firms with high levels of these external benefits. Localities can use tax incentives to help nurture 'industry clusters' which exploit 'agglomeration economies,' the increases in efficiency of production from the geographic concentration of related activities.

Joe Mattey, Senior Economist and Mark Spiegel, Senior Economist, Federal Reserve Bank of San Francisco, 'On the efficiency effects of tax competition for firms', The Region, Federal Reserve Bank of Minneapolis, June 1996

New Challenges to Developing Countries

Developing countries that are exporting international business services are currently facing considerable pressures for change from a number of initiatives coming from the OECD countries, including from its Harmful Tax Competition and E-commerce Initiatives. The Harmful Competition Initiative is focused on eliminating what the OECD determines to be 'harmful' practices in all geographically mobile services provided by all countries worldwide. This extends not just to financial services, but all geographically mobile services, including, but not limited to, shipping, distribution services, service industries, and company headquartering. The OECD is already taking steps to extend its work to e-commerce in developing countries, and its 1998 Report flagged that manufacturing industries in developing countries would be likely to have to be addressed later. Hence the OECD moves to eliminate harmful tax competition in financial services in non-OECD countries is part of a broader initiative to remove 'harmful' competition in a wide range of industry sectors, including e-commerce and manufacturing.

Tax Harmonisation

For the EU countries, these initiatives are part of a broader strategic objective to harmonise taxes within the EU. This is also an integral part of plans for an EU-wide tax that will give greater taxing powers to the EU bureaucracy in Brussels. However, harmonisation within the EU will not be sustainable if other major competitors are not also harmonising to EU rates, as there will be large-scale relocation of private investment to other countries and out of the EU. This therefore creates considerable pressure for the EU to ensure that other lower-taxing countries harmonise to its tax rates. The importance of low corporate tax rates for corporate investment inflows is demonstrated by the case of Ireland which has managed to achieve rapid economic growth for over a decade, assisted by a very low-tax environment for foreign corporations, now to be extended to all corporations, combined with a strong fiscal surplus.

Combating 'tax dumping' is one immediate priority; it is not acceptable for certain member States to practice unfair tax competition in order to attract international investment and offshore headquarters of European groups. Ultimately, the corporate tax system as a whole will have to be harmonised.

Mr Lionel Jospin, Prime Minister of France, Address on 'The Future of an Enlarged Europe', 28 May 2001, Paris

This raises concerns from an economic development policy perspective. At the OECD Forum on Harmful Tax Competition in June 2000, attended by 30 developing countries, a number of developing countries felt that action should also be taken against low-tax OECD regimes to prevent them 'poaching' developing country companies away from their home bases.

The WTO has observed that 'protectionism is not the first best choice to deal with fiscal challenges arising from trade liberalisation and globalisation'. In fact, governments are already responding to these challenges in more appropriate ways. High marginal income tax rates and corporate tax rates are coming down while consumption taxes rise. The WTO's 1998 Annual Report observed that tax harmonisation was being discussed in the EU and the OECD to deal with harmful tax competition, but noted:

This option, however, should be treated with considerable caution, as the fight against a 'race to the bottom' in tax rates may be used as a pretext for introducing a tax cartel.

The danger with the OECD Initiative is that the new global model will be a 'race to the top' for corporate tax rates, as countries harmonise to the highest common denominator and pressurise low-taxing countries to increase their tax rates.

A major concern is that the continental European welfare states face significant demographic problems over the next two decades due to ageing populations but, unlike the UK, have failed to develop adequate private pension provision. This creates a further risk of a global 'race to the top', driven by rising fiscal burdens in socialist Europe.

International Tax Competition

Competition among national governments in the public services they provide and in the taxes they impose is every bit as productive as competition among individuals or enterprises in the goods and services they offer for sale and the prices at which they offer them. Both lead to variety and innovation; to improvement in the quality of the goods and services and a reduction in their cost. A governmental cartel is no less damaging than a private cartel.

The principle of subsidiarity – that government services be provided, and paid for, so far as possible at the level of government closest to the citizen – would be violated by any attempt to impose from the center a uniform tax regime.

Milton Friedman, Hoover Institution, Stanford University, Emeritus Professor, University of Chicago and Nobel Laureate, May 2001

By lowering fiscal burdens and government intervention, countries grow quicker, resulting in stronger total tax revenues and government expenditures than in high-taxing countries. In sum, lowering the fiscal burden gives government a smaller percentage share of the economy, but of a much larger total pie. Moreover, it reduces the moral hazard that government bureaucracies create a culture of dependency on the state, particularly through political pork-barrelling by targeted handouts to various segments of the electorate. The continental European welfare state is an example of how such moral hazard results in economic rigidities such as inflexible labour markets and structural budget deficits, which impede economic progress.

For the Commonwealth, this is a key area for policy focus as developing countries search for more rapid economic growth and the path to economic success. While many forms of external assistance are possible, in the end a critical determinant of economic success lies in domestic economic management. Singapore and Ireland are among the leading fiscal models that other countries need to emulate if they are seeking to develop their industries and employment. Ireland has transformed its economy into one of the most successful in the world through a range of policy initiatives, of which low-tax regimes were a very important component.

India's 2001–2 Budget indicates how some major developing countries are beginning to recognise the importance of creating a favourable taxation regime that encourages entrepreneurship and the development of new industries. The Indian Budget cut the top rate of corporate and personal tax to 36 and 30 per cent respectively, both important steps towards creating a more dynamic economy. Savings incentives are also assisting in creating a fast-growing Indian mutual funds industry, creating a significant pool of domestic savings for equity and venture capital investments, including remittances from millions of non-resident Indians working in OECD and other countries.

However, the shift towards reducing the role of government is still budding in many developing countries after decades of socialist and communist economic philosophy which have resulted in economic stagnation and decline for many nations. Such shifts can easily be undone in a global tide towards a high-tax model, given the demonstrated inclination for governments to try to increase revenues in order to fund their expenditure programmes, rather than lowering spending in order to reduce tax burdens.

... the likelihood of maintaining a still satisfactory overall budget position over the longer run is greater, I believe, if surpluses are used to lower tax rates rather than to embark on new spending programs. History illustrates the difficulties of keeping spending in check, especially in programs that are open-ended commitments, which too often have led to larger outlays than initially envisioned. Decisions to reduce taxes, however, are more likely to be contained by the need to maintain an adequate revenue base to finance necessary government services. Moreover, especially if designed to lower marginal rates, tax reductions can offer favourable incentives for economic performance.

Alan Greenspan, *Federal Reserve's Semi-annual Report on the Economy and Monetary Policy*, Committee on Banking and Financial Services, US House of Representatives, 17 February 2000

The average tax burden in OECD countries has risen from 35 per cent in 1988 to an all-time high of 37 per cent of GDP in 1998, despite buoyant tax revenues, reflecting the tax and spend policies of many European countries.

... tax competition can even be helpful, not harmful, because it keeps governments in check. Tax competition can be a good spur for governments to keep to their core functions; to create a competitive business environment and not proliferate activities; to look for efficiencies and productivity gains, and to keep costs down.

Intervention by Singapore at Commonwealth Senior Finance Officials Meeting, September 2000

The WTO Annual Report for 1998 stated:

The empirical evidence does not provide convincing support for the claim that globalisation undermines governments' abilities to pursue their core functions.

Revenue has increased strongly in industrialised countries in recent decades. Only the structure of revenue collection is changing.

WTO Annual Report, 1998

According to Professor Devereux of Warwick University, average OECD corporate tax revenue as a share of total tax revenues has remained constant over the last 20–30 years. Indeed, the OECD's 1998 *Report on Harmful Tax Competition* states that 'the available data do not permit a detailed comparative analysis of the economic and revenue effects involving low tax jurisdictions' and 'preferential tax regimes'.

At least so far as taxes on corporate income are concerned, fears of an imminent collapse in government revenues may be overstated. In fact, for the EU as a whole, revenues from taxes on corporate income have increased over the last 20 years, both as a share of GDP and as a share of total tax revenue. Whilst there has been a downward trend in corporate tax rates, this has been accompanied by both a broadening of corporate tax bases and an improvement in underlying company profitability.

Institute for Fiscal Studies, *Corporate Tax Harmonisation in Europe*, November 2000

International Rule-making and Global Standards

There are a wide range of initiatives by various international organisations, other than the OECD initiative discussed above, to develop global standards which allow nation states to be bound voluntarily by entering into bilateral or multilateral treaties. However, there is growing concern among developing countries about the trend towards development of new international standards in international organisations where developing countries have little or no voice. Perhaps the most extreme example of exclusion of developing countries in international rule-making is the OECD, which is a club of 30 rich countries, comprising predominantly European nations bound by a commitment to the EU. Developing countries have no vote in the development of standards through this organisation.

Even in the IMF and World Bank, developing countries have only a small voice, with the majority of the voting rights being controlled by the OECD countries. For example, the 44 sub-Saharan African countries have just 4.5 per cent of the voting rights and only two Executive Directors at the IMF. The problem is accentuated by several unusual constituencies of large groups of developing countries headed by an OECD country in the Executive Directorship.

Developing countries need a greater voice in providing strategic direction to the Bretton Woods institutions to ensure greater effectiveness and credibility. ... We must ensure that we [developing countries] *can exercise ownership in a manner far beyond outdated formulae which currently govern quota distribution.*
Trevor Manuel, South African Finance Minister, IMF/World Bank Annual Meetings, Prague, 2000

The fear is that international standards developed by a handful of the richest nations can be used as new forms of protectionism, to block competition from developing countries in the fastest growing segments of international services trade where OECD countries have concentrated their own strategic economic focus.

In e-commerce, ICANN, the international organisation which manages internet space, has negligible developing country representation in an industry that is so critical to the future potential of developing countries to make a transition to a more rapid growth path.

So far, developing countries are only observers of the process. They do not participate on the boards of key organisations such as ICANN, which allow a minority to make decisions affecting their internet space. A lack of economical resources as much as awareness of the understanding of these strategic issues are the main reasons for non-participation.
'The Role of Domain Names', Rosa Delgado, Director, Société Internationale de Télécommunications Aeronautique (SITA), E-COMM 3, June 2001

These OECD initiatives in areas such as the Multilateral Agreement on Investment, the Harmful Tax Competition Initiative and the latest e-commerce initiatives are examples of how rule-making by the most powerful nations can erode the sovereign powers of developing countries. A key issue for small and developing countries is to ensure that they have an effective voice in the development of any international rules and standards.

If it is to reflect international realities, a globalised world requires more comprehensive institutions than the G-7 and a United Nations Security Council which comprises the victors of a war now more than half a century behind us. It requires active engagement with the two most populous countries in the world, China and India, rather than attempts to side-line or marginalise them. And it obliges us to develop international trade and financial organisations that reflect more fully the role of the developing world in the international economy and that take its interests into account. There has been talk about opening up the IMF and the World Bank, but it hasn't gone far enough.
Paul Keating, former Australian Prime Minister, 'Australia in a Globalised World', Melbourne, 14 July 1999

Creating A Shared Vision

A key challenge for Commonwealth nations is to work together to build a greater global consensus on how all nations can benefit from the opportunities arising in the fast-growing international business services industries. Important issues include how international standards should be set and how international organisations can facilitate this process. The need to achieve high standards of international prudential regulation and transparency are also critical objectives for Commonwealth countries.

Global Inclusiveness

It is essential that developing countries are fully included in any process of setting of international standards, whether for tax, environment, trade, labour standards or any other process of international standard-setting.

There are many positive ways in which developed and developing countries can work together to develop standards in many areas of international business services. The properly constituted international bodies that represent all regions already exist, in the form of the UN, the IMF and World Bank, as well as the WTO.

For example, in the area of e-commerce, a model law on e-commerce has already been developed by the UN. The Model Law on Electronic Commerce (MLEC), was adopted in 1996 by the UN Commission on International Trade Law (UNCITRAL). This provides a means by which all countries can rapidly address gaps in their legislation regarding e-commerce. Twelve countries had already adopted the MLEC by the end of 2000, with many others considering its adoption.

Similarly, the World Intellectual Property Organisation (WIPO), an intergovernmental organisation comprising 175 member nations, has developed two internet treaties. These are the WIPO Copyright Treaty, and the WIPO Performances and Phonograms Treaty.

These forms of globally inclusive and co-operative approaches to developing best practice have generated considerable enthusiasm from developing countries, which feel they are consulted and included in the development and management of these global standards. Many developing countries are then able to push for their adoption within their own legislative systems, since they have had inclusive participation in the development of these standards.

High Financial Standards

Strengthening regulation of the financial services industry worldwide is one of the key priorities for creating a more stable, dynamic global economy. The need for better regulation, strengthening of capital adequacy of financial institutions, development of high quality prudential regulation and implementing high levels of transparency and international best practice accounting standards are critical issues for all nations in the decade ahead. Many international business services centres already have very high standards of regulation and supervision, both within the OECD and in non-OECD jurisdictions. However, there needs to be a wider approach to improving transparency and regulatory standards than just focusing on the international business services segment of the business services industry.

All countries and territories in the Commonwealth can benefit by ensuring that they implement the highest standards of prudential supervision and regulation, as well as developing transparent accounting and management practices that meet international best practice and global standards. Financial disclosure and transparent practices are essential components of achieving high quality financial systems, combined with adoption of advanced risk management techniques. However, such initiatives cannot be ring-fenced to international financial services centres alone – they must encompass the full range of domestic financial institutions in all Commonwealth jurisdictions, as well as financial systems in all developed and developing countries. The recent domestic financial sector crises in three of the OECD countries – Japan, Korea and Turkey – which according to some estimates will cost over US$600 billion of taxpayers funds, highlight the critical importance of establishing well-regulated, properly supervised financial systems that are transparent, meet international accounting best practice and international capital adequacy standards.

While the OECD is pursuing small states with offshore financial centres to increase transparency of their banks, some OECD countries lack even the barest transparency in their own domestic sectors. For example, Turkey, an OECD member country, is currently experiencing a major macroeconomic and financial markets crisis stemming from the bad debts hidden within its state-owned banks, which control 40 per cent of the nation's banking assets. These banks have long been protected by Turkish laws that remove requirements for disclosure or investigation of bank balance sheets and exposure of non-performing loans, let alone compliance with international accounting standards.

Three of the Turkish state banks alone have accumulated estimated bad debts of US$20 billion, equivalent to 20 per cent of Turkish GDP.
'Turkey's state-owned banks present a litany of problems',
Wall Street Journal, 30 April 2001.

In the case of Korea, Standard & Poors stated in February 2001:

Three years after the start of Korea's financial crisis, and notwithstanding over Won 140 trillion of capital infusions, credit quality of Korean banks remains alarmingly weak …

… the disclosure standards at Korean companies, however, are often substandard. Last year a string of foreign suitors broke off planned tie-ups with Korean companies after starting their due diligence, presumably after uncovering severe discrepancies between the expected and actual financial health of the target. The message for investors is that transparency continues to be insufficient at Korean companies, even after three years of reform.
Standard and Poors, 'Korean reversal on reform buoys short term credit',
13 February 2001

In France, the bailout of then state-owned Credit Lyonnais was estimated to cost taxpayers US$15 billion, with a government inquiry started in 1996. Further problems have surfaced in recent months.

… the bank is at the epicenter of a scandal that won't go away, the legacy of a fateful purchase of California's failed Executive Life Insurance Co. in the early 1990s. Claiming Crédit Lyonnais fraudulently gained control of Executive Life, California and the state's powerful Insurance Dept. have launched a civil suit against the bank. And in Washington, the Justice Dept. is winding up a grand jury investigation that could result in the bank's criminal indictment. The U.S. Federal Reserve could also levy fines or even lift Crédit Lyonnais' U.S. banking license.

'The sword over Lyonnais – can the French state rescue the bank?',
Business Week, July 30 2001

Mexico, another OECD member, has only recently begun to recover from a massive banking sector crisis in the mid-1990s. According to *The Banker*, the estimated cost of the bank rescue operations resulting from the Tequila Crisis in 1994–95 was estimated at 18 per cent of GDP and even as late as January 2000 it was announced that one of the banks would cost an extra $1 billion to clean up.

One of the worst cases of poor banking regulation is Japan, whose huge banking sector has enormous bad debts by global standards, posing a potential systemic risk to the world financial system. As Brink Lindsay, Director of the Cato Institute said before the US House Sub-committee on Trade of the House Committee on Ways and Means, the extent of Japan's banking sector crisis is enormous.

Putting the matter bluntly, Japan's economy is in a mess. The 1990s has been a lost decade, with growth since 1992 averaging 1 percent a year. A recession, and perhaps a serious one, is now under way. Unemployment is at record highs. A black hole of bad debt has sucked the life out of the banking sector.

Brink Lindsay, Director, Cato Institute, July 1998

Do something. Anything. That has been the plea of global investors to Japan's rulers and financial mandarins for years, as the country's banking industry turned into one of the great black holes in the history of money.

Business Week, 15 October 2001

A decade after the Japanese asset bubble burst, banks are still estimated to have bad debts equivalent to 20 per cent of Japanese GDP. Furthermore, an estimated US$700 billion are on the watch list, and the Japanese Financial Services Authority has projected that another US$50 billion will go bad each year up to 2004. Japan also appears to have insufficient numbers of regulators; 10,000 US government employees worked on the US savings and loans crisis, compared with just 1,000 Japanese officials employed by the Japanese Resolution & Collection Corporation to date.

Japan's bureaucratically guided capitalism also demonstrates an increasing propensity to corruption. While the collusiveness of the political economy may be conducive to efficiency under certain circumstances, the private benefits increasingly outweigh the public, and the mire of mutual corruption deepens. There should be no need to spell out the details of the many scandals of recent years, indeed of twenty years since the Lockheed and Grumman scandals of the 1970s. They have involved top figures in the key central government agencies, provincial governors and city mayors, top corporate executives, bankers and securities company heads. The Ministry of Finance, which is the majordomo of the Japanese government, is now enmeshed in a series of scandals involving the combination of collusion and loose or inadequate supervision, as in the Jùsen or Housing Loan scandal which involved trillions of yen of mostly small investors' funds or the Daiwa bank affair, in which that bank's New York branch somehow 'lost' $US1.1 billion, but at a deeper level this Ministry bears much of the responsibility for deliberate inflation of the bubble of the 1980s, through its cheap money and inflated land and stock price policies, and for the diversion – and in the long run almost certainly the destruction – of much of the country's savings by funneling it into the construction sector. The Ministry of Finance provided the lungs that blew out the bubble, its favoured beneficiaries fattened, while the rest of the country was left spattered with debris when the bubble burst.

Where once it would have been said that in the Asian region only Japan was modern, efficient, and not-corrupt, now it might be said that the corruption is nowhere more deeply entrenched than in Japan. In the single month of November, four major financial institutions, including the regional Hokkaido Takushoku Bank and Yamaichi Securities, the country's Number Four securities firm, collapsed. Confidence in the institutions supervised by the Ministry of Finance, including the banks, plummeted, the withdrawal of deposits and their transfer to foreign banks and securities companies began to gather pace. Manufacturers of steel safes reported unprecedented demand, which presumably meant that individuals were shifting their money out of the banking system altogether. When people begin to feel it wiser to lock their money in vaults and safes rather than entrust it to banks, something is seriously wrong. From being the wonder of the world in the 1980s when Vogel's book [Japan As Number One, Harvard University Press, 1979] appeared, top Japanese bureaucratic and financial institutions have become a sort of laughing stock, even, in a sense, worse than 'nothing'.

'From Number One to Number Nothing: Japan's Fin de Siècle Blues', Professor Gavan McCormack, Department of Pacific and Asian History, ANU, Canberra

Whether the Bretton Woods institutions are contributing to improved global financial standards is also questioned by some observers. Gerald O'Driscoll and Brett Schaefer of the Heritage Foundation have argued that the IMF has exported poor banking practice in many countries.

The IMF exports poor banking sector practice by example. It damages the international financial system when it continues to lend to countries like Russia, a financial black hole.

'The IMF Promotes Poor Banking Practices', O'Driscoll and Schaeffer, Heritage Foundation, April 1999

There have also been significant concerns about the moral hazard issues related to bail outs.

... One of the reasons we have Asia [the East Asian Crisis] is that we bailed out Mexico. We signaled to creditors around the world that you could feel free to lend in Asia, and the U.S. Treasury and the IMF would bail you out if you got in trouble. Now if we bail this one out, we'll have established a second precedent, and the next time, it will be bigger and arguably something we can contain less easily.

Lawrence Lindsay, American Enterprise Institute and former Federal Reserve Governor, *Washington Post*, 22 December 1997

Therefore, although the OECD has been focusing its efforts on offshore financial centres, the largest global problems in financial regulation and systemic risk to the global financial system appear to be in onshore centres, particularly in a number of OECD countries, such as Japan, Korea and Turkey. The scale of bad debts estimated for these three coun-tries exceeds US$600 billion, even after hundreds of billions of bad debt write-offs in recent years, and may be far greater, with new bad debts fore-cast to grow by US$50 billion per year in Japan alone, according to Japanese government estimates. This dwarfs any concerns expressed by the OECD about how well-regulated offshore centres are, with many of the best run offshore financial centres having very high quality regulatory standards compared with Japan, Korea and Turkey. Indeed, the Channel Islands has consistently refused to allow Japanese banks permission to open offices in their jurisdictions as they do not meet the high prudential standards required for the Channel Islands.

There are no Japanese banks here. Japan's central bank, some say, doesn't regulate vigorously enough. Japanese banks get into trouble more quickly and they can't get support. Many banks in Japan have applied to set up in the Channel Islands but all have been refused. The Channel Islands policy requires a large capital base and strong regulation.

Ben Bendelow, Group Executive, Basle Trust Corp and Past President of the Offshore Institute, Jersey, 2001

High standards of corporate governance and accounting practices, there-fore, including a high degree of transparency, are critical for all companies and financial institutions, not just for offshore financial centres. Such standards are also critical for an efficiently operating domestic financial system, which underpins a dynamic economy. Well-managed offshore financial centres such as the Channel Islands and the Isle of Man might be justifiably sceptical of criticisms of their financial regulation coming from the OECD, whose member countries include some of the worst global examples of financial sector regulation and banking sector bad debts, such as Japan, Korea and Turkey.

Summary

As with other major global industries, international business services will remain subject to a high level of global competition, not only in the market-place but in the global arena of international law, trade and investment regulation and global standards, as countries vie with each other to obtain the greatest competitive advantage for their own financial services sectors.

All Commonwealth countries need to give urgent attention to ensuring that their financial systems meet the highest international standards to ensure the future success and competitiveness of their own economies. At the same time, globalisation is about international competition and developing competitive advantage. The benefits of globalisation accrue to the most competitive and efficient segments of industry – international business services are no exception.

International business services is a rapidly growing, high value adding market segment globally, and a sector that many countries wish to strategically position themselves in in order to establish or maintain a global market leader position. At a time when many countries are suffering from high dependency on commodity exports with declining terms of trade, and when even manufacturing is suffering from intense price competition and overcapacity globally, traded services is the new frontier that is a key focus for national competitiveness strategies.

Developing countries must strengthen their capacity for effective representation in international negotiations on traded services, in order to protect their right to compete in this key global export industry. Traded services has the potential to play a leading role in the economic development of many developing countries, as well as in bridging the digital divide and transforming these nations into knowledge economies.

The OECD and the Captive Insurance Industry: The OECD Report Re-examined

Trevor A. Carmichael QC[1]

Introduction and Overview

The report by the OECD, *Towards Global Tax Co-operation: Progress in Identifying and Eliminating Harmful Tax Practices,* has produced a wide-ranging reaction in the economic, financial, political and popular literature.[2] Commentaries on the subject have been supplemented by a wider-ranging political and diplomatic movement which too has sought to place the report within an equitable and developmental perspective. One focus area which may add to this response lies in a sectoral examination of the report, determining how it impacts on specific areas such as banking insurance. This brief paper will explore this sector of insurance including captive insurance, an industry which is present in both the offshore financial centre and the metropolitan financial centres.[3] Insurance is a useful category for examination not only because of its presence in both types of centres but also because it represents a business sector which positively responds to issues within the report such as transparency and substantial business activity.

Captive insurance started in the second half of the twentieth-century essentially as a means of giving companies the ability to provide their

---

1 Dr Trevor Carmichael QC is the Principal of Chancery Chambers, a Barbados law firm specialising in international business, environmental and charity law. He has served as UN Consultant to the Seychelles and as one of eight Organisation of American States experts engaged in drafting an OAS Convention on International Contracts.

2 A major body of this work has been undertaken on a continuous basis by Richard Hay whose most recent article, 'US Destabilises Assault on Offshore Centres', in *Tax Planning International Review,* Vol. 28, No. 9, September 2001, is a comprehensive review of the subject. Bruce Zagaris has also presented substantial contributions on the subject, as well as serving as a member of the Heritage Foundation, an organisation which was in the forefront of pointing out the weaknesses in the OECD Report.

3 A useful survey on insurance and reinsurance is to be found in the *Special International Financial Law Review* 1999 Supplement published by Euromoney Publications. Articles on Barbados, Canada, Germany, The Netherlands, UK and USA represent a useful compendium of the captive and non-captive jurisdictions.

own insurance. Its development was linked with the concept of facilitating the insuring of risks for which coverage was not available in the open market; in this regard it became synonymous with the implementing of self-insurance programmes. Captive insurance, however, extended its reach by giving companies the efficiency of bringing all of their insurance programmes into one company and accessing the worldwide reinsurance market. The facilitating environment of the captive insurance company has been so welcoming that many reinsurance companies themselves have structured some of their own corporations as captive insurers.

Development of Captive Insurance in Financial Centres

The captive insurance industry began as a way of providing attractively priced self insurance in a well-regulated jurisdiction. Pioneered by Bermuda in the mid-Atlantic, and Guernsey and Jersey in Europe, it rapidly spread to a number of offshore financial centres and subsequently to the USA and within Lloyds of London itself (see Table 1 and Figures 1 and 2). It is a fast-growing industry which provides protection to a single parent captive, as in the case of a single business, as well as to group or association captives as, for example, in the case of a group of emergency physicians or automobile dealers. The growth of the industry in different jurisdictions has been the result of specific policies; it is useful to isolate some of the jurisdictions and the macro- and micro-measures which have influenced and shaped individual policies.

In Bermuda the growth of the captive insurance industry was part of the overall planned development of international business from as early as the 1940s. It started through the introduction of 'captives' as essentially self-insurance schemes for non-Bermudian businesses which did not want to pay liability insurance premiums in the open market or which, for one reason or another, were uninsurable. It led the market continuously, and it also consistently introduced variations on the main theme. Hence, by the end of the 1990s, it had developed a carefully nurtured class system for insurance companies with varying levels of sophistication and complexity. At the most simple level, it continued to host the pure 'captive', merely insuring its own parent company together with the next level of captive taking on third party risks. However, it advanced into the area of the 'captive' loosely defined, acting as traditional reinsurer and most recently engaging in catastrophe risk and the more esoteric finite risk product.

Bermuda entered the captive catastrophe insurance business when it

Table 1. Captives by Domicile

Domicile	Number of captives	Domicile	Number of captives
Non-US Western Hemisphere		**US Onshore**	
Bermuda	1,405	Vermont	381
Cayman Islands	535	Hawaii	73
Barbados	237	Colorado	21
British Virgin Islands	184	Georgia	14
Turks & Caicos	63	Illinois	14
Bahamas	25	Tennessee	14
British Columbia	17	New York	12
Curaçao (Netherlands Antilles)	15	US Virgin Islands	7
Panama	2	Delaware	5
St Lucia	0	Florida	5
Subtotal	*2,483*	Kansas	4
		Rhode Island	4
Europe and Asia		Virginia	4
Guernsey	370	Maine	2
Luxembourg	175	Nevada	2
Ireland	178	South Carolina	2
Isle of Man	173	Washington DC	2
Singapore	54	Guam	1
Switzerland	32	South Dakota	0
Jersey	27	West Virginia	0
Gibraltar	12	*Subtotal*	*567*
Hong Kong	8		
Liechtenstein	2	Other US States	115
Lloyds	1		
Aland Island	1	All other non-US	162
Labuan	0		
Mauritius	0	***Total***	***4,458***
Subtotal	*1,131*		

created a regulatory climate to take on the business which had traditionally been the province of Lloyds of London but which had suffered serious financial losses as a result of property disasters such as Hurricane Andrew. It nevertheless provided the necessary regulatory environment by, among other things, requiring a property catastrophe company to provide capital and surplus of $100 million together with a solvency margin of at least 50 per cent of net premiums written.

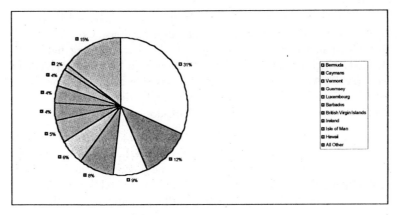

Figure 1. Captives Worldwide Statistics

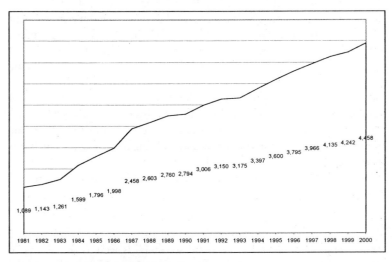

Figure 2. Long-term Growth in Captives

Barbados, as the sixth largest captive insurance domicile in the world, introduced legislation in 1983 to complement its old international business companies legislation (1965) and offshore banking, legislation (1979), and to make better use of its double tax treaty arrangements. Although Barbados' most active overall treaty use is with Canada, its captive insurance industry was given an original impetus by way of the Federal Excise Tax Exemption under its treaty with the USA. For the ability to establish a Barbados captive with a 'permanent establishment' and managed in Barbados allowed the US captive-owner the ability to be exempt from the federal excise tax under the treaty. It saved considerable costs. This treaty provision, if used sensibly with a managed Barbadian entity, became so attractive that eventually a Technical Corrections Bill was passed in the USA in an effort to level the playing field with Bermuda which had also signed a Tax Information Exchange Agreement with the USA. Nevertheless, Barbados was able to retain some major insurance entities which could justifiably, under the Double Tax Treaty, claim a 'permanent establishment' in Barbados.

Barbados has also remained the domicile of choice for Canadian interests through the Canada–Barbados Double Tax Treaty. In such a case, the captive must be resident in Barbados, and income generated from related foreign affiliates in the captive will avoid being considered Foreign Accrued Property Income and remains tax free until repatriated to Canada.

The British Virgin Islands, as one of the more recent jurisdictions with captive-insurance legislation, carefully fashioned its 1994 statute so as to allow effective regulation within a friendly business environment. It sought thereby to mirror the Bermuda and Barbados regimes, as well as the many other existing captive-insurance jurisdictions. Its financial services secretariat recognised that as a zero tax jurisdiction with a favourable climate of client confidentiality and with the fastest worldwide IBC growth rate, the need to stress the regulatory element was paramount. Hence the 1994 insurance legislation provided information access to foreign regulators and law enforcement officials in cases where there was suspicion of specific criminal offences. While the legislation still sought to ensure that it was attractive enough to capture offshore insurance and reinsurance companies, it nevertheless, maintained a respect for effective regulation.

In ensuring such regulation, like the other captive jurisdictions, it required that yearly audited financial statements for each company be filed with the regulatory authorities. It also gave to the Governor the right to approve merges and portfolio transfers, as well as the ability to suspend or cancel an insurer's licence. Further, the legislation allowed the transfer of long-term insurance business in whole or in part only if sanctioned by the Court.

When Ireland introduced its captive-insurance legislation, it sought to carve a special market niche by way of the direct writing captive. It courted and achieved success as a result of the ability to write insurance on a service basis – 'direct' – throughout the EU, thereby reducing the expense of fronting fees. This business opportunity was enhanced by the adoption of the Second Non Life Directive (88/357/EEC) and the Third Non Life Directive (92/49/EEC) which allowed the setting up of a single insurance entity in Dublin, with the ability to write directly in most EU countries.

Ireland has adopted the main regulatory features present in the older jurisdictions, such as Bermuda, Barbados and Guernsey, particularly in the licensing procedures for captive-insurance companies. As with all of the jurisdictions, regulation starts *ab initio* with the initial application for licensing by the captive. At that stage, a detailed application document must include all details on the proposed company's activities by way of a business plan with *pro forma* financial projections, copies of policy wordings, justification for premium ratings, claims handling and reinsurance particulars, copies of the company's management agreement, biographical details of the proposed directors and sample copies of the proposed corporate constating documents. As with the other captive jurisdictions, the licence application must also specify the classes of insurance which the captive proposes to write.

One challenge which is a by-product of the direct writing captive is the need for regular and detailed financial reporting to be made available to regulators. However, the Irish experience has been good in that requests from local country regulators are dealt with by one regulator to the other regulator and not by the company's managers. The ongoing financial reporting and the need to keep acceptable levels of solvency, common in the other captive jurisdictions, is also a feature of the Dublin regulatory framework.

Ireland's example was followed, from a business and regulatory perspective, by Gibraltar when in 1996 it introduced re-domiciliation legislation allowing it to attract existing captives already established in other jurisdictions. This feature buttressed the ability of Gibraltar domiciled captives, like their Dublin counterparts, to write direct insurance in the European Union. As a dependent territory of the UK, and part of the EU under Section 227(4) of the Treaty of Rome 1973 and the Act of Succession 1973, it enacted legislation allowing compliance with EU directives, including those dealing with insurance.

There is an implied sanction of Gibraltar's regulatory regime, for its insurance legislation was reviewed by the UK's Department of Trade and Industry. Such acceptance by the UK is a recognition of captive insurance as an industry, and an approval of the direct writing of insurance by Gibraltar's captives. It is an acceptance which is multilaterised by virtue of its practice within the EU. In this regard, it is a multilateral governmental acceptance not dissimilar to the same recognition given by Barbados captive insurance through its double tax treaty with such partners as Canada and the USA.

The captive-insurance domiciles therefore reflect a balance between aggressive insurance business development within a framework of self imposed and externally sanctioned industry regulation. It is a dynamic industry which gives rise to a continuing set of complex business arrangements, and which is represented by the novel forms of insurance and reinsurance practised by both offshore and onshore jurisdictions.

A Dynamic Multilateralised Industry

It is possibly in the area of reinsurance and alternative risk financing that the offshore captive insurance industry has made welcomed incursions into the global insurance market. While it is now readily accepted that some of the traditional captive jurisdictions are hosts to some of the most important reinsurance entities and are also in the vanguard in the development of new reinsurance products, it is nevertheless necessary to conceptually explore reinsurance so as to better understand the transparent industry convergence in this area between the offshore and the onshore.

Reinsurers assume risks from insurers – namely primary insurers or ceding companies – who have sold policies to the insureds. Within the concept of reinsurance, coverages are included which are placed 'on top of' a particular firm's self insured retention. While it is referred to as direct excess reinsurance, it is not in essence true reinsurance. It does create a situation that resembles reinsurance arrangements since the retention by an organisation is like the primary insurer's risk retention. Reinsurance is either 'facultative' or 'treaty'. The former gives protection to the primary insurer for individual risks and accordingly is written on a policy specific basis. Treaty reinsurance provides cover for a class of insured or a block of business.

The insurance industry and its derivative, the reinsurance industry, are by their nature dynamic, since risk is not static and exposure, while not necessarily infinite, must however be managed and controlled within safe financial limits. The recent development whereby the insurance markets and the capital markets have been judiciously used in joint enterprises has had at its core the need to extend the insurance product to its maximum feasible capacity. In this regard, the offshore captive insurance jurisdictions have been important components in transactions which seek to obtain this elasticity of investment and better insurance utilisation. In particular, the jurisdictions of Cayman Islands, Bermuda and Barbados have been critical components within such novel structures.

To place this trend within a theoretical framework, it must be recognised that different types of insurance liability will require different levels of capitalisation. It is a truism that the greater the risk which is assumed, the more capital and reinsurance an insurer will need so as to be able to write the related risk premium. The traditional position has been that the assets in insurer's insurance funds have had to be liquid and placed in very highly rated securities. The trend has changed, however, and with the help of some captive insurance jurisdictions insurers now seek to match their insurance fund assets to their claims liabilities as they develop.

The use of captives is now particularly effective in the novel area of securitisation of insurance risks. This new practice encompasses the grouping of a portfolio of similar risks to be underwritten in a corporate vehicle. It is in turn then able to issue debt or equity securities to investors in exchange for their cash investment in the corporate entity. The investor, therefore, is able to make a corresponding, although indirect, investment in the financial results of the particular insurance risks.

The captive jurisdiction takes on a special significance, since conventional reinsurance may be too costly or inflexible, thereby making probable the use of the special purpose entity or existing reinsurance company. In this regard, securitisation of insurance risk must be distinguished from making an investment in an insurer's stock. For in the case of an insurance investment, there is an inherent limitation since the assets of an insurer will generally be limited to certain categories of investment. Such investments will carry a fairly well defined performance within the context of contemporary capital markets. For investment in the shares of an insurance company will only offer a significant return if the company makes an above average underwriting profit net of expenses.

The advantage of securitisation is the versatility which it affords in avoiding the duplication of exposure to similar risks within an investor's existing investments with those present in the securitising insurer's own investment portfolio. The investor has the ability to focus on the parts of the insurer's portfolio of insurance risks which the investor views as likely to generate the greatest pure underwriting profit, while at the same time not sharing in the wider operational and investments risks of the insurer. Hence, with securitisation the insurer may select the particular insurance business which requires particular investment effort. The use of securitisation, for example by way of offering to institutional investors of securities issued by a catastrophe reinsurer, has been successfully deployed by way of a Cayman Islands 'special purpose vehicle'. It is the flexibility of the Cayman legislation as a captive insurance jurisdiction which gives scope to such effective use of a global financing instrument such as securitisation.

While securitisation represents a novel and current basis for the formation of captive insurance structures, the more conventional reasons remain as compelling characteristics in facilitating insurance cover of a multilateralised structure. Japan is useful as a pedagogical analysis since as a very dynamic economy within jurisdiction which is small in size, it is easy to dissect its captive anatomy. Since 1953, a Japanese captive has been established for insurance of one of its oil companies; in the 1970s Japanese shipping companies with substantial international operations also set up captive insurance structures. In the 1980s and 1990s, as Japanese trading and manufacturing companies expanded their operations in new directions, including insurance and reinsurance, they established captives in the jurisdictions with favourable legislation such as Bermuda, Singapore, Ireland, Vermont and other US domiciles, Luxembourg and Guernsey.

The Japanese captives have been formed in an effort to secure greater control of risk financing; to encourage risk management and develop risk financing; to obtain insurance cover not available on the Japanese market; to transform cost centres into profit centres; and to directly access the reinsurance market with its increased capacity, information and education. They have also availed themselves of the new techniques such as securitisation to obtain cover for high exposure risks such as with earthquakes or petrochemicals. While tax is an important factor, it is not the sole factor and it is not the main *raison d'être* in the formation of the Japanese captive – a feature which is virtually the same in all captive insurance structures. In the case of Japan, its companies are taxed on their worldwide income when repatriated to Japan. Provided that the captive pays income tax in excess of 25 per cent, the remainder of its income is not taxed unless and until it is repatriated to Japan. This tax regime has some similarities with the Canadian and American captive structures established in Barbados where the presence of a double tax treaty allows for greater flexibility.

The multilateralised captive structure is accordingly one which takes optimal advantage of the prevailing legislation, regulation and taxation in a captive insurance domicile while at the same time facilitating the orderly development of global insurance arrangements. This predominant and positive feature of the captive has been given such favourable recognition by the fact that within the captive domiciles themselves there is increasing activity for formation of captives in other captive insurance domiciles, as for instance in the case of the Caribbean electric utility companies considering the scope for structuring a group captive in a Caribbean captive insurance jurisdiction.

The positive features of the captive have also received the imprimatur of US regulatory authorities recognised by the inward movement of establishing captive insurance domiciles within the USA itself. American captive insurance jurisdictions such as Vermont, Illinois, Arizona, Colorado, New York, Hawaii, Massachusetts, Ohio and US Virgin Islands now complement the older offshore jurisdictions such as Bermuda, Cayman Islands and Barbados. Furthermore in Europe, even though Ireland may be considered a tax encouraging domicile, it is Germany which acts as a captive insurance jurisdiction to some of the world's Fortune 500 Captives. The captive insurance company is, therefore, increasingly a creature which may be nurtured offshore or onshore – a feature which recognises its legitimate business purpose. Its increasing multilateralised focus is also represented in the fusion of captive and non-captive legislation, as in the case of the recent Barbados legislation which allows for setting up of offshore and onshore insurance structures under one umbrella statute and further utilisation, if available, of tax credits under applicable double tax treaty legislation.

The captive insurance industry meets the standards of substantial business activity set out in the OECD report. Not only does it encapsulate very dynamic international insurance business activity as represented in conventional and non conventional uses, but it is also one which is substantially managed in the various captive insurance jurisdictions. Major international insurance brokers and intermediaries have established offices in these jurisdictions. While Bermuda represents an extreme case, with every major insurance entity having established a real presence in that country, Barbados, Cayman Islands, Guernsey and others also manifest varying levels of substantial business activity. In the case of Barbados, the industry employs over 200 people directly and a much larger number indirectly. It also adds significantly, as in the case of Bermuda, to the Barbadian tourism industry where many people make frequent visits to attend statutory meetings as well as meetings which are set up for pure business planning, development and execution. The insurance industry also transfers technology so that many professionals learn new skills in international insurance and more generally innovative financial service products.

The Challenge of Regulation

The OECD report considers the issues of transparency and regulation as critical to an orderly world financial order. The captive insurance industry manifests regulation and suspension at a micro level within the particular jurisdictions, and at a macro and more discrete level by way of participation in the various international bodies specifically established for the purpose of ensuring greater supervisory oversight.

All the captive jurisdictions carry very comprehensive procedures for the licensing of an insurance company and equally elaborate requirements for its ongoing operations. All the initial licence applications call for detailed information about the proposed directors and shareholders, as well as carefully spelled out business plans with *pro forma* financial projections for at least five years. These plans also spell out net and gross premiums income as well as the reinsurance programme (if applicable) by class. These licence applications are buttressed by legislation in all of the jurisdictions which sets out margins of solvency which must be maintained throughout the life of the captive. Hence, there is an implied ongoing legislative oversight which is complemented by the requirement, in all the jurisdictions, to file annual financial statements with the regulatory authority. Furthermore, all the captive jurisdictions do not allow fundamental corporate or financial changes without the approval of the regulators, even if, in some cases, the requirement is one of mere notification. It is, therefore, not surprising that the level of insurance insolvencies in captive insurance jurisdictions is low.[4] Indeed, where those insolvencies have taken place, the cause cannot with justification be attributed to insufficient regulation.

Regulation of the captive is also evidenced at the macro level through the supervisory activities of the International Association of Insurance Supervisors (IAIS) and the Offshore Group of Insurance Supervisors. In the case of the Offshore Group, its principal objects are carefully spelled out in its charter and include the establishing of standards for supervision and the facilitating co-operation between Supervisors of offshore insurance business. It makes as a condition of membership the need for the new member to agree to be supervised in accordance with the standards by the Group. Furthermore, elaborate provisions call for the presence of an Evaluation Panel which acts as a screen for new membership applications, and the Group has established standards for the supervision of insurance business to be adhered to by all members.

The International Group naturally has a larger membership and resources. Many of the offshore captive jurisdictions are represented. Furthermore, it extends observer status to a wide range of international insurance businesses, national insurance associations, international governmental organisations and international law firms as well as international accounting firms and leading research institutes. It has established a shared Supervisory Standard on Licencing and in October 2000 developed a very comprehensive Licensory Textbook. In 2001 it launched an Insurance Regulation Database. This body is very keenly involved in training of staff from various insurance regulatory agencies and its Technical Committee is in the vanguard of developing and main-

---

4 See the very useful text *Cross Frontier Insolvency of Insurance Companies* by Gabriel Moss QC (Sweet & Maxwell, London 2001) and, in particular, the article on Bermuda by Ian Kawaley and on Barbados by Trevor Carmichael.

taining standards in accounting, reinsurance and disclosure. A critical feature of its work is the multilayered involvement of critical persons within the international insurance industry as was evident in the Tripartite Insurance Fraud Conference organised jointly with the Association of British Insurers, the Association of Chief Police Officers and the International Association of Insurance Fraud Agencies. It attracted at least 80 delegates from 17 countries and the offshore captive insurance jurisdictions were to a large degree represented.

Captive insurance regulation is strong within the jurisdictions themselves through the various supervisory offices as well as in the broader international context through the vibrant oversight organisations. The regulation within the jurisdictions is within the licensing procedures as well as the ongoing statutory solvency and reporting requirements and is complemented by the discrete supervision exercised by the international regulatory bodies. The mix of internal and external regulatory forces have ensured the healthy development of the captive insurance industry, a regime which had its origins in the offshore financial centre and is now also strategically present in some of the 'onshore' OECD jurisdictions.

The Aftermath and Beyond

The captive insurance industry as practised in the offshore financial centres is clearly not in conflict with the principles and spirit of the OECD report. The nature of the industry, its extension to OECD, some jurisdictions, the substance of the industry generated from within the particular domiciles, and the overall domestic and international regulation and supervision, all contribute to insulating the captive insurance industry from the criticisms within the report.

Appearing before the Permanent Subcommittee on Investigations of the Senate Committee on Governmental Affairs, the US Treasury Secretary expressed concern about the ability of one country or a group of countries to interfere in another country's methods of structuring its own tax system. The OECD itself has agreed to three modifications to the repor: that coordinated defensive measures would no longer be taken against perceived offending jurisdictions; that the text of 'substantial activities' would no longer be applicable; and that the time for offending jurisdictions to commit to 'transparency' and 'exchange of information' would be extended to 30 November 2002.

The OECD published a new report on 11 July 2001 entitled 'A Report on the Misuse of Corporate Vehicles for Illicit Purposes', put together by its Steering Group on Corporate Governance. It calls, among other things, on intermediaries engaged in forming corporate entities to maintain information on beneficial ownership or undertake investigations on such ownership where suspicious behaviour is apparent. It has also extended the period for jurisdictions to make a commitment to transparency and regulation from 31 July 2001 to 28 February 2002.

Irrespective of the reports, it is clear that there is a need to examine such reports in a sectoral sense as has been undertaken in relation to captive insurance within this chapter. When one considers that the scope of the insurance industry and the banking industry has become less obvious as a result of features such as securitisation, it is evident that matters such as transparency and regulation need to be considered also in an industry specific sense to the degree that it is possible.[5] It is, therefore, not surprising that industry bodies including the International Actuarial Association are examining such issues. Such an examination will seek to establish that the concerns of the OECD reports are neither purely jurisdiction specific nor industry specific, particularly where the boundaries of industry and jurisdiction are no longer best viewed in the earlier conventional sense of the twentieth century.

---

5 The Report of the Working Group on Offshore Centres of the FSF recognised that the growth of London as the largest offshore banking centre was directly related to regulations placed on the US banking sector. London has also been a leading insurance and reinsurance centre and epitomises the insurance/banking fusion common to both the offshore captive and the onshore reinsurance company.

The World Trade Organisation and Fiscal Competition

WTO Compatibility of the OECD 'Defensive Measures' against Harmful Tax Competition[1]

Roman Grynberg and Bridget Chilala

Background

As a result of a mandate granted by the OECD ministers[2] in 1996, the OECD Secretariat prepared a report on harmful tax competition[3] which outlined the features of taxation systems that the Secretariat viewed as distorting global taxation and finance decisions.[4] The report identified two separate types of regimes that are deemed to be harmful, those that are tax havens[5] and those that have preferential elements.[6] Subsequent to the 1998 Report the OECD has prepared a second report in June 2000 which has named 35 jurisdictions as being tax havens and unless these jurisdictions sign memoranda of understanding with OECD they shall be listed as unco-operative tax havens by 31st July, 2001.[7]

---

1 This paper was originally published in the *Journal of World Trade Investment*, Vol. 2, No. 3, September 2001. Permission to reproduce it is gratefully acknowledged. Dr Roman Grynberg is Deputy Director and Bridget Chilala is Senior Policy Officer in the Economic Affairs Division of the Commopnwealth Secretariat.

2 OECD Ministerial Communiqué, May 1996.

3 OECD, *Harmful Tax Competition: An Emerging Global Issue*, Paris, 1998. The original OECD members include Austria, Belgium, Canada, Denmark, France, Germany, Greece, Iceland, Ireland, Italy, Luxembourg, Netherlands, Norway, Portugal, Spain, Sweeden, Switzerland, Turkey, the UK and the USA. The new members include Japan, Finland, Australia, New Zealand, Mexico, Czech Republic, Hungary, Poland and Korea.

4 OECD, *Towards Global Tax Co-operation: Report to the 2000 Ministerial Council Meeting and the Recommendations by the Committee on Fiscal Affairs*, Paris, June 2000.

5 The OECD report indicates that tax havens can be identified by four characteristics: they have no or only nominal taxes; they lack effective exchange of information; they lack transparency; firms registered in the tax havens tend to have no substantial activity in the jurisdiction. OECD, 2000, *op.cit.*, p. 23.

6 The OECD defines harmful preferential elements as those with no or low effective tax rates, 'ring-fencing' of domestic and offshore regimes, lack of transparency and lack of effective exchange of information. Ibid., p. 27.

7 Six countries, Bermuda, Cayman Islands, Cyprus, Malta, Mauritius and Netherlands Antilles, the so-called advanced commitment jurisdictions, have already made written public commitments to the OECD. Two other jurisdictions, San Marino and Isle of Man, have sent letters but the commitments and undertakings in those letters appear to fall far short of OECD demands.

Those jurisdictions failing to sign memoranda may then be subject to defensive measures, in effect economic sanctions, which can be instituted collectively or bilaterally by OECD members against those tax havens.[8] These proposed defensive measures and their compatibility with WTO rules are the subject of this paper.

The OECD is proposing to eliminate preferential tax systems amongst non-members as well as the OECD members which also maintain such measures. However, while preferential tax measures maintained by tax havens are defined unambiguously as harmful, the OECD employs the precautionary adjective 'potentially' harmful when describing OECD measures.[9] The OECD is also embarking on a global dialogue with numerous jurisdictions in Asia and Latin America where preferential tax regimes are deemed to exist. The OECD expects that all remedial measures by OECD and non-OECD jurisdictions in regard to preferential tax regimes will be fully implemented by 2005. Again, the difference in treatment being afforded to internal OECD preferential tax measures and non-tax haven measures will become significant in light of various exemption provisions of the GATT and GATS.

The paper considers several different areas of potential legal interface between the OECD punitive sanctions and WTO rules. This, however, is done in a context where the precise nature of those sanctions are unknown. The analysis considers the type of sanctions suggested and, briefly, possible violations of GATT and, more extensively, GATS rules. In the case of GATS several types of possible WTO violations are considered. These include violations of service sector commitments on mode 1 and 2 by OECD countries, Article XI.1 violations and possible violations of Article II (Most Favoured Nation) obligations and possible non-violation disputes. The defence under WTO rules of the proposed OECD sanctions is also considered.

Proposed Defensive Measures

The OECD in its 2000 Report has indicated that defensive measures which are tantamount to punitive sanctions would be applied on a col-

---

8 At the time of writing the OECD has not completed the six application notes regarding transparency/exchange of information; transfer pricing, ring-fencing, holding companies, fund management and shipping. These application notes will define commitments that those jurisdictions that the OECD deems to be tax havens will have signed by 31 July 2001. Thus, affected jurisdictions are expected to undertake commitments to implement measures that have not been clearly defined. Given that the applications notes will not be ready before OECD members can apply defensive measures, this renders the process all more contentious.

9 The OECD has identified 17 OECD tax jurisdictions which are deemed to have potentially harmful features. See OECD, 2000, ibid., pp. 12–14.

lective or bilateral basis against those jurisdictions that did not co-operate with the OECD initiative or agree to the terms of the Memorandum of Understanding. The defensive measures that have been proposed by the OECD against those jurisdictions they define to be 'unco-operative' include actions:[10]

i)   To disallow deductions, exemptions, credits or other allowances related to transactions with unco-operative tax havens or transactions taking advantage of their harmful tax practices;

ii) To require comprehensive information reporting rules for transactions involving unco-operative tax havens or taking advantage of their harmful tax practices, supported by substantial penalties for inaccurate reporting or non-reporting of such transactions;

iii) For countries that do not have controlled foreign corporations or equivalent (CFC) rules to consider adopting such rules, and for countries that have such rules to ensure that they apply in a fashion consistent with the desirability of curbing harmful practices;

iv) To deny any exceptions (for example reasonable cause) that may otherwise apply to the applications of regular penalties in the case of transactions involving entities organised in unco-operative tax havens or taking advantage of their harmful tax practices;

v)   To deny the availability of the foreign tax credit or the participation exemption with regard to distributions that are sourced from unco-operative tax havens or to transactions taking advantage of their harmful practices;

vi) To impose withholding taxes on certain payments to residents of unco-operative tax havens;

vii) To enhance audit and enforcement activities with respect to unco-operative tax havens and transactions taking advantage of their harmful tax practices;

viii) To ensure that any existing and new domestic defensive measures against harmful tax practices are also applicable to transactions with unco-operative tax havens and to transactions taking advantage of their harmful tax practices;

ix) Not to enter into any comprehensive income tax conventions with unco-operative tax havens, and to consider terminating any such existing conventions unless certain conditions are met;

10 Ibid., p. 25.

x)   To deny deductions and cost recovery to the extent otherwise allow-
     able for fees and expenses incurred in establishing or acquiring
     entities incorporated in unco-operative tax havens;

xi) To impose 'transactional' charges or levies on certain transactions
     involving unco-operative tax havens.

The nature of the measures outlined by the OECD fall into three broad
categories: those that apply to income derived from a particular jurisdiction (measures i–vii); those, overlapping slightly with the first category,
which are aimed directly at various types of transactions involving that
jurisdiction (measures i and xi); and measures of a general nature that
would have no immediate trade or commercial impact (measures viii and
ix). The OECD has also recommended that members review non-essential
aid to such jurisdictions.[11] While this may be a particularly severe form of
sanction, it is significant to note that its application appears not to violate
any particular WTO provision.

WTO Compatibility

Under GATT rules the defensive measures are not normally actionable
until such time as they are announced by particular OECD/WTO members. Their announcement and implementation should in itself constitute
grounds for consultation at the WTO should the measure be perceived to
violate WTO rules or they nullify or impair the rights of other WTO
members.[12] All OECD members are also members of the WTO and ten of
the affected tax haven jurisdictions are members of the WTO.[13] Until an

---

11 OECD, 2000, Ibid., p. 26.

12 The GATT jurisprudence on whether a WTO member is in a position to seek formal
consultations prior to the application of the measure is ambiguous. The most recent case, the
1990 panel on the 'EEC Regulation on the Import of Parts and Components, 'L/6657, found
that: '... the mere existence of the anti-circumvention provision in the EEC's anti-dumping
Regulation is not inconsistent with the EEC's obligation under the General Agreement'.
Earlier GATT jurisprudence indicated that the existence of mandatory laws made it possible
for WTO members to take action prior to the implementation of an action. GATS
definitions of 'measures' that nullify or impair rights include decisions under GATS, Article
XXVIII (a). It is uncertain whether a panel would view a decision by OECD Ministers to be
actionable under GATT or GATS rules prior to its implementation by individual OECD
members.

13 The following affected jurisdictions are also members of WTO: Antigua and Barbuda
(became a member on 01.01.95), Bahrain (01/01/95), Barbados (01/01/95), Belize
(01/01/95), Dominica (01/01/95), Grenada (22.02.96), Maldives (31/05/95), Panama
(06/09/97), St Vincent and the Grenadines (01/01/95) and Liechtenstein (01/01/95). The
following have observer status at the WTO: Samoa, Seychelles, Tonga and Vanuatu.

actual defensive measure is announced it is unlikely that there would be a basis for a WTO consultation but whether any subsequent WTO challenge would be successful would rest upon precisely what type of measures were applied. It is assumed in this paper that three types of punitive sanctions or defensive measures could be applied:

i)   A tax or administrative measure based upon all or selected transactions involving the sale of a good or service of a WTO member;

ii) A tax or administrative measure that would penalise the income of a company, domestic or foreign for trading in goods and services with a WTO member;

iii) A measure designed to place pressure on unco-operative tax havens but with no direct trade distorting impact.

WTO Rules Pertaining to Direct Tax Matters

GATT Provisions

In the unlikely event that the OECD defensive measure or sanction that is ultimately imposed after July 2001 is in the form of a more general withholding tax targeted against a wide range of goods transactions in the so-called 'un-co-operative jurisdiction', i.e. option (i) above, then there are a number of GATT 1947 provisions that would be relevant to both the defensive measure and any litigation predicated upon a possible violation of WTO rules. Measures vi and xi described in section 2 above could well be such general tax measures. This section deals with potential violations as they pertain to the trade in goods only. This constitutes only one part of a potential defence against OECD punitive sanctions. In reality, most of the proposed OECD sanctions will be against various service providers or will involve service sector transactions, as has been the case with EU measures so far. Potential GATS violations will be discussed in the following sections.

The GATT and the WTO have a long history of dealing with income and other direct tax matters. Those who drafted the original 1947 GATT agreement were of the view that income tax matters did not fall within the proper purview of the GATT and that the disciplines referred only to taxes directly on the good itself.[14] This raises a very serious definitional

---

14 At the Havana Conference which considered Article 18 of the charter (national treatment), it was stated that the sub-committee on Article 25 (XVI) 'had implied that exemptions from income taxes would constitute a form of subsidy permissible under Article 25 [XVI] and therefore not precluded by Article 18'. It was agreed that 'neither income taxes nor import duties came within the scope of Article 18 (national treatment) since this article refers specifically to internal taxes on products'.

problem. Clearly Articles I and III were not intended to deal with taxes on income but on goods.[15] While the intention of the GATT draftsmen may well have been not to impose disciplines on income taxes, the reality of the subsequent jurisprudence has been that GATT panels have demonstrated a willingness to consider income tax provisions as violations of particular GATT obligations. This section is predicated upon the imposition by OECD countries of a withholding tax on trans-actions with jurisdictions which the OECD deems to be un-co-operative. However, if these withholding taxes are imposed on a wide range of trans-actions with a particular jurisdiction, and are based on the value of those transactions, then they are in effect ad valorem taxes. The fact that these ad valorem taxes are intended to be withholding taxes in lieu of income taxes may not alter the perception of a panel as to whether they should be treated as taxes on goods or income derived from the sale of those goods.

The first case that has a bearing in this area is the Belgian family allowance case[16] of 1952 that any violation of Most Favoured Nation (MFN) obligations based on differentiation of tax and benefit regimes of the Contracting Parties is not GATT compatible. A second complaint was brought by Austria in the same year against income tax remissions granted by Italy.[17] These disputes were followed by the four so-called 'DISC disputes'[18] of the 1970s, all relating to the trade distorting effects of the application of various income tax measures. The subsequent pas-sage of the US Foreign Sales Corporation legislation stemmed in large measure from early US attempts to deal with the GATT incompatibility of the DISC legislation.

---

15 Article III.2 states, *inter alia*: 'The products of the territory of any contracting party imported into the territory of another contracting party shall not be subject, directly or indirectly, to internal taxes or other internal charges of any kind in excess of those applied to like domestic products'.

16 The 1952 panel report on 'Belgian Family Allowances' discusses a Belgian system of tax exemptions for products imported from countries considered to have a system of family allowances similar to that of Belgium, in relation to Article 1 G/32 adopted 7 November, 1952, IS/59.

17 L/875. See SR 13/12, SR 15/17, SR 16/9, SR 17/5.

18 *EC v. USA – Income Tax Legislation*. In this case, the claim was that the 1971 DISC Legislation, by allowing a deferral of income taxes on certain portion of export income for an unlimited period and without interest, constituted export subsidy in violation of Article XVI: 4. The Panel ruled that by not taxing export income equally with income from domestic sales, the US DISC law in some cases had effects that were not in accordance with US obligations under article XVI: 4. BISD 235/98, 285/114. The subsequent series of DISC tax cases which followed were USA v. Belgium BISD 23S/127, USA v. France BISDF 23S/114, USA v. Netherlands BISD 23S/137.

The most recent 1999 FSC case,[19] while driven by other trans-Atlantic trade frictions, is a result of the earlier, non-WTO compatible changes to the DISC legislation by the US Congress. Thus there is a long history of GATT and WTO panels dealing with the trade implications of direct tax measures.

There are several important provisions in the GATT rules that refer directly or indirectly to internal taxation measures. These include the provisions of Article I.1 (MFN), Article III.2 (National Treatment) and XVI (Subsidies) and Article XX(d) (Exceptions). As has been argued above, the GATT jurisprudence indicates that panels have consistently seen direct tax measures that have trade effects as being within the proper purview of the GATT and the WTO. However, in the past, GATT panels that have considered taxation-related issues have by and large dealt with aspects of taxation regimes as possible subsidies to exports. Any WTO panel created to consider the application of OECD defensive measures would be considering taxation issues in a manner quite different from previous panels.

GATS Provisions

The reality of the application of any as yet undisclosed defensive measures is that OECD members will attempt to avoid broad ranging discriminatory taxes and administrative measures against goods transactions precisely because such measures are of highly questionable GATT legality. The experience with EU measures, along with Controlled Foreign Corporation legislation,[20] indicates that tax jurisdictions which impose punitive or discriminatory measures tend to target income or service transactions on a selective basis, as outlined in the second option above. Even selective measures against transactions with what the OECD calls 'un-co-operative jurisdictions' that violate GATS Article II (MFN) provisions may be potentially actionable.

The problem that arises with the proposed OECD defensive measures against savings and income-related transactions with un-co-operative jurisdictions is that these transactions, while being income transfers, are simultaneously banking or financial sector transactions. Thus a measure

---

19 The recent decision of the WTO Panel and Appellate Body in the EU-US Tax treatment for Foreign Sales Corporations is noteworthy. This decision stated that the foreign sales corporation provisions of sections 921–927 of the Internal Revenue Code constitute an illegal subsidy of US exports. WT/DS108/AB/R (24 February 2000), para. 7.34 and footnote 602.

20 Controlled Foreign Corporation (CFC) rules stipulate that certain income of a CFC is attributed to and taxed currently in the hands of its resident shareholders.

which imposes a withholding tax on savings to a particular jurisdictions may constitute a violation of GATS depending on the nature of the transaction and the service sector commitments that have been made by the jurisdiction imposing the tax measure. If, for example, a particular OECD country has made commitments in banking and other financial service sectors in modes 1 and 2,[21] a withholding tax on a banking transaction with another jurisdiction may constitute both an Article XVII violation (National Treatment) and GATS Article II (MFN) violation, as well as a violation of sector specific commitments.

GATS Article XIV(d) – Tax Carve-Out Provisions

GATS Article XIV (d) provisions provide what appears to be a clear and incontrovertible national treatment tax carve-out.[22] The tax carve-out states:

... nothing in this agreement shall be construed to prevent the adoption or enforcement by any member of measures:

(d) inconsistent with article XVII, provided that the difference in treatment is aimed at ensuring the equitable or effective imposition or collection of direct taxes in respect of services or service suppliers of other Members

Uruguay Round negotiators recognised that tax measures differentiating between nationals and foreigners could be construed as a violation of GATS National Treatment obligations. The relatively loose language employed in the tax carve-out differs sharply from that found in GATT Article XX exemptions in that the measures envisaged suffer from none of the strict Article XX chapeau requirements that they be 'necessary to assure compliance'.

However, even the GATS national treatment tax carve-out which appears to be ironclad is subject to the Article XIV chapeau provisions which mimic those of GATT Article XX. Thus the measures that are applied must not 'constitute a means of arbitrary or unjustifiable discrimination between countries where like conditions prevail'.[23] An example may be worth considering. The application of a withholding tax on a

---

21 Mode 1 means supply of services from the territory of one member into the territory of any other member. Mode 2 refers to the supply of services in territory of one member to the service consumer of any other Member. GATS Article 1.2

22 Footnote 6, GATS, Article XIV (d) stipulates in detail what type of measures are in violation of Article XVII provisions.

23 This particular portion of the GATS Article XIV chapeau differs only by one word from the GATT Article XX chapeau which the uses the word 'same conditions' as opposed to 'like conditions'.

transaction with, say, Tonga which has had no finance centre activity since 1988, but is nonetheless listed by the OECD as a tax haven, along with the failure to apply a similar tax on an identical domestic transaction would be difficult to sustain. The potential violation of the chapeau provisions will be more evident when we come to consider the MFN violations.

GATS Article XIV(c) Provisions

OECD punitive sanctions or defensive measures that violate either MFN or National Treatment provisions of the GATS could be justified under the provisions of GATS Article XIV(c) provisions allowing measures:

necessary to secure compliance with laws or regulations which are not inconsistent with the provisions of this agreement, including those relating to ... the prevention of deceptive practices ...

This provision is identical to its GATT antecedent and could be used in a similar manner for GATT MFN or Article III violations.[24] It could be argued that the OECD defensive measures are aimed at preventing such deceptive measures and indeed much of the recent thrust of the OECD work programme in this area has been aimed at three aspects of the tax systems of tax havens that the OECD feels to be particularly harmful, i.e. the absence of transparency, discrimination between onshore and offshore activities and the absence of an effective exchange of information between jurisdictions. While the language of the OECD demands appears deceptively reminiscent of the principles underlying the multilateral trading system, this is only so at a superficial level. In fact GATS provides for the protection of commercial confidentiality[25] and GATS provisions which permit discrimination between nationals and non-nationals on tax matters.[26] Thus the apparent similarity between the most recent OECD demands from tax havens and the principles of the multilateral system is apparent rather than real.

There are several legal questions that arise from a defence of sanctions based on GATS Article XIV(c). First, is the use of a finance centre for the avoidance of tax within the gamut of what is normally defined as 'deceptive practices'? The OECD has been clear that these defensive

---

24 GATT Article XX(d). The GATT provision is somewhat broader, covering customs measures and enforcement of monopoly not relevant to the context of the GATS.

25 GATS Article III bis.

26 GATS Article XIV(d).

measures are aimed at dealing with both criminal and civil tax matters.[27] There is little jurisprudence in this regard, but that which does exist suggests that the deceptive practices were intended to refer to commercial fraud rather than civil tax matters. It should also be noted that the tax haven jurisdictions are in general willing to co-operate on matters pertaining to criminal tax fraud but in general reserve their sovereign rights on civil tax issues.

Second, the jurisprudence on interpretation of GATT Article XX(d) on this issue suggests that the measure must be taken to prevent a particular practice. Panels have strictly interpreted these as enforcement measures rather than as punitive measures.[28] The strict interpretation of Article XX(d) provisions in this regard is further supported by the shift in language used in the 1946 Suggested Charter for an International Trade Organisation which used the phrase 'to induce compliance' as opposed to the stricter GATT phrase 'to secure compliance with'. In this light the proposed defensive measures may be difficult to support under the provisions of Article XX(d) or GATS Article XIV(c) as none actually secure compliance with tax laws, but rather attempt to induce such compliance and thus fall within the precedents already established by GATT panels. Moreover, a panel may not view the use of finance centres in tax havens as deceptive practices in light of the existing but limited jurisprudence.[29] A defence of the OECD sanctions based on either GATT XX(d) or GATS XX(c) might prove difficult to sustain.

Potential Violations of Service Sector Commitments by OECD Countries

It must be reiterated that any challenge to the GATS compatibility of defensive measures by OECD countries can be predicated upon a violation of market access commitments provisions or based on a general or sector specific MFN violation. In the case of the former the success or otherwise will rest on which service sector commitments have been

---

27 OECD 'An Agreed Interpretation of the three broad principles of Transparency, Non-Discrimination and effective Exchange of Information', Paris, January 2001. The OECD has requested that the tax haven jurisdictions abide by these three principles. In its definition of 'Effective Exchange of Information' the OECD includes both criminal and civil tax matters. It defines the latter to include all matters 'pertaining to the determination, assessment, collection and enforcement of all tax matters'.

28 Panel Report 'EEC Regulation on Imported parts and Components', L/6657, adopted on 16 May 1990, 37/s 195–19,7 paras 5.14–5.18.

29 At the London Session of the Preparatory Committee the discussions indicated that the words 'deceptive practices' were broad enough to cover cases of false geographical markings. EPCT/C.II, pp. 5, 9; EPTC/C.II.54/Rev.1, p. 37. Other limited references include similar fraudulent practices.

made and the limitations that exist to those commitments. If mode 1 or 2 commitments are unrestricted for banking and other financial services, then a withholding tax measure, one of the more probable defensive measures, may be inconsistent with GATS obligations because national treatment provisions are subject to the offers in the service sector schedules.[30] It may also violate more general MFN obligations. The success or otherwise of a challenge to punitive sanctions or defensive measures will rest upon the nature of individual OECD service sector commitments. Table 1 in the Annex outlines the sector specific commitments made by WTO members in one important sector, banking and other financial services, in the relevant modes of supply.

It would appear from the above sample that the most important OECD members have left unbound their market access commitments in mode 1 in the banking and other financial services sector. This means they are at liberty to introduce new measures with regard to the supply of banking and other financial services from the territory of another member into own territory. However, OECD countries have generally imposed few market access limitations on mode 2, i.e. supply of a service in the territory. Thus, if an OECD service consumer which is purchasing banking services in a listed tax haven which is deemed to be an unco-operative jurisdiction has a discriminatory withholding tax imposed on their financial transactions inside an OECD country, then this could be viewed as a limitation of mode 2 market access, as well as a more general MFN violation. Any challenge to the WTO compatability of the sanctions will rest crucially on a definition of what constitutes mode 1 and mode 2. While the WTO Secretariat has produced important explanatory notes on the subject, an accepted and unambiguous definition of mode 1 and 2 in a world of electronic commerce does not yet exist. A challenge to sanctions based on violations of sector-specific commitments would necessitate a panel deciding on a clear and unambiguous definition of precisely what constitutes mode 1 and 2 in the financial services sector.[31]

While the provision of banking and financial services constitute the most significant part of economic activity of many finance centres there are other important areas of service-sector activity that are particularly important to tax havens and could be the subject of OECD sanctions or punitive measures. The provision of insurance and reinsurance services by tax havens is one of the most important sources of commercial activity.

---

30 GATS Article XVII.1.

31 WTO, Committee on Trade in Financial Services, 'Technical Issues Concerning Financial Services Schedules', S/FIN/W/9. Derestricted 22 April 1997.

Under the terms of the Understanding on Commitments on Financial Services some 31 members of the WTO have entered into the more disciplined commitments under the terms of the understanding which governs trade in insurance services.[32] If the OECD countries impose sanctions through measures nullifying or impairing the rights of WTO members under their mode 1 and 2 in insurance and reinsurance there may also be the basis for a challenge. Significantly, in the trade in insurance services the commitments of OECD members on mode 1 are far stronger than in the banking and financial services sector.

There exists another important issue pertaining to the application of defensive measures that relates to the stipulated limits of measures that can be taken by WTO members with regard to payments and transfers in sectors in which they have made specific commitments. The provisions state:[33]

Except under the circumstances envisaged in Article XII [Balance of Payments], *a Member shall not apply restrictions on international transfers and payments for current transactions relating to its specific commitments.* (Parentheses added.)

Should OECD countries impose sanctions that are based on withholding taxes on banking and other financial services transactions with uncooperative jurisdictions, as outlined in measure xi in section 2 above, then these could be viewed as violating GATS Article XI.1 provisions. However, the provision is more likely to temper the choice of OECD sanctions rather than be a basis for litigation. It will, however, severely restrict the OECD's choice of effective measures.

There are several caveats in regard to the comments made on the OECD commitments as they pertain to the terms of the GATS. Several MFN exemptions may be relevant in relation to this question and some OECD members, as we shall see, have imposed horizontal MFN limitations which may justify some of the threatened defensive measures. (See Table 2 in the Annex.)

Violations of GATS MFN Obligations on Taxation Matters
GATS Article XIV contains no general provisions for an MFN carve-out for taxation purposes unless these happen to be part of a double taxation agreement.[34] Members may limit the extent of the MFN coverage of their

---

32 Paragraphs 3 and 4 of *The Understanding on Commitments on Financial Services* contain relatively strict disciplines on cross-border trade in insurance services in mode 1and 2.

33 GATS Article XI.1.

34 GATS Article XIV(e).

service sector offer by providing a schedule of Article II Exemptions which supplement the WTO members' obligation to extend Article II MFN treatment to the services and suppliers of other WTO members. This applies to all service sectors. However, the GATS MFN exemption is in effect a negative list, whereas the national treatment obligations are in the form of a positive list. Countries which did not notify MFN exemptions during the Uruguay Round or upon accession may not introduce new measures. Thus, unless a particular sector or activity is listed in a country's MFN schedule, the MFN obligation exists irrespective of whether or not the WTO member has undertaken sector-specific market opening commitments.

A WTO member may maintain measures that are inconsistent with the obligation to accord immediate and unconditional treatment that is no less favourable to the services and service suppliers of other members than the treatment extended to the services and service suppliers of any other country. The Annex permits WTO members to breach, under prescribed conditions, one of the basic tenets of the GATS and provides members with the flexibility to withhold liberalisation commitments from those members that fail to offer reciprocal market access.

The lists submitted pursuant to the Annex are derogations from the MFN principle and the trade liberalising spirit of the GATS. Thus, exemptions are normally narrowly interpreted to advance the object and purpose of the GATS. The burden of establishing that a measure maintained or introduced is within the member's Article II exemption should be on the member asserting the exemption. While the Annex on Article II exemptions states that these exemptions should normally be of ten-year duration, there are abundant examples of MFN exemptions of indefinite duration.[35] A member that has determined that the need exists to exercise an exemption from its Article II MFN obligations may also be a member that has extended extensive market-opening commitments in its schedule. Of significance in this regard is the indefinite MFN exemption found in the US schedule which provides for measures of indefinite duration which are intended to foster efficient international taxation policies. These MFN exemptions include:[36]

measures permitting less favourable taxation of citizens, corporations or products of a foreign country based on discriminatory or extraterritorial taxes, more burdensome taxation, or other discriminatory conduct.

---

35 Annex on Article II Exemptions.

36 USA – List of Article II (MFN) Exemptions (GATS/EL/90), 15 April 1994.

Even by the relatively lax standards of Uruguay Round GATS offers, not renowned for their discipline, this particular MFN exemption is exceptional in terms of its effective denial of the most fundamental WTO rights and obligations. This, in effect, means that any challenge to the WTO compatibility of defensive measures imposed by the USA which violates either MFN or national treatment obligations in the service sector would be difficult to sustain. No similar general MFN limitation exists in the schedules of other OECD members. The US negotiators foresaw that in order to implement legislation such as controlled foreign corporation legislation it would be necessary to carve-out MFN for taxes in their service sector commitments. Nevertheless the US schedule of MFN exemptions does not extend to measures that affect the taxation of goods,[37] so general taxation measures which are discriminatory and which nullify or impair the rights of members to trade in goods remain open to GATT challenge as discussed above.

The only other possible justification for the defensive measures can be found in the carve-out for prudential measures which authorises each WTO member to establish 'prudential' regulatory measures to protect purchasers and beneficiaries of financial services, as well as its domestic financial system. Whether a panel would view so broad a use of the prudential carve-out to facilitate MFN violations for the purpose of dealing with harmful tax measure, especially when those measures are only applied to what the OECD deems to be non-co-operative tax havens, is questionable.[38] Indeed, given that exemptions for tax measures are dealt with under the tax carve-out to Article XIV, then the use of the prudential carve-out would be very difficult to sustain for application of taxation or defensive measures.

Non-Violation Disputes under the GATT and GATS
OECD members can be expected to consider at length the WTO compatibility of any defensive measure that is applied after 31 July 2001.

---

37 The US carve-out refers to measures on 'products', which normally include goods and services, but as this MFN limitation is annexed to a service sector offer it cannot be deemed to apply to GATT provisions.

38 Once a WTO member extends recognition to another country's prudential measures, the member must afford adequate opportunity for other interested members to negotiate their accession to such agreements or arrangements, or to negotiate comparable ones. If recognition has been afforded autonomously, WTO members must be afforded the opportunity to establish that similar circumstances exist in their countries warranting recognition of their prudential measures. Measures deemed prudential are not precisely defined but may include measures taken for 'the protection of investors, depositors, policy holders or persons to whom a fiduciary duty is owed by a financial service supplier or to ensure the integrity and stability of the financial system'.

Nevertheless, even if the punitive sanction that is imposed is not inconsistent with WTO obligations, there remains the potential for non-violation dispute if WTO members feel that a measure has nullified or impaired the benefits accruing under an agreement.

Both GATT[39] and GATS provisions[40] provide for the possibility of non-violation disputes. These disputes, in the case of the trade in goods, relate to the nullification and impairment of members' rights even where there has been no violation of GATT rules. The jurisprudence in this area is relatively expansive and indicates that the intention of GATT Article XXIII(1b) was to protect the balance of tariff concessions.[41] The question arises as to whether a punitive tax measure, in the form of a withholding tax or other discriminatory measure designed to lower the net income derived by those trading with a particular jurisdiction that is considered to be practising harmful tax competition, would be seen by a panel as altering, directly or indirectly, the balance of tariff concessions and thereby nullifying or impairing benefits of a WTO member.

Read in the light of the sector-specific commitments of WTO members, the GATS provisions pertaining to non-violation disputes tend to limit the extent to which WTO members can use non-violation disputes. These are limited to the nullification and impairment of a 'specific commitment of another member under Part III ... '. Clearly, the need to resort to such non-violation disputes is diminished under the GATS as sector-specific obligations limit the policy flexibility of individual members and thus disputes can arise from measures pertaining to sector-specific commitments.

The Chapeau of GATS Article XIV and GATT Article XX

Defensive measures that may be applied against tax havens can be justified by the exemptions contained in GATT Article XX and GATS Article XIV, as has been discussed above. However, all defensive measures are subject to the chapeau provisions of both articles which are similar but not identical. The chapeau provisions of the GATT Article XX constitute the guiding principles of exceptions to GATT rules and have been interpreted strictly in the past. The chapeau provision states, *inter alia*, that:

Subject to the requirement that such measures are not applied in a manner which would constitute a means of arbitrary or unjustifiable discrimination

---

39 GATT Article XXIII(1b).

40 GATS Article XXIII: 3.

41 BISD 37S/86.

between countries where the same conditions prevail, or a disguised restriction on international trade ...

The only significant difference between the GATS and GATT provisions, as mentioned above, is the use of the word 'like' in the GATS chapeau in the place of 'same' which implies a lower standard of similarity between situations. As we shall see, much of the jurisprudence is involved in determining whether an action is arbitrary or discriminatory behaviour. Few useful guides exist on the interpretation of the chapeau of GATS Article XIV. There is substantial jurisprudence on the chapeau of GATT Article XX and this would almost certainly be called upon by any panel reviewing whether or not the proposed OECD defensive measures violate the chapeau provisions.

Potential Sources of Discriminatory Treatment in the OECD Proposal

Perhaps one of the more difficult aspects of the OECD's position has been that some of its own members have displayed an apparent unwillingness to co-operate with the harmful tax iniative. In particular Switzerland and Luxembourg initially abstained from supporting the OECD recommendations[42] as a significant proportion of their economic activity rests upon what the OECD refers to as 'potentially' harmful tax competition. While both countries have now nominally agreed to support the OECD measures, their agreement has by no means been wholehearted. The subtle difference in language in the OECD report between its description of OECD members' preferential regimes as 'potentially' harmful measures[43] and of non-OECD measures which are deemed to be unambiguously harmful may be seen as the genesis of arbitrary and discriminatory behaviour which could sustain a WTO challenge to many of the defensive measures proposed by the OECD. The differential treatment in terms of the OECD and non-OECD jurisdictions practising harmful tax competition has no basis in economics or in taxation law. While the OECD members are practising potentially harmful tax measures, Tonga, for example which does have legislation but does not actually operate a finance centre is listed in the OECD study as a tax haven with a harmful regime. In any panel the OECD will have to offer a justification for such differential treatment.

In a field such as avoidance and evasion of income taxation, where information and economic analysis are, by the nature of the subject, in acutely short supply, it is worthy of note that Switzerland maintains a taxation

---

42 Recommendation of the OECD Council on Counteracting Harmful Tax Competition, 9 April 1998.

43 OECD *Towards Global Tax Co-operation – Report to the 2000 Ministerial Council Meeting and the Recommendations by the Committee on Fiscal Affairs*, Paris, June 2000, p. 12.

regime which has several potentially harmful preferential features.[44] Recently, in its negotiations with Switzerland, the EU has pursued co-operation on information exchange and has offered to impose withholding taxes on unco-operative jurisdictions that do not wish to exchange information.[45] The Swiss Bankers Association has publicly indicated that 'banking secrecy is non-negotiable' and that they would be likely to accept the withholding tax regime, but only once EU member states and associated territories have dealt with their own regimes.[46] Switzerland is reported to have total bank deposits of Euro 1,970 billion – an estimated Euro 1,056 of which is for non-Swiss clientele.[47]

The difficulty the EU confronts with Switzerland is replicated with other jurisdictions where OECD compliance consultations are not as advanced as those on the tax haven jurisdictions. At the time of writing OECD consultations on harmful tax matters with WTO members such as Singapore, Hong Kong, China and Latin American jurisdictions have only recently begun. Thus an element of arbitrary and discriminatory behaviour would appear to exist in the application of measures against the harmful tax practices of tax havens as opposed to the deferral of any measures against those jurisdictions which practise 'potentially harmful' measures.

The Swiss-EU discussions raise several issues and also point to ways forward to the resolution of the harmful tax issue. First, WTO members which face withholding taxes similar to those of Switzerland may have a basis for a WTO dispute based upon the EU market access commitments for banking and other financial services. The imposition of a withholding tax on a banking sector transaction by a Swiss banking service consumer in the EU may constitute a violation of the EU's mode 2 commitments found in the EU banking and other financial services commitments.

Second, and more significantly, the question of how such a bilateral system of withholding taxes would work in practice where there is the potential for financial flows through third parties is entirely unclear. Moreover, how, if the EU defensive measure is intended only to be a tax on savings, could it effectively be enforced without becoming a more

---

44 Switzerland maintains an administrative companies regime which results in preferential regimes for financing and the establishment of headquarters. OECD, 2000, pp. 13 and 14. The potentially harmful features of the Swiss system covered by the OECD are by no means exhaustive and there are other aspects of the system that may prove to be harmful.

45 Directive on Taxing Savings Income, EU Finance Council, 27 November 2000.

46 European Report, 13 December 2000, p. 12.

47 Ibid., p. 13. This includes the Channel Islands and the Caribbean islands.

generalised tax upon all transactions and, hence, of the most doubtful WTO compatibility? An effective and non-discriminatory tax regime is only likely to be resolved within a genuinely multilateral and co-operative context.

Relevant Jurisprudence on the Chapeau of GATT Article XX

One of the most significant WTO panel reports pertaining to the interpretation of the chapeau of GATT Article XX is the US-Shrimp-Turtle Case[48] where the Appellate Body was of the opinion that the chapeau of Article XX, interpreted within its context and in the light of the object and purpose of GATT and WTO Agreements, only allows members to derogate from GATT provisions so long as in doing so they do not undermine the WTO multilateral trading system and thus abuse the exceptions contained therein. Such undermining and abuse would occur when a member jeopardises the operation of the WTO Agreement in such a way that guaranteed market access and non-discriminatory treatment within the multilateral framework would no longer be possible. The Appellate Body found that when considering a measure under Article XX, one must determine not whether the measure on its own undermines the WTO multilateral trading system, but whether such a measure, if it were to be adopted by other members, would threaten the security and predictability of the system. Market access for goods could become subject to an increasing number of conflicting policy requirements that would lead to the end of the WTO multilateral trading system.[49]

The US imposed a Section 609 measure which the Appellate Body said constituted 'unjustifiable discrimination' between countries where the same conditions prevail and thus did not fall within the scope of the WTO Agreement.[50] In the US Gasoline[51] case, the Appellate Body also pointed out that the chapeau of Article XX:

by its express terms addresses, not so much the questioned measure or its specific contents as such, but rather, the manner in which that measure is applied. The Panel noted that where a member has taken unilateral measures, this could put the multilateral trading system at risk and could therefore constitute 'arbitrary and unjustifiable discrimination where the same conditions prevail.

The Appellate Body in this case said 'it is important to underscore that the purpose and object of the introductory clauses of Article XX is gen-

---

48 WT/DS58/AB/R, 12 October 1998.

49 Ibid., para. 112, Panel Report, paras. 7.44–7.55.

50 Panel Report, para. 7.49.

51 WT/DS2/AB/R, 20 May 1996, Panel Report, para. 7.60.

erally the prevention of the abuse of the exceptions'.

There exists only one significant drafting difference between the chapeau of GATT Article XX and GATS Article XIV. Whereas the former refers to the same conditions, the GATS exception contains the proviso that 'like' conditions prevail. This difference implies that drafters of the GATS agreement were requiring a higher level of discipline with regard to the exemptions under GATS than those of the GATT, as the demonstration of the same conditions prevailing is generally more onerous than like conditions.

Unjustifiable Discrimination

In the Shrimp-Turtle case, the Appellate Body recognised that the most conspicuous flaw in the application of the measure by the USA relates to its intended and actual coercive effect on the specific policy decisions made by foreign governments, members of the WTO. The WTO Appellate Body saw the Section 609 measures as an economic embargo that requires all other exporting members, if they wish to exercise their GATT rights, to adopt essentially the same policy.[52] Clearly, the USA negotiated with some, but not all, other members. This is, in effect, discriminatory and in the view of the Appellate Body unjustifiable. This was a unilateral measure, which the Appellate Body saw as disruptive and discriminatory with the potential to influence and underscore the policies of other members.[53]

There are parallels with the OECD's defensive measures. Here, the imposition of uniform and unilateral taxation rules with limited negotiations with selected WTO members could be seen to closely parallel the precise situation of the Shrimp-Turtle case and could be viewed as unjustified discrimination within existing precedent.

Arbitrary Discrimination

The US Section 609 measure was seen as 'rigid' and 'unbending' and did not inquire into the appropriateness of the programme for the conditions prevailing in exporting countries. Furthermore, it was said that there was little or no flexibility in how officials made the determination for certification pursuant to these provisions. It was, therefore, concluded that the US measure was applied in a manner that amounted not just to 'unjustifiable discrimination', but also to 'arbitrary discrimination' so that it was

---

52 Appellate Body Report, para. 161.

53 Ibid., para. 172.

contrary to the chapeau of the GATT provision.[54]

Again, the parallels with the case of the OECD defensive measures support the argument of arbitrary discrimination. The OECD's delineation between those WTO members who practise harmful tax practices, i.e. tax havens, and those who apply 'potentially harmful' preferential measures has no foundation in economics or in taxation law. Moreover, the OECD has presented no empirical evidence for such a delineation. Sanctions will only be imposed on those WTO members who are deemed un-co-operative by the OECD deadline . However, the OECD has just begun work on those Latin American and Asian jurisdictions outside the OECD that practise what are deemed to be harmful tax practices but are not tax havens. Moreover, no sanctions are imposed on OECD jurisdictions that practise harmful tax measures.[55] It will remain for a panel to decide whether the proposed OECD defensive measures fall within the precedent on 'arbitrary discrimination'. This will rest in part on whether a panel considers the distinctions created and ensuing differences of treatment to be arbitrary.

Necessary Measures

A GATT Panel examined the issue of 'necessary measures' in the case *Thailand – Restrictions on Importation of and Internal Taxes on Cigarettes.*[56] In considering the provisions on general exceptions, the panel said that 'parties cannot justify a measure inconsistent with other GATT provisions as "necessary", in terms of Article XX(d)', if an alternative measure which could reasonably be expected to employ and which is not inconsistent with other GATT provisions is not reasonably available, a contracting party is bound to use, among the measures reasonably available to it, that which entails the least degree of inconsistency with other GATT provisions. The panel commented that there was no reason why, under Article XX, the meaning of the term 'necessary' under paragraph (d) should not be the same as under article (b). It said that the same objectives were intended in both paragraphs.

Here too there are parallels with the proposed OECD defensive measures. As discussed in the introductory sections of the paper, the OECD has itself outlined several measures (measures viii and ix), including with-

---

54 Ibid., paras. 177, 184.

55 The OECD views acceptance of the 1998 Report by its members as equivalent to the signing of an Memorandum of Understanding by tax havens. However, this does not cover harmful tax measures of non-OECD countries which are not tax havens.

56 DS10/R adopted 7 November 1990, 37S/200, paras. 70–80.

holding aid, which, while potentially quite severe in terms of their economic repercussions on tax havens, are entirely compatible with the WTO obligations of individual OECD member states. The existence of clearly WTO compatible defensive measures will, in light of the WTO jurisprudence requiring that Article XX measures be the least trade distorting, make it difficult for OECD members to impose other measures without violating their WTO obligations.

Conclusion

It is difficult to speculate as to whether the proposed OECD defensive measures, which may be applied collectively or individually by OECD members, will be in violation of their WTO obligations and will involve nullification and impairment of the rights of affected WTO members. There exist punitive measures that are WTO compatible, such as the termination of aid. Moreover, as only ten jurisdictions are WTO members, a policy of targeting these for agreement would minimise the OECD's risk of possible WTO disputes. General withholding taxes on transactions with tax havens will probably be the measures most likely to be viewed as violating GATT or GATS obligations. Sector-specific measures, which are the most likely and most common form of defensive measure, could also be violations of GATS obligations. The legality or otherwise of specific defensive measures will depend upon the sector-specific, as well as horizontal service sector commitments, of particular WTO members. In the case of WTO members such as the USA, its MFN carve-out on taxes will permit precisely such measures against others.

The resolution of the question of harmful tax competition can only be found through multilateral dialogue. At present the OECD remains steadfastly opposed to such an inclusive and reciprocal multilateral process and prefers instead a tax forum run by the OECD without peer review. In a world of hyper-mobile capital, international tax issues will only be resolved through genuine multilateral co-operation. The current OECD process is instead based on threats of punitive sanctions against those refusing to comply with the OECD's demands. There is no desire in the global community to set up yet another international organisation, yet there exists a clear demand for international governance in this area. Here either the IMF or the World Bank, working with other relevant international organisations such as the OECD and the Commonwealth Secretariat, could provide an appropriate and inclusive, but ad hoc, international forum for resolving global tax issues. Unless such an inclusive approach is taken to the resolution of this dispute then two outcomes are possible. Either a confrontation will occur in July 2001 or the affected jurisdictions will grudgingly comply. In the event of the former, the credibility of the OECD will be eroded. In the event of the latter, the credibility of the process of globalisation as an inclusive and consultative process will be further undermined.

There are, however, two very significant issues that are of far greater importance than the issue of sanctions against small WTO members. First, if the sanctions are brought before the WTO, then a panel at the WTO will adjudicate on the decisions of another international organisation, albeit one with limited membership.[57] To those who have watched the steadfast opposition, since the Singapore Ministerial Conference of the WTO, of the developing world to the introduction of new issues onto the agenda of the multilateral system, the possibility of a WTO panel sitting in judgement on the decisions of the OECD should surely resonate with those concerned about the possibility of the WTO sitting in judgement over trade aspects of the rules and standards of the International Labour Organisation or on Multilateral Environmental Agreements. Paradoxically, it may be the developing world that opens up an entirely new area of international public law with quite unintended and possibly undesirable consequences.

Second, and perhaps more significant, is the fact that the OECD clearly has a much larger tax and capital market agenda than just harmful tax competition. This was made abundantly clear in the 1998 Report where the OECD indicated that incentives on the movement of physical capital are also on their agenda.[58] Given the nature of its tax and regulatory programme, the OECD has a long-term strategy of imposing its standards and regulations on the movement of capital in a wide range of areas. Following the relative success of the widely accepted interventions of the Finance Action Task Force in dealing with money laundering and criminal issues, if the harmful tax initiative succeeded without a major political confrontation, the next step would be to move to international tax regulations that will prove far more politically intrusive and will have more serious implications for the ability of developing countries to attract capital through the use of tax incentives.

---

57 Strictly speaking this is not entirely unprecedented. The WTO panel on the Canada/Brazil subsidy case held that they had the right to review the OECD's Export Credit Arrangement.

58 OECD Report, 2000, p. 8: 'The Report focuses on geographically mobile activities, such as financial and other service activities, including the provision of intangibles. Tax incentives designed to attract investment in plant, building and equipment have been excluded at this stage, although it is recognised that the distinction between regimes directed at financial and other services on the one hand and at manufacturing and similar activities is not easy to apply. The Committee [the Fiscal Affairs Committee of the OECD] intends to explore this issue in the future'.

Annex

Table 1. Selected Sector-specific Commitments in Banking and Financial Services

WTO/OECD Member	Sector or Sub-sector	Modes of Supply	Limitations on Market Access
USA	Financial services limited to banking and other services and excluding insurance	Mode 1	Unbound
		Mode 2	Michigan limits, according to the country of their home charters, the bank in which corporate credit unions may place deposits.
European Union	Banking and other financial services excluding insurance	Mode 1	Unbound
		Mode 2	[Limitations are applied in Germany, Greece, Italy, Finland, Portugal, Sweden and the UK].[59]
New Zealand[60]	Banking and other financial services (excluding insurance and related services)	Mode 1	Unbound
		Mode 2	None

59 Text in parenthesis is a summary of the wording in the schedule.

60 Has no commitments on provision and transfer of financial information.

Table 1. Selected Sector-specific Commitments in Banking and Financial Services (continued)

WTO/OECD Member	Sector or Sub-sector	Modes of Supply	Limitations on Market Access
Japan	Banking and other financial services (excluding insurance and related services)	Mode 1	Unbound
		Mode 2	Overseas deposits and trust contracts denominated in foreign currencies, the sum of which are over 100 million yen value, and those denominated in yen are subject to approval. Business corporations which satisfy the standards of in-house systems relating to legal affairs, risk management and financial management set out by the Ministry of Finance may be given an approval effective for an indefinite period of time with respect to overseas deposits denominated in foreign currencies 1 million yen value for the purpose of the portfolio investment subject to only ex post reporting.
Australia	Banking and other financial services (excluding insurance and related services)	Mode 1	Unbound
		Mode 2	None
Canada	Banking and other financial services (excluding insurance and related services)	Mode 1	Unbound
		Mode 2	None, other than: Trading in securities and commodity futures – persons (all provinces): there is a requirement to register in order to trade through dealers and brokers that are neither resident nor registered in the province in which the trade is effected.

Table 2. Selected MFN Exemptions

Country with Exemption/Sector	Countries to which Measure Applies	Duration	Description of Measures Indicating its Inconsistency with Article 11
Australia/Financial services (securities)	All countries	Indefinite	Members of foreign stock exchange who wish to become members of the Australian Stock Exchange are only able to do so if the foreign stock exchange provides access to Australian Stock Exchange members on terms and conditions which are reasonable and not more onerous than those applying to applicants for membership of the Australian Stock Exchange.
USA/All sectors taxation measures	All	Indefinite	Differential treatment under direct tax measures at the federal level.
			Sub federal tax measures affording differential treatment to service suppliers or to services when the differential treatment is based on a number of identified criteria
			Sub-federal measures substantively incorporation provisions of federal law subject to an MFN exemption under the GATS agreement.
USA/financial Services	All	Indefinite	Differential treatment of countries due to application of reciprocity measures or through international agreements guaranteeing access or national treatment.

Table 2. Selected MFN Exemptions (continued)

Country with Exemption/Sector	Countries to which Measure Applies	Duration	Description of Measures Indicating its Inconsistency with Article 11
Banking and other financial services excluding insurance	Canada	Indefinite	A broker-dealer registered under US law that has its principal place of business in Canada may maintain its required reserves in a bank in Canada subject to the supervision of Canada.
Canada/Financial services, including lending of all types and trading for own account of certain securities by loan and investment companies	Great Britain and Northern Ireland, Republic of Ireland	Indeterminate	Preferential treatment in Quebec for allocation of licences is provided by the Province of Quebec to loan and investment companies incorporated under the laws of the Parliament of the United Kingdom and Ireland for purpose of obtaining a licence to carry on business.
Air and maritime transport – exemption from tax	All countries	Indeterminate	Exemption from taxes on income and capital of a non-resident person earned in Canada from the operation of a ship or aircraft in international traffic on the basis of reciprocity with the country in which the person resides.
European Community/ Financial services	States in Central, Eastern and South-Eastern Europe, and all members of the Commonwealth of Independent States	10 years	Measures granting favourable tax treatment (offshore regimes) in Italy to service suppliers trading with the countries to which the measure applies.
Japan			No MFN exemptions.

Potential WTO Claims in Response to Countermeasures under the OECD's Recommendations Applicable to Alleged Tax Havens

Stephen J. Orava[1]

Introduction

In 1998, the OECD issued a report, *Harmful Tax Competition: An Emerging Global Issue*. In the report, the OECD made recommendations intended to counter the perceived harm caused by the operation of so-called 'tax havens'.[2] In 2000, the OECD followed this up with its Report to the 2000 Ministerial Council Meeting and Recommendations by the Committee on Fiscal Affairs – *Towards Global Tax Co-operation: Progress in Identifying and Eliminating Harmful Tax Practices*. The 2000 Report provided a list of tax havens and set out a range of 'possible defensive measures' that could be imposed on them in order to remedy the 'harmful' tax competition attributed to them.

In late June 2001, after objections from the USA, the OECD significantly scaled back its proposals, generally limiting its approach to aspects of information exchange intended to facilitate greater scrutiny of accounts used to shelter fraud, tax abuse, money laundering and other criminal practices. The OECD's new position, however, does not in any way preclude individual countries from following the OECD's earlier recommendations and proceeding with defensive measures at a national level.

Apart from the OECD process, the challenge to tax havens has recently received a new momentum in the context of the global fight against terrorism. Following the terrorist attack on the USA on 11 September 2001, many governments are taking a closer look at ways to uncover and shut down terrorist financing, including new sanctions and enhanced rules on money laundering. The EU is also reportedly relying on the new anti-terrorism initiatives to inject new life into its fight against tax havens and so-called 'harmful' tax competition. One EU official is quoted

---

1 Stephen J. Orava is a Senior Associate in the WTO Global Practice of Baker & McKenzie.

2 The term 'tax haven' is used in this article, although the more appropriate term would be 'low-tax jurisdiction', i.e. countries that apply no or only nominal tax rates.

as saying: 'Politically it is now going to be very difficult to defend the continuation of tax havens, no matter where they are in Europe.[3] Even in the current context, however, it remains obvious that a balanced approach is necessary in order to ensure an effective fight against terrorism, while respecting both the legitimate tax policies of sovereign nations and international legal obligations.

This article provides a preliminary analysis of possible claims that alleged tax havens may have under the rules of the World Trade Organisation when another WTO member imposes a particular countermeasure. The analysis will be limited to claims relating to financial services under the General Agreement on Trade in Services, which is the primary source for relevant WTO obligations. At present, it is unclear whether any particular OECD member has imposed a specific countermeasure explicitly or implicitly in accordance with the OECD recommendations. The following overview of potential issues remains, therefore, necessarily abstract and to some extent speculative. However, it may nonetheless serve to highlight the specific issues that countries that consider imposing such measures may encounter. Without prejudice to individual circumstances in individual cases, this analysis demonstrates that following the OECD recommendations may lead to claims of WTO inconsistency, especially if the measure is not carefully tailored to address legitimate objectives.

Background

The 1998 Report introduced certain criteria to identify tax havens and harmful preferential tax regimes. This article is limited to issues relating to tax havens.

The definition of a tax haven has proved somewhat elusive in the past. As stated in the 1998 Report, the OECD concluded in an earlier report in 1987 that 'a good indicator that a country is playing a role of a tax haven is where the country or territory ... is generally recognised as a tax haven'. Thus, the OECD essentially concluded that a tax haven is defined as a tax haven. In its 1998 Report, the OECD moved on from this rather circular 'reputation test' to a slightly more substantive definition, i.e. that a tax haven was a country with no or nominal taxation, usually coupled with a reduction in regulatory or administrative constraints.

The OECD's proposals are based on the claim that tax havens lead to harmful tax avoidance, because entities have incentives to migrate to jurisdictions with lower tax rates and less burdensome regulatory or

---

3 'Brussels Sees Need to Focus on Tax Havens', *Financial Times*, 25 September 2001.

administrative requirements. The OECD concludes that this migration has an adverse effect on the home country's tax base and contends that such tax-rate-based competition is unfair.

Apart from the philosophical and political question of whether this effect should be considered a detriment or a necessary consequence of desirable global competition, it is clear that when the Uruguay Round negotiations on the GATS concluded in 1994, the existence of tax havens was known to the negotiators and was considered a condition of competition in the market for financial services. Thus, WTO member commitments, both in 1994 and following the financial services negotiations in 1998, were conducted in full knowledge of the effect that tax havens have on the financial services market.

GATS Claims

In assessing the possible WTO inconsistencies of specific countermeasures, it is important to recognise the fundamental point that only WTO member countries are bound by WTO obligations. Moreover, only countries that are WTO members have the right to challenge whether measures taken by other WTO members are consistent with their WTO obligations. As an international organisation, the OECD is not itself subject to WTO rules, although its individual members are subject to WTO obligations in their capacity as WTO member countries.

For the purposes of this analysis, consider the following scenario: a WTO member country, relying on the OECD recommendations, imposes a countermeasure affecting an alleged 'tax haven' which is also a WTO member. The threshold question for a valid claim by the affected 'tax haven' (the 'Complainant') is whether the GATS applies to the particular countermeasure imposed by the other WTO member (the 'Defendant'). Assuming that the Defendant has applied a 'measure' subject to the GATS, the next question is whether such a measure is inconsistent with the Defendant's WTO obligations, and/or causes, or has caused, the nullification or impairment of benefits that could reasonably have been expected to accrue to members based on the Defendant's relevant WTO obligations.

Jurisdictional Issues

The GATS, in principle, covers virtually all measures relevant to the international rendering of services. GATS Article I:1 provides that the GATS 'applies to measures by Members affecting trade in services'. The drafters of the GATS clarified the meaning of this very broad statement by providing, *inter alia*, the following definitions.

♦ 'Trade in services' is defined to include the supply of a service through the four 'modes' of supply. (GATS Article I:2) The analysis in this article is limited to the following 'modes' of supply, which are the most relevant to possible GATS claims:

  – from the territory of one member into the territory of any other member ('cross-border supply' or Mode 1); and

  – in the territory of one member to the service consumer of any other member ('consumption abroad' or Mode 2).

♦ 'Measure' means 'any measure by a Member, whether in the form of a law, regulation, rule, procedure, decision, administrative action, or any other form'. (GATS Article XXVIII:a)

♦ 'Measures by Members' means primarily measures taken by 'central, regional or local governments and authorities'. (GATS Article I:3(a))

The Panel in *European Communities – Regime for the Importation, Sale and Distribution of Bananas* ('*EC – Bananas*') removed any doubts about the broad coverage of GATS when it stated:

The scope of the GATS covers any measure of a Member to the extent it affects the supply of a service regardless of whether such measure directly governs the supply of a service or whether it regulates other matters but nevertheless affects trade in services.[4]

The Appellate Body affirmed this finding of the Panel.[5]

Thus, it is safe to conclude that virtually any government measure that affects a WTO member's financial service providers is likely to fall within the scope of GATS disciplines.

Domestic Countermeasures
The OECD identified the following 'range of possible defensive measures' in its 2000 Report:

♦ To disallow deductions, exemptions, credits, or other allowances related to transactions with unco-operative tax havens or to transactions taking advantage of their harmful tax practices.

♦ To require comprehensive information reporting rules for transactions involving unco-operative tax havens or taking advantage of their

---

4 Report of the Panel, WT/DS27/R/USA, para. 7.285 (22 May 1997).

5 Report of the Appellate Body, WT/DS27/R/AB, para. 220 (9 September 1997).

harmful practices, supported by substantial penalties for inaccurate reporting or non-reporting of such transactions.

♦ For countries that do not have controlled foreign corporation or equivalent rules to consider adopting such rules, and for countries that have such rules to ensure that they apply them in a fashion consistent with the desirability of curbing harmful tax practices. (Recommendation 1 of the 1998 Report)

♦ To deny any exceptions (for example, reasonable cause) that may otherwise apply to the application of regular penalties in the case of transactions involving entities organised in unco-operative tax havens or taking advantage of their harmful tax practices.

♦ To deny the availability of the foreign tax credit or the participation exemption with regard to distributions that are sourced from unco-operative tax havens or to transactions taking advantage of their harmful practices.

♦ To impose withholding taxes on certain payments to residents of unco-operative tax havens.

♦ To enhance audit and enforcement activities with respect to unco-operative tax havens and transactions taking advantage of their harmful practices.

♦ To ensure that any existing and new domestic defensive measures against harmful tax practices are also applicable to transactions with unco-operative tax havens and to transactions taking advantage of their harmful tax practices.

♦ Not to enter into any comprehensive income tax conventions with unco-operative tax havens, and to consider terminating any such existing conventions unless certain conditions are met. (Recommendation 12 of the 1998 Report)

♦ To deny deductions and cost recovery, to the extent otherwise allowable, for fees and expenses incurred in establishing or acquiring entities incorporated in unco-operative tax havens.

♦ To impose 'transactional' charges or levies on certain transactions involving unco-operative tax havens.

The above 'possible' countermeasures are phrased in very general terms. However, virtually all of these countermeasures when implemented in the domestic laws, regulations and/or practices of particular OECD members would constitute measures to which the GATS would apply. In other words, consistent with the definitional provisions of the GATS cited above, they would constitute actions by central governments that affect trade in services, in particular financial services.

Notwithstanding broad GATS coverage in principle, the Complainant would need to be selective in choosing the specific measure(s) to challenge, as certain countermeasures (especially those with clear discriminatory aspects) are more likely to be inconsistent with WTO obligations.

OECD Recommendations

At present, only the OECD's recommendations are in effect, and no OECD country has (at least formally) imposed a countermeasure. Thus, the first issue is whether the GATS applies to the OECD's recommendations themselves.

Based on the above definitions, an argument could be made that the OECD's recommendations constitute a 'measure' because they fall within the very broad definition of a 'measure', including a measure 'in any form', and because they reflect a decision by the central governments of the individual OECD members (i.e. were formally adopted by OECD governments). Moreover, these recommendations are likely to have 'affected trade in services, as evidenced by a likely decline in deposits or other effect on the demand for financial services by the Defendant's consumers from or within the affected tax havens.

While tax havens could attempt to take pre-emptive actions against OECD member countries based on the above argument, it would be difficult to sustain such a challenge in formal dispute settlement proceedings. Past practice under GATT and WTO panels generally provides that panels will not find that discretionary legislation, i.e. legislation that the executive authority has discretion whether or not to apply, is inconsistent with GATT or WTO obligations.[6] The same logic would be likely to apply here, given that the OECD member governments are not obliged, under international or domestic law, to apply any counter or defensive measures whatsoever as a consequence of their decision to adopt the OECD's recommendations. The 2000 Report expressly states that 'member countries retain the right to apply, or not apply, defensive measures unilaterally to any jurisdiction'. Thus, it would be very unlikely for a WTO panel to rule that the OECD recommendations must be applied by

---

6 See, for example, Report of the Appellate Body, United States – Anti-Dumping Act of 1916, WT/DS136/AB/R-WT/DS162/AB/R, para. 88 (adopted 26 September 2000); Report of the Panel, United States – Measures Treating Export Restraints as Subsidies, WT/DS194, para. 8.9 (adopted 23 August 2001); United States – Measures Affecting the Importation, Internal Sale and Use of Tobacco, Panel Report, BISD 41S/131, para. 118 (adopted 4 October 1994).

WTO members who are also OECD members, i.e. that such measures are 'mandatory', and thus that such recommendations themselves are measures that are inconsistent with relevant WTO obligations.

Notably, however, in *United States – Measures Treating Export Restraints as Subsidies* (*'US – Export Restraints'*), adopted in August 2001, the Panel found that it was not precluded from first assessing whether particular 'measures' were inconsistent with relevant WTO obligations and, secondly, determining whether the 'measures' were mandatory or discretionary.[7] In other words, the Panel found that it could issue findings on the substance of the matter without first answering the threshold question of whether the alleged measures were mandatory. In effect, the Panel determined that the 'measure' at issue was inconsistent with WTO obligations if it were ever to be applied in the future, a quasi-conditional ruling that is in many respects similar to an advisory opinion.

Although a far more speculative case, given the absence of domestic legislative or regulatory actions implementing specific countermeasures, a similar approach could theoretically be used to challenge the OECD recommendations. If a WTO panel were to follow the same approach as the Panel in the *US – Export Restraints* case, it could first assess whether the OECD's recommended countermeasures, or a carefully selected subset thereof, would violate relevant WTO obligations and then determine if such recommendations were 'mandatory'. Under this approach, the complaining WTO member(s) could, theoretically, obtain findings that certain OECD-recommended countermeasures could not be applied because they are WTO inconsistent. The absence of specific details of any particular countermeasure, however, would be likely to limit the possibility of success under this approach, although this would not necessarily preclude achieving certain political and/or diplomatic objectives in highlighting the potential WTO implications for the future imposition of countermeasures.

It remains, however, highly unlikely that a panel would go so far to analyse the WTO consistency of such potential measures based solely on the existence of the OECD recommendations and the Defendant's OECD membership, in the absence of any further 'hard evidence' (such as draft legislation) indicating that the Defendant actually intended to act on these recommendations. The circumstances of the *US – Export Restraints* case seem to mark the outer limits of panels' courage to venture into the field of speculation.

---

7 *US – Export Restraints*, para. 8.14.

Although the issue of mandatory versus discretionary measures could be used to refuse formal consultations under the WTO's dispute settlement procedures, a tax haven WTO member could take steps under the transparency provisions in the GATS. GATS Article III:4 states that '[e]ach Member shall respond promptly to all requests by any other Member for specific information on . . . international agreements within the meaning of paragraph 1'. Paragraph 1 of Article III states that '[i]nternational agreements pertaining to or affecting trade in services to which a Member is a signatory shall also be published'. Thus, a tax haven WTO member could request specific information from an OECD member regarding its intentions with respect to the OECD recommendations. Certainly, these recommendations satisfy the broad standard of 'affecting trade in services', especially financial services.

GATS Article III:5 also permits a WTO member to notify 'measures' that it considers 'affect the operation of this Agreement' to the Council for Trade in Services. The standard in this provision appears primarily self-determinative, i.e. that the member itself 'considers' whether such affect exists. Thus, a tax haven WTO member could also notify the OECD recommendations to the Council for Trade in Services.

The approaches above under GATS Article III could be used to facilitate discussions outside the auspices of the OECD and may arguably assist in providing a more level playing field for reasonable dialogue among the affected countries.

Violation Claims under GATS

The following is a discussion of potential GATS claims that a Complainant tax haven could raise to challenge a countermeasure. Given the broad scope of potential measures, this article only discusses possible claims in general terms as well as certain issues that it will be critical to evaluate in order to support such claims.

For purposes of the discussion below, we have assumed that services suppliers in the Complainant's territory provide financial services to (1) the Defendant's consumers in the Defendant's territory (cross-border supply) and (2) the Defendant's consumers in the territory of the Complainant (consumption abroad). Substantial debate has taken place regarding how to differentiate financial services supplied under mode 1 (cross-border supply) and services supplied under mode 2 (consumption abroad).[8] This

---

8 See, for example, Technical Issues Concerning Financial Services Schedules, Note by the Secretariat, S/FIN/W/9 (29 July 1996).

article does not address the precise distinctions between the two modes, although such distinction may be critical where obligations differ based on mode of supply. To facilitate the analysis, this article uses the example of the imposition of a countermeasure by France as a member country of the EU.

Article II – Most-Favoured-Nation Treatment

The first likely line of challenge against countermeasures directed specifically against tax havens would be that the measures are inconsistent with the so-called most-favoured-nation obligation. The MFN obligation under GATS is set forth in Article II:1 and provides that:

[E]ach Member shall accord immediately and unconditionally to services and service suppliers of any other Member treatment no less favourable than that it accords to like services and service suppliers of any other country.

This provision applies to all services covered by GATS, but does not cover services expressly listed as exempted by certain members.

Accordingly, if the Defendant imposed a countermeasure that allowed a third country's financial services suppliers to provide financial services on a more favourable basis than the Complainant's suppliers, the Complainant could claim that the Defendant is violating its MFN obligation under GATS Article II. The general test is whether the particular measure creates less favourable conditions of competition between the Complainant's services suppliers and like suppliers of third countries.[9] Thus, if the Defendant (in its action against the tax haven) applies the same tax treatment both in law and in fact, regardless of the origin of the financial services supplier, the Defendant would not violate its MFN obligation.

For example, assume that France has imposed a particular countermeasure that provides, either in law or in fact, more favourable treatment for its consumers depositing funds with financial services providers in Switzerland than it does for consumers depositing funds with financial services providers in the alleged tax haven, i.e. the Complainant. Assuming that the French countermeasure created competitive conditions that were less favourable for the Complainant's financial services suppliers compared to Swiss suppliers, the French measure would appear to be inconsistent with France's MFN obligation. Many of the general countermeasures listed in the 2000 Report (see above) would be likely to

9 See, for example, Report of the Panel, EC – Bananas, W/DS27/R/P, para. 7.385 (22 May 1997); Report of the Appellate Body, EC – Bananas, para. 248 (9 September 1997).

change the competitive conditions under which financial services suppliers of tax havens operate in their dealings with clients from other WTO members. Moreover, the services that are compared (i.e. those offered to French consumers by the Complainant's suppliers and by the Swiss suppliers) would probably be considered 'like' services and thus the subject of valid comparison in the MFN analysis.

However, the Complainant must be cautious in asserting an MFN-based claim, because significant exemptions may apply. For example, if the USA imposed the same countermeasure as France in the previous example, the finding of an inconsistency would be subject to a number of MFN exemptions relating to tax measures that the USA scheduled during negotiations. For example, the US MFN exemptions include '[d]ifferential treatment under direct tax measures at the federal level' regarding:

measures permitting less favorable taxation for citizens, corporations or products of a foreign country based on discriminatory or extraterritorial taxes, more burdensome taxation, or other discriminatory conduct.[10]

Thus, to the extent that the countermeasure falls within the scope of one of the exemptions, a panel would not find that the USA acted inconsistently with its MFN obligation under GATS Article II, although the same panel could find that the identical French measure was WTO inconsistent.

Apart from such country-specific MFN exemptions, additional exceptions, both specific and general, may apply. The general, sector-specific and security exceptions under GATS are addressed further below. With regard to MFN obligations, GATS Article XIV(e) specifically provides:

nothing in this Agreement shall be construed to prevent the adoption or enforcement by any Member of measures:

(e) inconsistent with Article II, provided that the difference in treatment is the result of an agreement on the avoidance of double taxation or provisions on the avoidance of double taxation in any other international agreement or arrangement by which the Member is bound.

Thus, if the relevant countermeasure falls within this exception relating to double taxation (and conforms to the other requirements for relying on a general exception discussed below), the Defendant may escape an adverse decision that it acted inconsistently with its WTO obligations. In most instances, however, this narrow exception could not be used to justify an MFN incompatible countermeasure targeting so-called 'harmful' practices of alleged tax havens.

---

10 United States of America, Final List of Article II (MFN) Exemptions, GATS/EL/90 (15 April 1994).

Specific Commitments

Part III of the GATS covers obligations of members relating to market access and national treatment. Part III represents a 'bottom-up' approach to services commitments because WTO members can voluntarily choose those sectors and sub-sectors to which the relevant obligations will apply and may schedule further limitations on the scope of such commitments.

By contrast, the Understanding on Commitments in Financial Services (the 'Understanding') provides for a 'top-down' approach to scheduling specific commitments in financial services. Under a 'top-down' approach, members commit to the application of obligations to all subsectors and under all circumstances, except where specific exemptions are scheduled. A number of WTO members, including most OECD members, agreed to schedule their financial services commitments in accordance with the Understanding.

The provisions of the Understanding apply on an MFN basis to all other members. In other words, France must comply with its obligations under the Understanding equally with respect to other members that use the Understanding and with respect to all other WTO members, including alleged tax havens.

Market Access

Cross-border Trade

GATS Article XVI (Market Access) generally provides that members are prohibited from imposing the restrictions listed in paragraph 2 for a particular service if they have scheduled a specific commitment not to do so and have not placed any relevant limitations on such commitment (either horizontal or sector-specific). The 'specific commitments' are made by sector or sub-sector and by mode of supply.

The Understanding, however, takes a supplemental approach and, in certain instances, more or less fully opens the markets of those members using the Understanding. Paragraph B.3 states, in relevant part:

Each Member shall permit non-resident suppliers of financial services to supply, as a principal, through an intermediary or as an intermediary, and under terms and conditions that accord national treatment, the following services: (c) ... advisory and other auxiliary services, excluding intermediation, relating to banking and other financial services as referred to in subparagraph 5(a)(xvi) of the Annex.

For consumption abroad, paragraph B.4 of the Understanding states:

Each Member shall permit its residents to purchase in the territory of any other Member the financial services indicated in:

(a) *subparagraph 3(a)*;

(b) *subparagraph 3(b)*; *and*

(c) *subparagraphs 5(a)(v) to (xvi) of the Annex.*

The services listed in subparagraph 5 of the GATS Annex on Financial Services (the 'Annex') include a wide range of generally-defined financial services, including accepting deposits, lending of all types, financial leasing, payment and money transmission services, trading, money brokering, asset management, and settlement and clearing services.

Thus, rather than narrowly preventing limitations on the number of financial service suppliers or the type of legal entity as provided under GATS Articles XVI:2(a) and (e), paragraph B.4 of the Understanding provides much broader obligations, especially regarding consumption abroad, i.e. that the relevant member 'shall permit the purchase in the territory of any other Member' of the wide range of services identified in the Annex.

Consider again the example of a proposed French countermeasure. The EU's schedule of specific commitments, which applies to France, states the following:

1. *The Communities and their Member States undertake commitments on Financial Services in accordance with the provision of the 'Understanding on Commitments in Financial Services' (the Understanding).*

2. *These commitments are subject to the limitations on market access and national treatment in the 'all sectors' section of this schedule and to those relating to the subsectors listed below.*

3. *The market access commitments in respect of modes (1)* [cross-border supply] *and (2)* [consumption abroad] *apply only to the transactions indicated in paragraphs B.3 and B.4 of the market access section of the Understanding respectively.*

If the French measure does not permit French residents to, for example, purchase financial services involving the making of deposits in banks within the territory of the Complainant tax haven, France would appear to be acting inconsistently with its WTO obligations as reflected in the Understanding. Notably, France has not scheduled (through the EU) any other limitations on market access that would limit its obligations under the Understanding. Thus, a countermeasure may be especially susceptible to attack under this provision of the Understanding, depending on the circumstances.

Non-discriminatory Measures

In addition to the general GATS obligations and standard market access commitments, the Understanding contains additional specific market access obligations relating to measures that are not discriminatory, but nevertheless have an adverse effect on market access for financial services. Paragraph B.10 of the Understanding states:

Each Member shall endeavour to remove or to limit any significant adverse effects on financial service suppliers of any other Member of:

(a) non-discriminatory measures that prevent financial service suppliers from offering in the Member's territory, in the form determined by the Member, all financial services permitted by the Member;

(b) non-discriminatory measures that limit the expansion of the activities of financial service suppliers into the entire territory of the Member;

(c) measures of a Member, when such a Member applies the same measures to the supply of both banking and securities services, and a financial service supplier of any other Member concentrates its activities in the provision of securities services; and

(d) other measures that, although respecting the provisions of the Agreement, affect adversely the ability of financial service suppliers of any other Member to operate, compete or enter the Member's market.

Depending on the facts, a particular countermeasure could readily fall within the above categories. Although the chapeau language 'shall endeavour to remove' limits the effectiveness of this provision, it may still be used to establish the context under which specific commitments were made and to support a claim that measures adversely affecting the ability of other Members' financial services suppliers to compete should not be maintained.

GATS Article XVII – National Treatment

Article XVII of GATS applies the national treatment principle to trade in services, stating that 'each Member shall accord to services and services suppliers of any other Member, in respect of all measures affecting the supply of services, treatment no less favourable than that it accords to its own like services and services suppliers'.[11] The national treatment obligation, however, only applies when a Member has scheduled a specific

---

11 The national treatment provisions in the Understanding only address national treatment with respect to financial services suppliers established in the territory of the relevant Member, i.e. mode 3 of supply covering commercial presence. This mode of supply does not fall within the scope of this article.

commitment in the relevant services subsector and when any scheduled limitations do not apply. Thus, to establish a violation, the Complainant must demonstrate that the Defendant: (1) has treated the Complainant's service suppliers less favourably than its own 'like' suppliers; (2) has made specific commitments in the relevant sector; and (3) has not scheduled relevant national treatment limitations.

Using the example of France, the first step is to determine whether the countermeasure violates national treatment. If France imposes a counter-measure that accords less favourable tax treatment to the use of financial services supplied from the territory of the Complainant tax haven compared to the tax treatment applied to the same financial services supplied by French providers, France's countermeasure may violate the national treatment provision under Article XVII.

To sustain this case, however, the Complainant must also show that France made a specific commitment in the relevant financial service and that no limitations apply to the relevant mode of supply. In the case of France, the EU made specific commitments in the financial services sector and entered 'None' (i.e. no limitations to the application of national treatment in the sector) under modes 1 and 2 in its schedule. In addition, the EU's schedule does not contain any relevant horizontal limitations, i.e. limitations applicable to all sectors.

Even assuming that a panel were to find that the Defendant acted inconsistently with its WTO obligations under GATS Article XVII, the Complainant's case must still survive the potential assertion of general, sector-specific and security exceptions under GATS. The less specific exceptions will be discussed below. The general exception under Article XIV(d), however, specifically addresses national treatment and taxation. It allows for measures:

… *inconsistent with Article XVII, provided that the difference in treatment is aimed at ensuring the equitable or effective [footnote omitted] imposition or collection of direct taxes in respect of services or services suppliers of other Members.*

Footnote 6 of GATS defines the scope of (d) very broadly and includes measures that, for example:

◆ Apply to non-residents or residents in order to prevent the avoidance or evasion of taxes, including compliance measures; or

◆ Apply to consumers of services supplied in or from the territory of another Member in order to ensure the imposition or collection of taxes on such consumers derived from sources in the Member's territory.

Given the broad language of this exception, it is clear that a significant array of measures may be justified, including countermeasures against tax havens as suggested by the OECD, provided that additional requirements applicable to 'general exceptions' (see below) are met.

General, Sector-Specific and Security Exceptions

The obligations contained in the GATS are subject to the general exceptions under GATS Article XIV. In addition, paragraph 2(a) of the GATS Annex on Financial Services (the 'Annex') establishes a sector-specific exception applicable to financial services regulation, the so-called 'prudential carve-out'. Finally, GATS Article XIV *bis* provides certain security-related justifications for measures that would otherwise be inconsistent with WTO obligations.

If one of these exceptions applies, a panel will not find that the Defendant has violated its WTO obligations in imposing the countermeasure. Importantly, however, the Defendant has the burden of proof to demonstrate to the panel that an exception applies. The final question addressed below is whether these exceptions are applicable to measures that are inconsistent with the obligations in the Understanding.

General Exceptions

Based on practice under GATT Article XX applicable to goods, analysis of the general exceptions involves a two-step process. First, the Defendant must demonstrate that one of the subparagraphs of GATS Article XIV applies. Second, the Defendant must demonstrate that the chapeau, or introductory section, of Article XIV would not otherwise preclude reliance on the exception.

The specific exceptions to Article II, the Most Favoured Nation obligation, and Article XVII, the national treatment obligation, under Articles XIV (e) and (d) were addressed above. Provided that their specific requirements apply, a measure would also have to meet the requirements of the chapeau.

The other potentially relevant subparagraph within Article XIV for this analysis seems to be subparagraph (c), which allows for measures:

... necessary to secure compliance with laws and regulations which are not inconsistent with the provisions of this Agreement including those relating to:

(i) the prevention of deceptive and fraudulent practices.

The chapeau of Article XIV provides that the relevant measures must not be

... applied in a manner which would constitute a means of arbitrary or unjustifiable discrimination between countries where like conditions prevail, or a disguised restriction on trade in services.

The Defendant (France in the example) would need to demonstrate that the relevant countermeasure directed against the Complainant tax haven falls within (c) and meets the test in the chapeau of Article XIV. Depending on the measure, the 'necessity' test under (c) is often difficult to overcome because it must be shown that no other less trade-restrictive measure was reasonably available to achieve the objective. Moreover, in this case, depending on the justifications used for the measure, it may be difficult for the Defendant to argue that it meets the relevant standard, i.e. is intended to secure compliance with laws relating to deceptive and fraudulent practices, especially given that the OECD reports focus more on avoiding 'harm' from tax competition rather than on enforcing measures for the prevention of fraud of any kind.

Provided one of the subparagraphs applies, the question whether the countermeasure contravenes the chapeau would depend on the facts of the case. An 'honest' and open countermeasure directed against tax havens is likely to pass the test of not being a disguised restriction on trade. However, whether such a targeted measure would pass the requirement of non-discrimination between 'countries where like conditions prevail' is an open question that, ultimately, will have to be decided by a panel and the Appellate Body based, *inter alia*, on the parameters taken into account to establish 'likeness'. The OECD's apparent distinction between the harmful measures of non-OECD Members and the 'potentially' harmful measures of OECD Members suggests that an argument of non-discrimination may be difficult to maintain.

Paragraph 2(a) of the Annex on Financial Services – Prudential Measures

The Annex applies to measures affecting the supply of financial services. Paragraph 2(a) of the Annex states:

[n]otwithstanding any other provision of the Agreement, a Member shall not be prevented from taking measures for prudential reasons, including for the protection of investors, depositors, policy holders or persons to whom a fiduciary duty is owed by a financial service supplier, or to ensure the integrity and stability of the financial system. Where such measures do not conform with the provisions of the Agreement, they shall not be used as a means of avoiding the Member's commitments or obligations under the Agreement.

Due to its prominence and broad coverage, this 'prudential carve-out' is likely to be asserted as an affirmative defence to any claim regarding a particular countermeasure specifically affecting trade in financial services. However, the Defendant will again have the burden of demonstrating that the particular countermeasure is a prudential measure within the meaning of the provision and is not being used as a means of avoiding its commitments or obligations.

Depending on the facts, the Complainant could argue that such provision is irrelevant to the consumption of financial services in the consumption abroad mode of supply, i.e. outside the territory of the defendant. This could be supported with reference to the heading of paragraph 2, which indicates that it applies to 'domestic regulation'. It also appears illogical for prudential measures, which generally apply to domestic supervision and licensing, to apply to purchases from foreign services providers, especially outside the territory of the regulating member. However, the reference to ensuring 'the integrity and stability of the financial system' in paragraph 2(a) could be used to justify measures with extraterritorial effect. Regardless of this, the Defendant must still demonstrate, based on specific information and evidence, that it imposed the countermeasure for these legitimate reasons, and not simply to address conditions of competition known at the time that its financial services obligations were negotiated.

Security Exceptions

While the general exceptions and the prudential carve-out for financial services regulation are relevant for possible justifications of restrictive measures based on the political and economic rationale of the OECD recommendations, measures motivated by the present 'war against terrorism' may find a basis in the GATS security exceptions, embodied in Article XIV *bis*. The provision reads in relevant part:

1. Nothing in this Agreement shall be construed:

(…)

(b) to prevent any Member from taking any action which it considers necessary for the protection of its essential security interests:

*(…)*197

(iii) taken in time of war or other emergency in international relations (…)

This provision is modelled quasi-verbatim on GATT Article XXI, and thus related case law would seem to provide helpful interpretative guidance. However, despite its 54 years of existence, GATT Article XXI has only been invoked in a handful of cases, none of which has been allowed to proceed to clear panel pronouncements on the substance of the provision. Moreover, members have been very reluctant to discuss security matters in a trade forum. This was demonstrated most recently by an agreement between the USA and the EU to suspend their WTO dispute over the US imposition of sanctions on Cuba. Therefore, while measures affecting trade in services that are inconsistent with WTO obligations may be justified on national security grounds, it is important to bear in mind that WTO members involved in a dispute over security measures are likely to seek solutions outside the formal WTO dispute settlement system.

The GATS security exception provides a wide degree of discretion to WTO members. A member relying on the exception would only need to demonstrate that the measure was taken during a war or 'other emergency in international relations'; that it was taken to protect 'essential security interests'; and that it was considered necessary to protect such interests.

First, the present situation involving the 'war on terrorism' may qualify as a 'war' under classical definitions in international law. In any case, an 'other emergency in international relations' clearly exists. Taking a speculative look into the future, however, this requirement may be harder to fulfil once a reasonable degree of peace and security has been restored, i.e. once the actual use of military force is discontinued and no terrorist attacks have been carried out for a reasonable period of time. In any event, members would appear to have substantial discretion to assess whether a 'war' or 'other emergency' exists and to assess the duration of such a situation.

Second, the Defendant will enjoy a significant margin of discretion in defining its own 'essential security interests', considering the subjective nature of such interests. At the same time, however, the Defendant is not entirely free to identify any interest as an essential security interest. Economic interests, for instance, would not qualify.

Third, the Defendant must demonstrate that it 'consider[ed]' that the measure was 'necessary' to protect its essential security interests. The language again accords the Defendant a wide margin of discretion in 'considering' for itself whether the measure is necessary, although such discretion is not limitless. Just as in the case of general exceptions, a determination that a countermeasure is 'necessary' would require the absence of less trade restrictive measures that are equally effective at protecting the legitimate security interests. However, as the language ('considers') suggests, a member is not required to take significant risks and may choose stronger measures if they provide more security, provided a certain degree of 'reasonableness' is respected.

If a member attempted to justify a countermeasure against a tax haven based on the national security exception, such countermeasure would probably need to bear a clear relation to the fight against terrorism and would have to be at least to some degree demonstrably efficient in this regard. Moreover, the measures taken under this subparagraph of GATS Article XIV *bis* are considered 'emergency' measures, which would suggest that the provision does not justify the imposition of such measures for an indefinite period of time in the absence of continuous relevant circumstances. Thus, to counter the use of the security exception, tax havens could argue that the countermeasures imposed must have a direct relationship to the fight against terrorism (for example, money laundering and terrorist financing rather than 'harmful' tax competition). In addition, tax havens affected by countermeasures may, even if forced to accept them under the present circumstances, be able to secure their removal when and if conditions improve.

Would the Exceptions apply to the Understanding?

An interesting interpretative question is whether the general exceptions in GATS Article XIV, the prudential exception in the Annex and the security exception in GATS Article XIV *bis* would apply to the obligations in the Understanding.

Article XIV states that 'nothing in this Agreement' shall preclude the adoption or enforcement of measures under certain circumstances. Paragraph 2(a) of the Annex states '[n]otwithstanding any other provisions of the Agreement'. Article XIV *bis* states '[n]othing in this Agreement shall be construed'. There is no reference to the Understanding in the GATS or the Annex. Moreover, the Understanding appears to represent the plurilateral equivalent of other 'understandings' that apply to members and to clarify certain provisions of GATT, such as the Understanding on the Interpretation of Article XVII of GATT 1994 (State trading enterprises). In this instance, the Understanding supplements Part III of GATS.

The text of the preamble to the Understanding refers to the GATS, suggesting that the GATS is indeed a separate 'Agreement' from the Understanding. Moreover, the preamble provides that its provisions are applicable only to the extent that they do not conflict with the GATS, again re-emphasising that the Understanding is separate from the 'Agreement' (i.e. the GATS) as the term 'Agreement' is used in the exceptions. There is also no direct conflict between the GATS and the Understanding, i.e. both the GATS and the Understanding can be given full effect without reading the exceptions to apply to the Understanding. Finally, there is no indication in the text itself that any provisions of the

GATS, including the general, prudential and security exceptions, are explicitly or implicitly intended to apply to the provisions of the Understanding. Thus, notwithstanding the possible policy arguments, a strict legal interpretation of the relevant provisions could lead to the conclusion that the GATS general, prudential and security exceptions do not apply to measures found inconsistent with obligations under the Understanding.

An alternative interpretation, however, could be based on GATS Article XX:3, which states that '[s]chedules of specific commitments shall be annexed to this Agreement and shall form an integral part thereof'. The Understanding is intended to replace or supplement the approach from Part III of GATS. Thus, when a member expressly states in its schedule that it is making specific commitments in accordance with the Understanding, an argument could be made that it effectively includes the obligations in the Understanding as an integral part of its GATS schedule and as a replacement for the approach in Part III of GATS. Under such an interpretation, the general, prudential and security exceptions would apply to the Understanding in the same manner as they apply to other scheduled commitments under Part III of GATS.

Notwithstanding the lack of legal and textual clarity, it would be highly unlikely for a panel or the Appellate Body to find that the general, prudential and security exceptions would not be available for measures that are inconsistent with provisions in the Understanding. Rather, the object and purpose of the exceptions, together with the unique relationship between the GATS and the Understanding, would be likely to accord panellists sufficient flexibility to find that the exceptions would apply. However, any member seeking to rely on those exceptions to justify a countermeasure against a tax haven would still need to demonstrate that it has satisfied the requirements of such exceptions.

Non-Violation Claims under Article XXIII:3 of GATS

Under GATS Article XXIII:3, the Complainant could also assert that the application of the relevant countermeasure nullifies or impairs benefits that it could reasonably have expected to accrue to it under the Defendant's specific commitments, even though the measure does not conflict with the provisions of the GATS. If successful under this so-called 'non-violation' claim, the Complainant could be entitled to modification or revocation of the measure.

Using Article XX:III:1(b) of GATT 1994 as a guide, three elements must be satisfied:

(i)   the existence of a governmental measure;

(ii) nullification or impairment of a benefit accruing to the member that could not have been reasonably anticipated by it at the time when the relevant specific commitment was negotiated; and

(iii) an upsetting of the competitive relationship between foreign and like domestic services or service suppliers.[12]

Although experience suggests that succeeding with a non-violation claim is difficult, whether the Complainant could satisfy these elements will ultimately depend on the specific facts surrounding the countermeasure imposed.

Conclusion

OECD Members have developed a series of recommendations involving tax havens, including proposed countermeasures to remedy 'harmful' tax competition. Although the OECD's initiatives now appear more focused on information exchange, alleged tax havens must be vigilant against the imposition (either directly or indirectly) of countermeasures by activist OECD members seeking to improve their own tax competitiveness outside the context of further formal activity by the OECD.

The above discussion shows that the imposition of such countermeasures could result in claims that the particular OECD member is acting inconsistently with its WTO obligations, in particular with its financial services obligations under GATS. If a member decides to impose countermeasures, it should verify conformity with its WTO obligations, as the victims of such measures are likely to scrutinise them carefully and will be prepared to vindicate their WTO rights if the circumstances warrant.

The recent terrorist attacks have generated a well-justified call for tighter oversight over possible sources and avenues of terrorist funding, including a renewed effort to examine the role of alleged tax havens. The initiatives aimed at terrorist financing, however, can and should be carefully balanced to ensure that they are developed in a manner that is both effective in achieving their important goals and consistent with international legal rights and obligations, including those of the WTO.

---

12 See Werner Zdouc (1999). 'WTO Dispute Settlement Practice Relating to the GATS', *Journal of International Economics* L. 295, 302–308.

Export Processing Zones and the WTO Agreement on Subsidies and Countervailing Measures

David Robertson[1]

Introduction

Many of the Commonwealth's developing countries have established export processing zones (EPZs) as trade policy instruments designed to promote non-traditional exports. Typically, these programmes provide that if a company locates a manufacturing facility within a geographically delimited zone and exports all or most of its products it will be provided with a number of incentives. These incentives range from exemption from various direct and indirect taxes and customs duties to the provision of a number of free or low-cost services. EPZs located in developing countries typically provide the greatest number of incentives.

The WTO's Agreement on Subsidies and Countervailing Measures contains specific definitions, restrictions and implementation dead-lines in relation to the use of export subsidies. These rules may affect incentives granted to EPZ companies in Commonwealth developing countries that are currently WTO members or are contemplating accession.

This paper aims to highlight some of the potential conflicts between the SCM Agreement and EPZ incentives. It should be borne in mind, however, that each EPZ will have particular regulatory characteristics and that each Commonwealth WTO member may have differing bilateral or regional obligations. The comments made in this paper can, therefore, only be general in nature and should not substitute a case-by-case review of EPZ incentives.

Agreement on Subsidies and Countervailing Measures

The SCM Agreement came into effect on 1 January 1995 and builds on Article XVI of the General Agreement on Tariffs and Trade 1947 and the

1 David Robertson is an Associate in the WTO Global Practice of Baker & McKenzie.

earlier Agreement on Interpretation of and Application of Articles VI, XVI and XXIII. The SCM Agreement provides a more or less complete code in relation to the use of subsidies so that reference back to GATT1947 and the earlier Agreement on Interpretation is not necessary in most instances.

Definition of Subsidy

The rules contained in the SCM Agreement apply only to subsidies as defined within the Agreement. A subsidy is defined in Article 1 as a financial contribution by a government or any public body, including a direct transfer of funds (for example grants, loans and equity infusion), government revenue that is forgone (for example tax credits), provision of goods or services by a government, other than infrastructure, and income or price support.

This very broad definition is qualified by two provisos. First, to become subject to the rules in the SCM Agreement, a subsidy must confer a *benefit* on the recipient; second, it must be *specific*, i.e. available only to an enterprise or industry or group of enterprises or industries within the jurisdiction of the authority granting the subsidy. Article 2.2 specifically provides that 'a subsidy which is limited to certain enterprises located within a designated geographical region ... shall be specific'. Subsidies extended on the basis of administrative delineation would also be specific.

The general definition of subsidy is further refined by specifying two categories of subsidies: prohibited export subsidies and actionable subsidies. These two categories are also referred to as 'red light' and 'yellow light' subsidies. Until 2000 there was a third category of non-actionable subsidy, which has been discontinued.

Prohibited Export Subsidies

Prohibited export subsidies are those '... contingent, in law or fact ... upon export performance ... and those contingent ... upon the use of domestic over imported goods'. Prohibited export subsidies are described further by reference to Annex I of the SCM Agreement, which provides an illustrative list of Prohibited Export Subsidies. Annex 1 includes as prohibited export subsidies a number of the incentives that might be offered to EPZ companies including:

◆ Transport or freight charge subsidies on export shipment provided or mandated by the government;

- The provision by governments of export credit guarantees or insurance programmes at premiums that are inadequate to cover the long-term operating costs and losses of the programmes;

- The full or partial exemption, remission or deferral in relation to exports, of direct taxes or social welfare charges paid or payable by industrial or commercial enterprises. (Direct Taxes are defined as taxes on wages, profits, interests, rents, royalties, and all other forms of income, and taxes on ownership of real property.)

Developed WTO members are prohibited from granting or maintaining prohibited export subsidies. However, the SCM Agreement recognises that subsidies may play an important role in the economic development of developing countries. Accordingly, least-developed countries (as designated by the United Nations), and developing countries with a GNP per capita of less than $1,000, are exempted from the prohibition on prohibited export subsidies indefinitely, or at least for so long as their GNP remains below the specified level.

Developing countries, other than least-developed countries and those with a GNP below $1,000 per capita, are exempted from this prohibition until the end of 2002. However, they are required to phase out prohibited export subsidies within the eight-year implementation period, preferably in a progressive manner, and they may not increase their level of export subsidies.

If a developing country requires an extension of the period of exemption in relation to prohibited export subsidies, Article 27.4 of the SCM Agreement provides that it may enter into consultation with the Committee on Subsidies and Countervailing Measures ('the Committee') to determine whether an extension of the period is justified. These consultations must be initiated at least one year before the end of the exemption period, i.e. by the end of 2001. If, having taken into account all relevant economic, financial and development needs, the Committee is of the view that the extension is justified, then the subsidy will be subject to annual reviews from then on.

It is worth noting that developing countries may be reluctant to apply for extensions on the grounds that to do so could create unease amongst existing or prospective EPZ companies. The alternative is to develop a strategy for bringing the incentive packages within the SCM Agreement rules.

A further exemption is provided in relation to the prohibition against subsidies in the form of domestic content requirements or preferential treatment for domestic over imported inputs. Developing countries were exempted from this prohibition until 2000. Least-developed countries are exempt until the end of 2002.

Some Further Examples of Measures Likely to Constitute Prohibited Export Subsidies

Each of the following measures may, subject to the particular circumstances of the EPZ concerned, constitute a prohibited export subsidy:

◆ exemption from taxes on real estate;

◆ exemption from taxes on profits as well as of any other tax determined on the basis of gross or net income, dividends paid to shareholders or income or sales;

◆ income tax exemptions based on locating plant in areas of 'lesser development';

◆ income tax exemptions based on reinvestment in the host country;

◆ exemption from taxes on remittances abroad;

◆ provision of non-chargeable customs processing services;

◆ the provision of public administrative services to EPZ manufacturers on a non-chargeable basis, such as assistance in selection of personnel, advice regarding government regulatory requirements, and assistance with the housing and educational needs of personnel.

Actionable Subsidies

The second category of subsidies are actionable subsidies. These subsidies are defined by reference to the effect they have on another WTO member. Therefore, if a subsidy falls within the Article 1 definition of subsidy, confers a benefit on the recipient and is specific, but is not a prohibited export subsidy, then the following test will be applied to determine whether or not it is an actionable subsidy:

Article 5:

No Member should cause, through the use of any subsidy referred to in paragraphs 1 and 2 of Article 1, adverse effects to the interests of other Members, i.e.

(a) injury to the domestic industry of another Member;

(b) nullification or impairment of benefits accruing directly or indirectly to other Members ...

(c) serious prejudice to the interests of another Member.

Serious prejudice is deemed to occur in certain circumstances, namely where the total *ad valorem* subsidisation of a product exceeds 5 per cent of its value or where subsidies are paid to cover operating losses sustained by an industry. Where serious prejudice is deemed to exist, the burden of proof is on the subsidising member to show that the subsidies in question do not cause serious prejudice to the complaining member. This presumption of serious prejudice, however, only applies in relation to developed countries. For developing countries serious prejudice must be demonstrated by positive evidence.

Further, where a developing country maintains an actionable subsidy, i.e. one which causes adverse effects to the interests of other members as per Article 5, a remedy will only be granted where the subsidy in question also displaces or impedes imports of like products into that country, or injures a domestic market in another country. In other words, the threshold to be reached before a remedy will be granted in response to an actionable subsidy is raised for developing countries.

Some Examples of Measures Likely to Constitute Actionable Subsidies
The measures listed below may, depending on the particular circumstances of the EPZ concerned, constitute actionable subsidies.

◆ exemption from import charges on the importation of raw materials, machinery and any other components necessary for EPZ company manufacturing (where the same exemptions are granted to imports for the manufacture of like products for domestic consumption);

◆ exemption from municipal taxes;

◆ exemption from stamp duty or transaction taxes;

◆ exemption of sales and consumption taxes on purchases of goods and services.

Non-actionable Subsidies

The final category of subsidy recognised by the SCM Agreement is non-actionable. Article 8 provides that subsidies which are not specific and certain other specific subsidies, for example industrial research subsidies, assistance to disadvantaged regions and subsidies to implement environmental requirements, are non-actionable. Members relying on the exemptions in Article 8 must notify the Committee. However, Article 31 of the SCM Agreement provides that Article 8, amongst others, applied only for a provisional period of five years. The Committee was then faced with the task of deciding whether to extend Article 8's application. The Committee failed to reach a consensus on an extension before 31 December 1999. Accordingly, this exemption no longer applies and previously non-actionable subsidies will now be treated in the same way as other subsidies.

This raises the question of whether subsidies previously notified under Article 8 continue to enjoy their exempt status, and if so for how long.

Notifications

The SCM Agreement builds on the obligation contained in Article XVI of GATT 1947 that members must notify any subsidy that they maintain. Article 25 of the SCM Agreement requires members to notify any specific subsidy within the broad definition of Article 1, i.e. prohibited export subsidies, and actionable subsidies as well as any non-actionable subsidies. Notifications are to be submitted by 30 June each year and members may bring to the attention of the Committee any member's failure to notify.

Remedies

Where a WTO member maintains a prohibited subsidy, the aggrieved WTO member may initiate the SCM Agreement dispute settlement process, which includes an expedited timetable for action by the Dispute Settlement Body. If it is found that the subsidy is indeed prohibited, it must be immediately withdrawn. If this is not done within the specified time period, the complaining member may be authorised to take countermeasures.

It is worth noting that in the *Australia – Subsidies Provided to Producers and Exporters of Automotive Leather* case, a dispute between the US and Australian Governments resulted in a WTO panel ordering that the exporter concerned repay A$30 million of export assistance to the Australian Government. A sanction of this type passed through to a corporation clearly demonstrates the risks that EPZ companies will be evaluating in relation to the incentives they receive.

An alternative course of action open to the aggrieved WTO member, once a prohibited export subsidy is established, is to initiate a countervailing duty investigation with a view to imposing an additional import duty on the product or products concerned from the subsidising country. Before an aggrieved member may impose a countervailing duty, it must comply with the detailed obligations contained in the SCM Agreement regarding the conduct of a countervailing duty investigation and the findings of a subsidy, injury and a causal link between the two.

Affected members can take action against a member maintaining an actionable subsidy in the same way as for prohibited subsidies. In the event that it is determined that adverse effects as defined in the SCM Agreement exist, the subsidising member must withdraw the subsidy or remove the adverse effects. Alternatively, a countervailing duty investigation may be commenced once the existence of an actionable subsidy has been established.

The SCM Agreement provides that a countervailing duty investigation of a product originating from a developing country is to be terminated if it is determined that the level of the subsidies does not exceed 2 per cent (3 per cent for some developing country members) of the value of the product, or if the subsidised imports from the developing country concerned amount to less than 4 per cent of the total imports of the like product into the aggrieved country.

Finally, a countervailing duty investigation will also be terminated in circumstances where the amount of the subsidy is *de minimus*, or where the volume of exports or the injury is negligible.

Main Issues for Commonwealth Governments with EPZs
Illegal Prohibited Export Subsidies

Several of the preferential incentives typically provided to companies in EPZs fall squarely within the definition of prohibited export subsidy as described in Article 3 and the illustrative list in Annex 1. For example:

- ◆ the exemption or partial remission of direct taxes such as wage taxes, profit taxes, rents, royalties and property taxes;

- ◆ transport or freight charge subsidies on export shipment provided or mandated by the government;

- ◆ the provision of export credit guarantees or discounted insurance programmes.

It is important to note that the SCM Agreement is not targeting duty-free imports and exports. Rather, the Agreement targets the set of fiscal incentives, such as tax breaks and utility subsidies, which are offered on a preferential basis to exporters. If these measures were applied nationwide and to companies other than exporters, they would not be considered discriminatory and would probably not, therefore, be subject to WTO regulation. However, where these fiscal incentives are provided to EPZ firms on a preferential basis they become prohibited export subsidies (as described above) and are viewed as being an export subsidy for the EPZ companies' exported goods.

Therefore, developing Commonwealth countries with active EPZs and a per capita GNP of over US$1,000 technically have until the year 2003 to remove the prohibited subsidies or realign EPZ incentive schemes with national norms. Where this is not done, these countries face potential disciplinary actions and countervailing measures from trade partners.

As discussed above, the least-developed Commonwealth countries and those with a GNP per capita of less than US$1,000 are exempt from this restriction on prohibited subsidies.

Illegal Local Content Requirements

Prohibited export subsidies include both subsidies contingent on export performance and those contingent on the use of domestic over imported goods (Article 3.1(b)). The phase-out period for these local content subsidies is slightly different to that for export performance subsidies. Developing countries were required to remove all such subsidies by the end of 2000. Least-developed countries have until the end of 2002 to remove local content subsidies. Local content requirements may also conflict with a country's obligations under the WTO Agreement on Trade Related Investment Measures.

Introduced Prohibited Export Subsidies

It should be remembered that the eight-year period before developing countries are prohibited from maintaining prohibited export subsidies, i.e. until 2003, is intended to be a phase-out period. Article 27.4 of the SCM Agreement provides that a developing country 'shall not increase the level of its export subsidies'. Accordingly, where Commonwealth developing countries have increased, or are proposing to increase, the level of subsidies or introduce new subsidies, a careful assessment should be made as to whether the subsidy falls within the definition of prohibited export subsidy. Where such subsidies have already been introduced there is, of course, the possibility of retaliation from a trade partner.

Extended Time-limits for Specific Prohibited Export Subsidies

For all developing Commonwealth countries there is room in the SCM Agreement for a one-year extension of the exemption in relation to particular prohibited export subsidies, with annual consultations regarding further yearly extensions. These consultations must be initiated by the end of 2001.

Illegal Actionable Subsidies

Where a Commonwealth country maintains an actionable subsidy, i.e. one which causes adverse effects to the interests of another member and exceeds the *de minimus* thresholds, that country may become the focus of a direct challenge to the subsidy or a countervailing duty investigation, potentially resulting in the country being forced to withdraw the subsidy or remove the adverse effects or the country's exporters facing a higher duty on exports to certain foreign markets.

It should be noted that while least-developed countries or those with a GNP per capita below $1,000 are exempt from the restrictions on prohibited export subsidies, there is no exemption in relation to actionable subsidies. Therefore, if such a country were to export sufficient levels of subsidised product to pass the *de minimus* thresholds, an aggrieved country could take action against it.

Failure to Notify Subsidies

Article 25 of the SCM Agreement requires members to notify any subsidies being maintained by 30 June each year. This includes an obligation to notify that no subsidies at all are maintained.

New Round of Negotiations

The issues raised above all presume that the SCM Agreement remains unamended. However, developing countries, including Commonwealth developing countries, may decide that the export subsidy exemptions for developing and least-developed countries should be extended as part of any future negotiating round.

Regulatory Issues for Financial Centres

Getting the Domestic Financial Architecture Right

Winston Cox[1]

Introduction

The Asian crisis of 1997–98 highlights the importance of the financial sector to development. The loss of wealth and income that followed in the wake of the crisis underscored the nexus between robust financial systems and the reduction in poverty that is expected to accompany economic growth and development. The crisis, which capped those of the past two decades by its widespread domestic and international contagion, catapulted the architecture of the international financial system, and by implication that of the domestic system, to a position of prominence on the agenda of international economic issues. It also demonstrated flaws in the Shaw-McKinnon[2] thesis of financial liberalisation that was incorporated into the Washington consensus and that was accompanied by financial sector crises in developing countries during the 1980s and 1990s. The attention given to the financial architecture is intended to make the system more robust and less prone to crisis, and to ensure that financial intermediation supports steady growth and development. The initial concern with financial architecture has been with the international financial system, but since the international system includes a linked network of domestic financial systems, it was inevitable that the architecture of domestic financial systems would also come under scrutiny.

This paper examines the reforms of the domestic financial system in developing countries. It makes the case that developing countries must continue to strengthen their prudential regulation and supervision of the financial system or face endemic crises that will wipe out gains in poverty

---

1 Winston Cox is Deputy Secretary-General (Developent Co-operation) of the Commonwealth Secretariat. This paper is based on a speech given at the Overseas Development Institute, London, 28 March 2001.

2 McKinnon, Robert I. *Money and Capital in Economic Development*, Washington DC: Brookings Institute, 1973; *Financial Liberalisation and Economic Development: A Reassment of Interest Rate Policies in Asia and Latin America*, San Francisco: International Center for Economic Growth, 1988; and 'Financial Liberalisation in Retrospect: Interest rate Policies in LDCs' in G. Ranis and T.R. Schultz. *The State of Development Economics*, New York: Basil Blackwell, 1988; Shaw, Edward S. *Financial Deepening in Economic Development*, New York: Oxford University Press, 1973.

reduction. The paper is divided into four sections: the first examines the relation between the development of the financial sector and economic growth; the second reviews the structure of financial systems in developing countries; the third looks at prudential regulation in developing countries; the final section sets out what must be done to make the system work as intended.

The Financial System and Economic Growth

Empirical investigations have established a robust link between the evolution of the financial system and economic growth and development.[3] As Schmidt and Wrinkler observed: 'the positive correlation between the formation of financial assets and the rate of growth in per capita income is always significant, regardless of what combination of other macroeconomic policy variables are applied as further regressors' (Schmidt and Wrinkler, 1999, p. 5). The implication is that high levels of financial asset formation stimulate real capital formation and technological advances, which are key factors determining growth, and not the converse, namely that savings is a positive function of per capita income. Countries where the banking system exhibits a larger volume of liquid liabilities and a larger volume of credit issued to the private sector in relation to GDP, usually have higher rates of growth of per capita GDP. The evidence also shows that countries with more developed financial systems form more real capital and show greater technological innovation and progress.

Goldsmith (1969)[4] conducted the first major investigation into the relationship between the development of the financial system and economic growth on the basis of outstanding financial assets. By focusing on the financial inter-relations ratio (FIR), i.e. the ratio of the value of all outstanding financial assets in the financial sector of a given economy to the value of all outstanding real capital, Goldsmith was able to conclude that there is a 'positive though irregular association between the level of real national product per head and the FIR' (Goldsmith, 1969, p. 377). Later studies drawing on the work of Shaw (1973) and McKinnon (1973) use the relation between the monetary aggregate M2 and GDP rather than

3 Schmidt, Reinhard H. and Wrinkler, Adalbert. 'Building Financial Institutions in Developing Countries', Working Paper Series, Finance and Development, No. 45, Johann Wolfgang Geothe-Universität, Frankfurt am Main, November 1999 (p. 5); Brownbridge, Martin and Kirkpatrick, Colin, 'Financial Regulation in Developing Countries, Finance and Development Research Programme', Working Paper Series, No. 12, IPDM, University of Manchester, January 2000.
4 Goldsmith, R. *Financial Structure and Development*, New Haven, Connecticut: Yale University Press, 1969.

the FIR to establish the link between financial sector development and economic growth. Using cross-country regressions for 77 countries between 1960 and 1989, King and Levine[5] have linked real per capita growth in GDP, the growth in the capital stock, the investment share of GDP and a variable calculated to capture productivity growth, with financial asset formation in an economy to:

♦ the ratio of liquid liabilities, i.e. currency held outside the banking system plus demand and interest bearing liabilities of banks and non-bank financial intermediaries, to GDP;

♦ the ratio of credit issued by the banking system to private enterprises to GDP;

♦ the ratio of domestic credit issued by the deposit banks to domestic credit issued by deposit banks and the central bank; and

♦ the ratio of claims on the non-financial private sector to domestic credit.

Given the link between development of the financial sector and economic growth and development, one must ask why the financial sector in developing countries has remained underdeveloped relative to that of the industrial countries. The modern theory of finance suggests that because of the asymmetric nature of financial information among potential borrowers and lenders, it is rather difficult to organise an interpersonal and inter-temporal resource transfer due to the incentive information in any financial transaction. As institutions that play a role in financial intermediation they have to devise mechanisms to overcome these problems. This leads to the conclusion that the underdevelopment of financial institutions in most developing countries is caused by their inability or unwillingness to overcome the incentive-related problems associated with intermediation, a conclusion that is reinforced by the behaviour in developing countries of those financial institutions that have strong ownership and management links with a major partner in an industrial country. Empirical studies of bank failure in both industrial and developing countries reveal the main causes of failure to be poor risk evaluation and inadequate loan evaluation, both factors that reflect failure to overcome incentive-related problems associated with intermediation, and fraud.[6]

---

5 King, R.G. and Levine, R. 'Finance and Growth: Schumpeter might be Right', *Quarterly Journal of Economics*, Vol. 107, pp. 717–737, 1993.

6 BIS. *Credit Risk Modelling: Current Practices and Applications*, Basle Committee on Banking Supervision, Bank for International Settlements, April 1999; *Sound Practices for Loan Accounting and Disclosure*, Basle Committee on Banking Supervision, Bank for International Settlements, July 1999.

Accordingly, financial sector development has to be one of the key strategies for least-developed countries (LDCs) hoping to achieve sustainable growth in the long term. But building the financial sector has to go beyond the creation of new institutions; it must also include standards for prudential regulation and supervision, and training of staff to manage and regulate these institutions.

The Financial System

The financial system consists of providers and users of financial services. The typical financial system consists of a variety of institutions, instruments and markets that facilitate the flow of financial resources between borrowers and lenders. The institutions include pawnshops and money-lenders, banks, insurance companies, leasing companies, venture capital funds, mutual funds, pension funds, brokerage houses, investment trusts and stock exchanges. Financial instruments range from currency notes and coins, cheques, mortgages, corporate bills, bonds and stocks to futures, swaps and other complex derivatives. The markets for these instruments may be organised or may be informal. The users include households, businesses and the government.

Compared to that of an industrial economy, the financial system in a typical developing country may be characterised by the absence of one or more of the providers of services, the absence of many of the instruments and a lack of depth in the markets. The gaps are closing, however, because of a number of factors. One factor is the widespread acceptance of the Washington consensus and its emphasis on financial sector reform and modernisation, including the removal of restrictions on ownership of financial institutions by foreign investors, and the policy of some governments, when divesting their shares in the institutions that they owned, of employing the model of a strategic international partner who takes a significant equity position in, and management control of, the institution. Another factor helping to close the gap is the high level of co-operation between industrial and developing countries in combating financial sector crime, in supporting law enforcement by working together against money laundering and other financial sector crimes, and in improving supervision and the regulatory framework of financial institutions.

When developing countries began to modernise their financial systems most were characterised by branch banks or subsidiaries of international banks making self-liquidating loans mainly to enterprises engaged in some combination of natural resource exploitation and the distribution of goods imported mainly from the metropolitan country.[7] The first phase of modernisation usually began with the establishment of a central bank that was in a few instances converted into a monetary authority,[8] especially in the 1990s when dollarisation became the fashion. The next step in modernisation was the transfer of the former branches or subsidiaries of international banks to local ownership. This was also accompanied by the establishment of stock exchanges and additional specialised financial institutions such as Grameen-type banks and other institutions for lending to small and medium-sized enterprises, institutions for mortgages and other long-term lending, and for leasing, by either the private sector or, very often, by the government. The process of modernisation was often interrupted by systemic crises but, unlike the Asian crisis, they were limited to the local economy and had little or no international impact.[9]

Financial sector crises often exposed weaknesses that compromised the ability of the financial system to finance development. Among the more debilitating weaknesses are: directed credits and administered interest rates; lack of international standards; poor and non-transparent supervision; inadequate local markets for debt; a scarcity of equity;[10] and political interference in the management and operations of state-owned institutions. Directed credits and administered interest rates, usually through government-owned or government-influenced development financial institutions or commercial banks, relieved managers of responsibility for risk analysis in their credit decisions. They took the view that the corollary of government direction and influence was a government guarantee or at least a letter of comfort, which was often not worth the paper on which it was written. The result has been considerable portfolio losses, sometimes leading to a bail-out by the Treasury where it was fiscally affordable, or to recapitalisation using a financial sector loan from the International Financial Institutions (IFIs), and sometimes to the closure of many institutions, with little to show for the effort. The lack of standards, and poor and non-transparent supervision, meant that problems that

7 Newlyn, W.T. 'The Colonial Empire', in Sayers, R.S. (ed.). *Banking in the British Commonwealth*, Oxford University Press, 1952.

8 Around 128 central banks (excluding the European Central Bank and the Bundesbank) were established (or re-constituted) between 1945 and 2000, compared with 58 before 1944. See Chandavarkar, Anand. *Central Banking in Developing Countries*, MacMillan Press Ltd., 1996.

9 Antwi-Asare, T.O. and Addison, E.K.Y. *Financial Sector Reforms and Bank Performance in Ghana*, Overseas Development Institute, 2000; Bonnick, Gladstone. 'Storm in a Teacup or Crisis in Jamaica's Financial Sector', XIVth Adlith Browne Memorial Lecture, Caribbean Centre for Monetary Studies, 1998.

10 IFC. *Lessons of Experience No. 6 – Financial Institutions*, International Finance Corporation, Washington DC, 1998.

could be masked during periods of rapid growth were quickly exposed at the first hint of crisis in the financial sector or in periods of falling output. These shortcomings also make it possible for aberrant behaviour and conflict of interest involving directors and staff of the institutions to go undetected until it is too late.[11] These are the kinds of problems which need to be addressed by the redesign of the domestic financial architecture.

Financial Sector Regulation in Developing Countries

Several studies have found that liberalisation of the financial system in developing countries was accompanied by financial fragility and widespread distress affecting banks and non-financial institutions during the 1980s and 1990s.[12] These crises were triggered by liberalisation that was not properly sequenced and that preceded advances in financial system regulation. Liberalisation also took place in an environment of macroeconomic instability and rising fiscal deficits, which in turn resulted in penal interest rates that put highly leveraged corporations at risk. Weaknesses that were masked by rapid economic growth were later exposed by economic downturn. The policy justification for prudential regulation and supervision is to prevent systemic risk and to provide protection for small depositors – objectives that sometimes conflict. Banks and other financial institutions are subject to moral hazard and adverse selection can put their clients at risk, especially the numerous atomised depositors who have neither the incentive nor the expertise to monitor the institutions.

Before the 1980s, LDCs did not accord high priority to prudential regulation or supervision of their financial systems for two reasons. First, government policy emphasised economic regulation such as controls over interest rates and sectoral allocation of credit, because governments in LDCs were keen to use the financial system to promote economic, social and political objectives. Second, many developing countries had inherited banking and regulatory systems from colonial times in which the need for supervision by domestic regulators was limited because banks were owned by reputable and established foreign banks, were conservatively managed and subject to strict regulation by their parent institutions. However, the fragility that emerged in the 1980s exposed the inadequacies of the financial legislation and supervision in the face of changes in their financial

---

11 Bonnick, Gladstone, 1998, op. cit.

12 Brownbridge, Martin and Kirkpatrick, Colin, 2000, op. cit.

systems, notably changes in the ownership of their banks and relaxation of controls.

The reforms in the financial sector of developing countries in the 1980s were in many cases stimulated by financial crises or were part of broader reforms funded by the World Bank and IMF. Conditionalities related to financial sector regulation and supervision featured prominently in financial sector adjustment loans from the IFIs. Prudential reforms followed broadly similar patterns in LDCs, which adopted a model of regulation and supervision based on the Basle Committee's Core Principles of Effective Bank Supervision.[13] In this model, detailed prudential regulations were set out in banking laws and subsidiary legislation, with supervision undertaken by a public agency. Supervision entailed on-site inspections and off-site monitoring of banks based on the CAMEL principles, under which supervisors evaluate a bank according to its capital asset quality, management, earnings and liquidity. These principles are also extended to deposit taking non-bank financial institutions (NBFIs); supervisors aim to inspect institutions at regular intervals and institutions are required to submit regular financial reports to the supervisors. Many LDCs have adopted the Basle capital adequacy ratios. Prudential reforms in many countries have also included considerable institutional strengthening and some have adopted some type of insurance deposit.

Another source of regulatory support is the Financial Stability Forum (FSF), created in 1999. The purpose of the FSF is to promote financial sector stability through information exchange and international co-operation in financial supervision and surveillance. It brings together on a regular basis national authorities responsible for financial stability in significant financial centres, international financial institutions, sector specific international groupings of regulators and supervisors, and committees of central bank experts. Its major role has been to co-ordinate a set of codes and standards that are at the heart of the new international financial architecture. The IMF and other standard setting agencies, working together, have developed standards and codes covering a number of economic and financial areas, including data dissemination, fiscal, monetary and financial policy transparency, banking regulation and supervision, securities and insurance regulation, accounting, auditing, bankruptcy and corporate governance. The adoption of internationally recognized standards, or codes of good practices, can help to improve economic policy-making and strengthen the international financial system.

---

13 BIS. *Core Principles for Effective Bank Supervision*, Basle Committee on Banking Supervision, Bank for International Settlements, September 1997.

The burden of adjusting to the new codes and standards falls heavily on the developing countries and the time required to implement them should not be underestimated, even for large and relatively sophisticated countries like India and Brazil. But the attempt to set and universally apply standards and codes suffers from the inadequate participation of developing countries in the process, which violates Helleiner's principle of 'No harmonisation without representation'.[14]

Financial sector crisis also exposes the inadequacies of macroeconomic policy, especially with respect to the exchange rates and the financing of the fiscal deficit. Very often inadequate exchange rate policies may encourage external exposures that are not sustainable and cause financial resources to be directed to activities that carry an inherent exchange risk, for example property development for the domestic market, or that are not commercially viable. It is usually with respect to fiscal policy that the greatest weakness in the domestic financial architecture becomes evident. Until the IMF/World Bank-led financial sector reforms in the latter half of the last decade, deficit spending by government was often financed by borrowing from the central bank. Central banks, with their capacity to create liquidity were legally bound to purchase government paper and provide an overdraft (ways and means) to fund the fiscal deficit; they often did this with severe balance of payments and inflationary consequences. Some countries, to avoid repeating the excesses of money creation through borrowing from the central bank, have accepted dollarisation[15] and the replacement of the central bank with a monetary authority that does not have the capacity to create liquidity.

Making the Structures Work.

Although LDCs have made substantial progress in financial sector regulation and supervision, the real challenge is to make the regulations work in the way and for the purpose they were intended. If changes in the financial system are to be useful to LDCs, they should satisfy four criteria which Blackman has identified in relation to interest rate policy in Barbados between 1972 and 1987, but which have much wider applicability to the general condition of the financial sector. These conditions are: (i) the recognition of market imperfections in the financial sector;

---

14 Ocampo, José Antonio. 'Recasting the International Financial Agenda', *International Capital Markets*, Vol. 21, No. 1, Commonwealth Secretariat, London, February 2001.

15 Berg, Andrew and Borensztein, Eduardo R. 'The Pros and Cons of Full Dollarization', IMF Working Paper WP/00/50, March 2000; Terrones, Marco and Catao, Luis. 'Determinants of Dollarization – The Banking Side', IMF Working Paper WP/00/146, August 2000.

(ii) the imperative of economic development; (iii) the insulation of the economy against volatility; and (iv) the development of the financial markets themselves.[16] Sensitivity to these conditions should influence both the pace and scope of financial sector liberalisation and the architecture of the system.

Many LDCs suffered banking crises long after they had begun to implement prudential reforms. For example, Indonesia, Korea, Malaysia and Thailand suffered in the 1997–98 Asian crisis even though they had implemented reforms in the 1980s and 1990s. Kenya, which had also initiated reforms in the 1980s, suffered several bank failures in the 1990s. Although no prudential regulatory system or supervisory model can prevent bank failure, and zero tolerance of bank failure should never be the objective of financial sector regulation and supervision, events in many developing countries indicate that the systems are still prone to major weaknesses. Hanohan[17] has identified three sources of weakness: macroeconomic epidemics; poor management and other microeconomic deficiencies; and endemic crisis in a government-permeated banking system where political interference is the 'Achilles heel of any regulatory system'. In addition, other causes are weakness of the supervision office, deficiencies in the laws and law enforcement and migration of financial institutions or transactions from the more highly regulated and supervised to the less highly regulated and supervised part of the financial system.

The capacity of financial institutions to withstand macroeconomic shock varies, but since some institutions withstand the shock this suggests that others could also have done so. On the microeconomic side, unless the system is very concentrated, no one institution is likely to be large enough to cause an asset price boom and bust on its own. Rather, the microeconomic failures have more to do with management negligence, shortsightedness or fraud, which should be discovered by effective application of modern supervisory and regulatory techniques. Government influence on the banking system may take a combination of forms, including directed credits, excessive borrowing from the central bank, high reserve requirements, encouraging commercial banks to borrow abroad to ease pressure on the reserves, under-capitalisation and inadequate provisioning, especially by government-owned financial institutions. An additional twist is provided in a federal system where state gov-

---

16 Blackman, Courtney N. *Central Banking in Theory and Practice: A Small State Perspective*, Monograph (Special Studies) Series No. 26, Caribbean Centre for Monetary Studies, University of the West Indies, St Augustine, Trinidad, p. 102.

17 Hanohan, Patrick. *Banking Systems in Developing and Transition Countries: Diagnosis and Prediction*, BIS Working Paper No. 39, BIS, Basle, January 1997.

ernments may use the banks they own as sources of funding for their own borrowing needs.

The regulatory system will not live up to expectations if the financial sector legislation omits important prudential guidelines or includes provisions that are not precise enough. Examples of these omissions are the low levels of minimum capital requirements in many sub-Saharan African countries, overly lenient loan classification and provisioning rules and the omission of restrictions on excessive exposure to high risk sectors, for example real estate, exposed by the Asian crisis. Nor will the system deliver if there is weak enforcement of the prudential regulations by the supervisors – known as regulatory forbearance. Regulatory forbearance may be the result of political pressure on the regulatory authorities who may not wish to alienate the politicians who appoint them or it may be the result of 'regulatory capture'. This could take the form of the regulators being afraid that disclosure of problems may have the effect of a self-fulfilling prophecy, or may have an adverse effect on their career prospects. The fear of regulatory forbearance, however, should not be used as an argument to replace the judgements of mature and experienced officers by automatic disclosure. The system should always retain scope for supervisors to use their discretion not to disclose information in their early dealings with an institution that may be in difficulty, especially if there is a strong possibility that the institution could be saved by an injection of liquidity.

Institutions may also move transactions to that part of the financial sector which is least regulated, either in an attempt to evade detection or in an effort to be innovative. (Innovation in the financial sector is always ahead of regulation.) This migration highlights the need to regulate transactions rather than institutions, since one of the features of financial sector modernisation is the dissolution of boundaries between institutions. Some countries have attempted to resolve the issues created by the dissolution of boundaries between financial institutions by introducing a single regulator similar to the Financial Services Authority (FSA) in the UK. But this model offers no greater security to the architecture of the system because it has no intrinsic features that reduce regulatory forbearance, provide protection against interference or solve the skills shortage.

Given the weaknesses in the system of regulation and the causes of failure of financial institutions in LDCs, there must be considerable doubt about whether the model designed for industrial economies is appropriate for developing countries. Goodhart et al.[18] take the view that the devel-

---

18 Goodhart, Charles, Hartman, Phillip, Llewellyn, David, Rojas-Saurez, Lilliana and Weisbod, Steven. *Financial Regulation: Why How and Where Now?* London: Routledge, 1998.

oped country model is justified because 'the general analysis of, rationale for, and principles of, financial regulation are not fundamentally different in developing countries' (1998, p. 99). Caprio[19] questions the wisdom of exporting industrial country regulatory methodology to developing countries, especially since it has not in any event prevented bank failures. But such an argument only recognises that failure of financial institutions is impossible to prevent, even when the most sophisticated techniques of supervision and regulation are applied and even where markets are much better developed.

For developing countries to benefit from the positive effects of developed financial markets and institutions it is not sufficient for them to liberalise the financial system and become proficient at prudential regulation and supervision. Nor is it enough for them to participate in the development of and adopt internationally acceptable codes and standards and keep their financial sector open to foreign investment and the accompanying technology transfer, i.e. to get the architecture right. They must also have the human resources to make the system work. This implies heavy investment in training and emphasis on the principles and practice of good governance in financial institutions. The soundness of the financial system will ultimately depend on the quality of the personnel entrusted with the tasks of managing, regulating and supervising institutions.

Summary

Developing countries can benefit from the positive relationship between financial sector development and economic growth but to do so they must modernise and reform the financial sector and markets. While the first steps in financial sector reform concentrated on the creation of new and specialised institutions, endemic crises in the 1980s and 1990s, culminating in the Asian crisis of 1997–98, also highlighted the importance of prudential regulation and supervision. Even though the importance of regulation and supervision to the orderly development of markets and institutions is clear, developing countries have continued to experience setbacks in their implementation. To make prudential supervision and regulation work better, developing countries should not neglect the importance of sequencing financial sector liberalisation and prudential

---

19 Caprio, Gerrard. 'Bank Regulation: The Case of the Missing Mode', Policy Research Working Paper 1574, World Bank, 1996; 'Safe and Sound Banking in Developing Countries: We're not in Kansas Anymore', Policy Research Working Paper 1739, World Bank, 1997.

regulation. They should err on the side of higher capital requirements than those set out in the Basle Core Principles, impose tighter lending limits and financial restraints, have well-defined intervention rules that limit forbearance and reduce political pressure on regulators, and above all they should invest heavily in the training of staff needed to manage and regulate the financial system.

The Five Essential Issues Facing Offshore Financial Centres

Colin Powell OBE[1]

Introduction

This paper addresses the five essential issues now facing Offshore Financial Centres. In my view these can be listed as:

◆ ensuring there is an international level playing field;

◆ exchanging information and the protection of personal privacy;

◆ transparency;

◆ non-discriminatory tax regimes;

◆ maintaining a competitive advantage.

All five issues are interlinked; exchange of information, transparency, and non-discriminatory tax regimes are all elements for which an international level playing field is required if an individual jurisdiction's competitive advantage is to be maintained.

An International Level Playing Field

An overriding issue for Offshore Financial Centres is to ensure there is an international level playing field, applying, in particular, to all jurisdictions engaged in the provision of offshore financial services. As a starting point it would help if there was general agreement that, in setting international standards on financial regulation, money laundering and harmful tax competition and monitoring their compliance, there is no justification for focusing on OFCs separately from other jurisdictions. This is particularly important as whenever the subject of OFCs is discussed, a major problem is how they are to be defined.

If OFCs are to be defined by international organisations such as the OECD or the G7 Financial Stability Forum, with the threat of sanctions or 'defensive measures' being taken against those that do not comply

---

1 Colin Powell OBE is Chairman of the Jersey Financial Services Commission and Chairman of the Offshore Group of Banking Supervisors. This paper is based on a speech given at the Transcontinental Trusts 2001 Conference, Geneva, 18–19 June 2001.

with international standards, it is of utmost importance that the definition is one that embraces all the jurisdictions that are engaged in the same finance centre activities. Otherwise there is not a level playing field and business will simply migrate from jurisdictions that are threatened to those that are not.

The International Monetary Fund, in its working papers on OFCs, has tended to identify such centres as any centre that engages in the provision of cross-border financial services carried on in respect of non-residents. On this basis every major financial centre, including London, New York, Frankfurt and Tokyo, engages in the provision of offshore financial services, and indeed London is often described as the world's largest offshore financial centre.

In an attempt to narrow the focus, many have sought to define an OFC as a jurisdiction where the bulk of the financial service activity carried on is in respect of non-residents, notwithstanding that in absolute terms more 'offshore' business can be expected to be undertaken through London or New York than through the OFCs more narrowly defined. There are always difficulties with the treatment of centres such as Luxembourg and Switzerland who do not like to be considered 'offshore' (as they were by the G7 Financial Stability Forum). There are also substantial differences between well-established centres such as Hong Kong, Singapore, Jersey, Guernsey and the Isle of Man, which can be compared with Luxembourg and Switzerland in the range and level of financial services provided, and smaller centres which engage in providing financial services to non-residents on a much more limited scale and with a much narrower range.

This difficulty of definition is one of the reasons why the international initiatives undertaken by the Financial Action Task Force, the Financial Stability Forum and the OECD have been criticised for, among other things, their unfairness in not adopting a level playing field approach. The OECD, for example, produced an initial list of tax havens in 1998 apparently based on the contents pages of offshore year books but which then, without good reason, excluded Hong Kong, Singapore, Luxembourg and Switzerland.

One of the helpful outcomes of this difficulty of definition is that some international organisations such as the FATF and the Basle Committee on Banking Supervision have been persuaded that the focus should be not on whether a centre is properly described as 'offshore' or 'onshore' but on whether or not a centre complies with or co-operates in the implementation of international standards of financial regulation and anti-money-laundering. This message also appears to have registered with the

OECD Fiscal Affairs Secretariat but Frances Horner, when speaking at the Transcontinental Trust Conference held last December in London, while agreeing that it made good sense to address all jurisdictions equally in terms of whether they are co-operative or non co-operative, said that it could not be deflected from the OECD ministerial edict that a list of unco-operative tax havens, as opposed to unco-operative jurisdictions globally, should be produced.

The United Kingdom Government made its position very clear in March 2000, when congratulating Jersey, Guernsey and the Isle of Man for the way they had responded to the recommendations in the report on the review of financial regulation in the Crown Dependencies (the Edwards Report). A UK Treasury Minister stated:

The policy of the United Kingdom Government on offshore centres can be summed up as follows:

♦ *We have no problem, in principle, with centres who earn their living from providing financial services to non residents. This activity is not confined to offshore centres. Many onshore centres, including London and New York, do substantial non resident business;*

♦ *It is important that all financial centres comply with world standards regardless of whether onshore or offshore;*

♦ *We support the initiatives under way in various international bodies to encourage all jurisdictions to improve standards;*

♦ *We consider that the true distinction is not between onshore and offshore centres, but between centres which comply with international standards and those which do not.*

An international statement to this effect would be most welcome.

The OECD's view, which remains untested, is that 'tax havens' will not co-operate in meeting international standards unless threatened by 'defensive measures', and cannot be trusted to implement such standards without first agreeing their implementation plans with the OECD. Other jurisdictions can be trusted to engage in a self-assessment process. There is no level playing field between competing jurisdictions such as Jersey and Guernsey that fall into the first category, and Luxembourg, Switzerland, Hong Kong and Singapore that fall into the second.

There are clear signs, however, in all the international initiatives which focus on OFCs, of a growing recognition of the importance of a level playing field if the co-operation of these centres is to be secured. There is also a recognition that there are many jurisdictions outside the list of traditional OFCs on which attention needs to be focused as much as, if not more than, many of the OFCs.

Thus, in initiating its non-co-operative countries and territories exercise, the FATF included Russia and Israel, as well as a number of more traditional OFCs, in its first list of 15 non co-operative jurisdictions published in June 2000. The second batch of jurisdictions reviewed by the FATF also included many jurisdictions that would not be considered to be OFCs.

The European Union, in progressing its tax package embracing the proposed Directive on the taxation of savings income, has recognised that to preserve the competitiveness of European financial markets efforts are needed to draw non-EU jurisdictions into the adoption of 'equivalent' measures in the case of the USA, Switzerland, Liechtenstein, Monaco, Andorra and San Marino, or the 'same' measures in the case of dependent or associated territories such as the Channel Islands, Isle of Man and dependent or associated territories in the Caribbean. The EU clearly sees the need for a level playing field. However, when the same arguments are advanced by OFCs, they are often portrayed as an unreasonable or 'obstructive' condition.

For their part, individual non-EU jurisdictions have made it clear that they will not respond to the EU approaches until it is clear what the EU member states are going to do and what competing non-EU jurisdictions generally are going to do. A key player in this respect is Switzerland which appears to take the view that it does not want to facilitate 'avoidance' of any measures agreed by the EU member states, but at the same time is determined to preserve the privacy of law-abiding citizens. Accordingly, the Swiss have indicated that if they agree to join with the EU in seeking to establish a sound system of taxation of savings income, they will not adopt the exchange of information provisions in the EU proposal but will be prepared to apply a withholding tax to interest payments made by Swiss paying agents to individuals resident in an EU member state. Other non-EU jurisdictions may decide to follow a similar course. However, while the Swiss may have geopolitical reasons for wanting to work in harmony with the EU, this would seem to be far less the case with the USA; it will probably be more difficult to convince the USA that its interests will be served by the adoption of measures 'equivalent' to those to be adopted by the EU.

The OECD, in progressing its harmful tax competition initiative, has also given increasing recognition to the importance of a level playing field. To quote from an OECD document prepared by the Fiscal Affairs Secretariat earlier this year, 'the OECD member countries in themselves are not a large enough geographical grouping to achieve globally accepted international tax standards and to co-ordinate their dissemination, implementation of administration, and economies outside the OECD must be brought into this process'. In the 1998 Report on harmful tax competition, the OECD, in referring to 'harmful preferential tax regimes', emphasised that a co-ordinated approach, including dialogue by the OECD with non-member countries, is required to achieve the level playing field which the OECD stated is so essential to the continued expansion of global economic growth.

There is still a gap, however, between the preaching and the practice on the subject of level playing fields.

The OFCs that the OECD have been seeking to draw into commitments, with the threat of 'defensive measures' if they do not co-operate, have emphasised that they are willing to play a full part and to participate on an equal basis in a partnership programme through ongoing discussions in a global form involving OECD members and representative non-member jurisdictions. They have emphasised that it is of the greatest importance, if there is to be a global approach and an international level playing field, that all relevant countries should be integrated into the process of setting new international tax standards and in the detailed implementation of both existing and new international standards on harmful tax practices. This would include the terms and conditions for the effective exchange of information for tax purposes and the development of application notes which would be used to guide jurisdictions participating in such a global forum when seeking to eliminate harmful tax practices.

Jersey and Guernsey have made it clear that where legislative and policy decisions are required in order to respond to the OECD tax initiatives, these will be presented to their respective assemblies, having due regard to whether or not equivalent measures are to be adopted by OECD members, and by those non-member jurisdictions which are materially in competition with the Islands in the provision of cross-border financial services. It has also been made clear by the Islands that they will be as determined to protect their economic interests and fiscal autonomy as they expect OECD member and non-member jurisdictions to be.

An international level playing field is of overriding importance when considering the three broad principles that the OECD considers to be the key to a global approach to the removal of harmful tax practices:

- effective exchange of information
- transparency
- non-discrimination.

These principles in themselves have presented no difficulties for the quality OFCs. However, in the absence of clear evidence that a level playing field exists in the interpretation of these principles, and that they are being honoured equally by competing jurisdictions, including members of the OECD, it should not have come as a great surprise to the OECD that only a few 'tax havens' rushed forward to make the commitment requested of them.

Exchange of Information

The Channel Islands, for example, have no difficulty whatsoever in meeting the OECD's requirements for the exchange of information in respect of the investigation and prosecution of criminal tax matters. Existing legislation in respect of all crimes of money laundering, international cooperation and investigation of fraud means that in respect of criminal tax matters the Islands already cover the requirements for information exchange set out by the OECD, and in many cases this will extend to areas of information exchange which in other jurisdictions might be covered by civil rather than criminal proceedings. For this reason, among others, there is no good reason for the Islands to be considered 'non-co-operative' by the OECD and they are confident they will not be so considered. Indeed, it has been suggested that any list of 'non co-operative' jurisdictions that included the Islands would, in the eyes of many, lack credibility.

It is doubtful whether many of the OFCs, and certainly none of the quality OFCs, would have any difficulty in joining with the OECD member states in adopting the report on 'Improving Access to Bank Information for Tax Purposes' published in 2000 with its reference to allowing information to be provided to tax authorities upon specific request for the investigation or prosecution of criminal tax matters. Such procedures could be expected to be readily accommodated in any tax information exchange or mutual legal assistance, agreements or treaties to be negotiated.

There is, however, as yet no consensus about the exchange of information on civil tax matters. Switzerland and Luxembourg have clearly indicated that they will defend personal privacy where no crime has been committed, and the USA also has come down firmly in support of personal privacy in respect of those who are not alleged to be engaged in matters that might lead to criminal prosecution. There is also little apparent support outside the EU for the automatic exchange of information referred to in the proposals for a Directive on the taxation of savings income. Even within the EU countries such as Luxembourg and Austria have opted for the transitional withholding tax approach, rather than the exchange of information approach in respect of that Directive. The USA appears more likely to respond to specific requests for information within the framework of tax information exchange agreements negotiated on a country by country basis.

Jersey and Guernsey have indicated their willingness to engage in discussions on a global basis with a view to the development of a model exchange of information instrument concerning 'civil tax matters', and to join in discussions on the effective adoption and implementation by both OECD members and representative non-member jurisdictions of such an instrument. The OECD appears to have recognised, albeit with some apparent reluctance, that financial centres engaged in the provision of financial services to non-residents are in active competition with each other and that if one centre was required to take action ahead of the others the only result would be that the business would flow to those jurisdictions that were not so forthcoming. Thus, if a jurisdiction such as Jersey or Guernsey was to accept that the OECD tax initiative should extend to a commitment to exchange information on bank deposits held by individuals – and the Islands do not accept that the 1998 Report on Harmful Tax Competition, which refers to business taxation in respect of geographically mobile financial and other service activities, extends to such matters – then business could be expected quickly to flow to a jurisdiction such as Switzerland or Hong Kong where no such commitment had been made.

Transparency

Linked to the exchange of information is the OECD concept of transparency. According to the OECD, effective exchange of information depends on:

♦ The existence of relevant and reliable information;

♦ The legal ability of a state requested to provide information to obtain the information for purposes of transmitting it to the state requesting the information;

♦ A legal mechanism for providing the information to another state for tax administration purposes;

♦ Adequate safeguards to protect the confidentiality of the information exchanged; and

♦ Administrative measures to ensure that the exchange of information will function effectively.

Clearly tax information exchange agreements will be worthless if the jurisdictions concerned do not have information to exchange. Again, if an international level playing field is adopted, quality OFCs such as Jersey and Guernsey should have little difficulty in meeting the OECD's requirements (unlike some OECD member states). Information on beneficial ownership of companies, partnerships and other legal entities established in the Channel Islands, including managers of collective investment funds and trustees and beneficiaries of trusts, is information that is held within the Islands. The legislation for the regulation of company and trust company service providers recently enacted in both Jersey and Guernsey make provision for the licensing of individual business entities. This licensing process calls for business to be undertaken in a fit and proper way, and one of the central requirements in this respect is that those providing company and trust company services know with whom they are dealing. In this area it is the OFCs themselves that are setting the standards. The Offshore Group of Banking Supervisors has decided to set up a working group, and invite representation from relevant international organisations, with a remit to translate these standards into an international standard for general adoption.

It is also expected that there would be sufficient information available to enable those who are providing the financial services to understand the scope of the business activities of those they are serving, so that proper safeguards can be in place regarding anti-money-laundering activities and the provision of suspicious transaction reports under the relevant legislation. Hence, if specific requests are made for information in respect of the investigation or prosecution of criminal tax matters, there should be no difficulty for quality OFCs in providing the required information. Indeed, this is already current practice. It would not have been possible for Jersey, for example, to have received the congratulations it has received from judicial authorities, such as the US Department of Justice, on the co-operation that they have obtained in the pursuit of those engaged in organised crime if information was not both available and exchanged.

What is important, however, is that there should not be double standards. For example, it is possible for a company to be incorporated in the UK without information on beneficial ownership being made available to the Company Registry – something that is also possible in respect of Delaware Corporations in the USA but not in respect of the incorporation of a Jersey company. Many jurisdictions, including OECD member states, have taken steps to reduce the administrative burdens placed upon small companies in respect of the requirement to file or audit accounts, and it is doubtful whether in many jurisdictions financial information is available to the same extent as in the quality OFCs.

Non-Discriminatory Tax Regimes

The importance of an international level playing field also applies to the OECD tax initiative – and to the EU Code of Conduct on business taxation initiative – in respect of so-called harmful tax regimes.

Many are now questioning whether tax competition should ever be seen as harmful – and the recent pronouncements by the US Administration lend credence to this view. Other OECD member countries have also indicated that they fear that in attacking certain jurisdictions on the grounds that they are said to be engaged in harmful tax practices, financial services will be diverted to jurisdictions which are less well-regulated and therefore less reputable as far as financial regulation and anti-money-laundering measures are concerned.

Initially the OECD 'tax haven' exercise appeared to be focused on the so-called evils of any jurisdiction with no or nominal tax. However, the OECD has now accepted the zero tax regimes of the Cayman Islands and Bermuda, and has generally accepted that it has no right to seek to impose its will upon jurisdictions in the determination of their independent fiscal policies, providing there is no discrimination between resident and non-resident taxpayers.

The OECD has also accepted, in discussions with the Channel Islands, the logic of the argument that if zero tax regimes are acceptable, then it makes no sense to resist zero tax arrangements for particular areas of financial business activity (providing this is done on a non-discriminatory basis) because otherwise all that would happen would be that the business would migrate to the zero tax regimes. Accordingly, the principle of what has been described as 'salami' slicing has been taken on board. As a result, there should be no difficulty in the Islands or other jurisdictions maintaining favourable tax arrangements for areas of business such as collective investment funds and captive insurance where the removal of any discriminatory arrangements distinguishing between resident and non-resident tax payers can be undertaken without detracting from the Islands' competitiveness as a low-tax jurisdiction.

The Channel Islands have made it clear at all times, not only in respect of the OECD, but also in respect of the EU tax initiatives, that they support the principles of fair tax competition, but are not prepared to make commitments one result of which could be to leave the Islands competing for the provision of financial services with other relevant jurisdictions on an un-level playing field. While the EU member states, for example, see the need to act in unison in removing what they perceive to be harmful tax measures to ensure the effective functioning of the goods, services, capital and labour markets in the EU, so the Channel Islands see the need for an inclusive global response to so-called harmful tax measures if their economic interests are to be safeguarded. Above all, the view is taken that since the EU Code of Conduct on business taxation is designed to support the interests of the EU, member states should put their own houses in order before expecting other non-EU jurisdictions to participate. The Code of Conduct Group's report included a large number of footnotes reflecting the extent to which member states were in disagreement with the listing of individual tax measures, and their wish to enter reservations. For example, there is no apparent agreement on how the Dutch holding company regimes, or the Belgian co-ordination centres, are to be dealt with.

There is also criticism of the OECD initiative for focusing solely on geographically mobile financial and other service activities and for not applying their principles on harmful tax competition to business activities generally.

Under pressure from a number of quarters the OECD proposals on the removal of tax ring-fencing have been watered down. Increasingly, therefore, the main issue on which OFCs will need to respond is the matter of exchange of information. This arises from the requirements of customer due diligence for effective financial regulation, for anti-money-laundering measures, and for the fight against corruption, as well as for the investigation and prosecution of tax crimes.

Maintaining the Competitiveness of OFCs

In looking to the future, it has been suggested that even if OFCs pass the tests set by the international initiatives of the OECD or the FATF, and escape the threat of what has been described by the OECD as a common framework of defensive measures, they will still face the prospect of individual countries continuing to take defensive measures against individual OFCs. However, when considering the impact of any such defensive measures, as they have been identified to date, it is important to keep a sense of proportion.

Many jurisdictions already apply different regimes to financial transactions with low-tax jurisdictions (through controlled foreign corporation legislation or exclusion from double taxation agreements of specific favourable tax arrangements). In many cases jurisdictions will need to introduce legislation or amend international agreements to introduce measures to restrict, condition or even prohibit financial transactions with OFCs. In this context it is to be expected that no jurisdiction would want to act against its own best interests by introducing measures other than at the same time as other countries. For example, the City of London and UK financial institutions could be damaged if their competitive position was to be adversely affected by action being taken by the UK Government which was not also being taken by other countries. The US authorities appear to have recognised the force of this argument in their recent pronouncements.

Without doubt the international initiatives that are perceived to be directed at OFCs have given rise to some uncertainty about the future of some, if not all, of these centres. There is growing recognition, however, that there are quality offshore jurisdictions that are complying with international standards and can be considered partners rather than the enemy, that quality business is being attracted to these quality OFCs and that such centres have a future.

We return to the question of definition. No-one would suggest that the offshore financial services provided out of London, Zurich, Geneva, Luxembourg, Dublin, Singapore or Hong Kong are at risk of disappearing. There is, therefore, no reason why the quality OFCs that might more traditionally be so identified cannot continue to exploit niche market opportunities and have an appeal in the world financial market place.

Many of the reasons for the success to date of quality OFCs such as the Channel Islands will be unaffected by the international initiatives.

◆ The acceptance by the OECD of zero tax regimes, providing they are non-discriminatory is as good an indication as one could hope for that there is a future for tax differentials.

◆ The greater speed with which OFCs can enact legislation which meets the needs of the international financial market place will remain.

◆ The record of political and fiscal stability among many offshore financial centres will be sustained.

◆ The confidentiality offered to those engaged in legitimate business and who have legitimate reasons for protecting their privacy will remain.

◆ The greater flexibility of small jurisdictions will remain.

◆ The quality of the services provided and the expertise available will be maintained.

There will always be room in the market place for quality niche market operators. The advantages of OFCs which have been referred to in this paper, together with a continued growth in wealth worldwide and the globalisation of the financial market place, suggests there is every reason to expect that both small and large OFCs, working to international standards, will continue to find a place in the sun.

More international co-operation will be called for in the pursuit of those engaged in fiscal fraud and other criminal matters; this will manifest itself in requests for greater exchange of information in support of criminal investigations and prosecutions. The work of the Financial Action Task Force on money laundering, and of the Basle Committee on Banking Supervision on customer identification and customer due diligence, also points to the need for more openness. There is, however, no reason why companies engaged in legitimate business should face fewer opportunities for taking advantage of international tax differentials through OFCs, nor should investors engaged in legitimate activities fear for any loss of the privacy they have a right to enjoy and which they will be able to call upon human rights legislation to defend.

There is, therefore, every reason for optimism about the future of OFCs, whether they are being used by corporate bodies or individual investors, providing they are committed to and comply with international standards. This is a process that will require an international level playing field if it is to be fully effective in its application. What the Offshore Financial Centres ask for is that they should be recognised as partners in the application of international standards, and not as the enemy.

Offshore Financial Centres and the Supranationals: Collision or Cohabitation?[1]

Richard J. Hay[2]

Over the last three years the OECD, the world's club of rich countries, has demanded sweeping changes in the design and transparency of the world's Offshore Financial Centres (OFCs). The OECD seeks tax information exchange and threatens sanctions for offshore centres which refuse to comply with their demands. The Financial Action Task Force, a G7 chartered agency housed in OECD offices in Paris, has mounted a campaign with complementary objectives to combat money laundering. A number of other bodies, including the Financial Stability Forum, the IMF, the UN and the EU, have pursued similar initiatives to promote change in the world's financial system.

OFCs have voiced concerns that the fora most active in developing standards have elite memberships restricted to the world's rich and powerful countries. The initiatives conducted by the OECD and FATF, in particular, have been criticised for adopting an exclusionary and confrontational approach, ill-suited to securing the co-operation necessary to effect meaningful change.

OFCs are troubled by the fact that the standards sought to be imposed on them are not uniformly adopted by member states of the organisations tabling the demands, fuelling concerns that supranational bodies are proceeding with insufficient regard to fairness or the concerns of non-members.[3] In the absence of a commitment to ensure a level playing field for all participants, the supranational agencies, including particularly the OECD, are perceived to lack the moral high ground claimed by them in the attack on the offshore world.

The OECD project was thrown into disarray by a widely publicised with-

---

1 Copyright: Richard Hay 2001. This article was first published in the *Chase Journal*, Vol. V, Issue 2, August 2001.

2 Richard Hay is an international partner in Stikeman Elliott, an international law firm. He is admitted to practice in Ontario, New York and England.

3 Article 1 of the OECD Convention requires the OECD to promote the interest of its own members.

drawal of support for elements of the initiative by the new US Republican administration, articulated in a statement tabled by the US Treasury Secretary on 10 May 2001. Secretary O'Neill reiterated support for the core objective of the project – tax information exchange – in testimony before a Senate hearing on 18 July 2001.[4] However, he continued to express concerns about the 'condemnatory tone' of the OECD reports leading to 'unfair' treatment of non-OECD countries.

The narrowing support from the US Treasury has led to several important developments in the OECD project. First, the deadline for offshore centre agreements with the OECD has been put back from 31 July to 28 February 2002. Second, the prospect of sanctions (termed 'co-ordinated defensive measures' by the OECD) being imposed on OFCs has receded. Any such measures will be delayed in any event to 2003. Third, non-core elements of the initiative have been abandoned as the project has been narrowed to focus on information exchange for the purpose of enforcement of tax laws. Finally, the OECD has been placed under pressure to ensure that OECD member countries are held to 'standards and timelines at least as rigorous' as those sought to be imposed on OFCs.

This paper considers the current state of play in the complex and overlapping supranational initiatives proposing changes in the regulation of OFCs. The implications of the shift in the US position, in particular, are reviewed. The underlying rationales for change are considered, as are the likely and appropriate responses for the stakeholders in the offshore centres, including governments, financial institutions and clients.

The Appeal of Tax-Free Centres in an Increasingly Transparent World

Offshore Financial Centres are jurisdictions that attract a high level of non-resident financial services clients relative to the volume of domestically sourced business. The globalisation of business, enhanced mobility of individuals, increasing sophistication of the offshore world and the higher level of information available on planning opportunities have all increased the attraction of international and offshore financial services. OFCs now offer a level of expertise in many areas which exceeds that available in the major onshore money centres.

OFCs currently hold assets valued at US$6–8 trillion. The rapid expan-

---

4 Statement of Paul O'Neill before the Senate Committee on Governmental Affairs, Permanent Subcommittee on Investigations, OECD Harmful Tax Practices Initiative, 18 July 2001 (available at www.senate.gov)

sion of the world economy continues to increase global wealth, further enhancing asset growth in the offshore world.[5] This success is driven by institutions, corporate and individual clients voting with their feet to take advantage of the absence of tax and greater flexibility found offshore.[6]

There is a misguided perception in some quarters that the move to transparency in response to changing standards will lead to the demise of the offshore world. No doubt the appetite of some of the marginal users of the international financial system (tax evaders and money launderers) will be chilled by transparency. However, the main appeal of offshore centres is, and will remain, the ability of clients to transact in an income tax-free environment.

The OECD now accepts the legitimacy of income tax-free systems in the offshore world.[7] Accordingly, the opportunity to conduct business on a tax-neutral platform will continue in offshore centres, and the offshore world will continue to service constantly increasing client demand, despite the extensive changes underway. This is particularly true for those offshore centres which are using their tax-neutral platforms to conduct real and substantial activities in areas such as the following:

- establishment and administration of mutual fund companies and trusts;

- international tax and estate planning;

- structured debt and special purpose vehicles to support capital markets transactions;

- structures for management of political and personal risk;

- special purpose vehicles for securitisations;

- insurance and reinsurance products;

---

5 The 2000 Merrill Lynch Gemini study, for example, notes that the number of US dollar millionaires in the world economy has increased by 50 per cent over the last three years to a current total of approximately 7,000,000 millionaires.

6 As the FSF (*Report of the Working Group on Offshore Centres*) notes that the growth of London as the largest offshore banking centre has been linked directly to regulations imposed on the US banking sector: capital controls implemented through the Interest Equalisation Tax of 1964, the Foreign Credit and Exchange Act of 1965, cash reserve requirements on deposits imposed in 1977 and a ceiling on time deposits in 1979. By establishing foreign branches to which these regulations did not apply, US banks were able to operate in more cost-attractive environments (p. 8).

7 The OECD report, *Towards Global Tax Co-operation: Progress in Identifying and Eliminating Harmful Tax Practices* (26 June 2000) states that its project: 'is not intended to promote the harmonisation of income taxes or tax structures generally within or outside the OECD, nor is it about dictating to any country what should be the appropriate level of tax rates' (p. 5).

- international employee stock option and deferred compensation plans;
- shipping and aircraft financing structures.

Overview of the Principal Onshore Initiatives

The principal supranational agencies seeking change are:

- The Paris-based OECD which seeks greater transparency on tax matters through the Harmful Tax Competition Initiative. The main reports published by the OECD on its objectives are *Harmful Tax Competition* (27 April 1998), *Towards Global Tax Co-operation* (26 June 2000), *Improving Access to Bank Information for Tax Purposes* (24 March 2000) and the *Report on Misuse of Corporate Vehicles for Illicit Purposes* (29 May 2001);[8]

- The Financial Action Task Force housed in the OECD offices in Paris, charged with countering money laundering. The main reports published by FATF are the *Reviews to Identify Non-Co-operative Countries or Territories* (22 June 2000 and 22 June 2001) and the *Report on Money Laundering Typologies* (1 February 2001);[9]

- The Basle-based Financial Stability Forum, seeking enhanced standards for international banking regulation to address market integrity and prudential concerns. The relevant report published by the FSF is the *Report of the Working Group on Offshore Centres* (5 April 2000).[10]

Related initiatives include:

- EU efforts to impose effective taxation of savings through either a withholding tax or information reporting to support improved taxpayer compliance. This initiative culminated in the Feira Agreement on the taxation of savings reached in Portugal in June 2000.[11] Member states agreed to information exchange as the ultimate objective of EU policy, though members who currently impose withholding tax can still do so until 2009. Member countries have committed themselves to promote the adoption of similar information exchange policies in dependent and associated territories (for example the British Overseas Territories) and in the USA and Switzerland. The EU has recently

---

8 Available on the web at www.oecd.org.

9 Available on the web at www.oecd.org/fatf.

10 Available on the web at www.fsforum.org.

11 Santa Maria da Feira, European Council, Presidency Conclusions (19 and 20 June 2000).

abandoned plans to promote tax harmonisation amongst its members;[12]

♦ The US Program for Qualified Jurisdictions and Qualified Intermediaries, designed to facilitate monitoring of US taxpayers investing
back into that country through offshore structures. This initiative has
the (incidental?) effect of projecting US domestic regulation of financial intermediaries onto a global basis.

Implications of the Proposed Changes for Personal Financial Privacy

The complete record of an individual's financial transactions – now
sought on a global basis – forms a revealing insight into the intimate
details of one's personal life. The collection and sharing of such information, and the linkage of databases through the use of electronic tools,
poses many concerns for the privacy of individuals.[13]

The OECD report, *Improving Access to Bank Information for Tax Purposes*,
contains informative insights into the scope of existing financial disclosure in onshore countries. France, for example, requires financial institutions managing stocks, bonds or cash to report to the government on a
monthly basis regarding the opening, modification and closing of accounts
of all kinds. This information is stored in a central computerised database
which is used by French authorities for research, control and collection
purposes. Four other OECD countries – Hungary, Korea, Norway and
Spain – also maintain centralised databases.[14]

Scepticism concerning the ability of governments to resist the temptation
to access information for unauthorised purposes is rife, particularly as
there is, by definition, no opportunity to monitor unauthorised access.
Affluent taxpayers in at least one major OECD country also fear that tax

---

12 *Tax Policy in the European Union – Priorities for the Years Ahead*, European Commission,
23 May 2001. The report states at paragraph 2.4:

*It is clear that there is no need for an across the board harmonisation of Member States' tax systems.
Provided that they respect Community rules, Member States are free to choose the tax systems that
they consider most appropriate and according to their preference.*

13 The UN Declaration of Human Rights 1948 recognises and protects privacy as a basic
human right. Article 12 reads:

*No one shall be subjected to arbitrary interference with his privacy, family, home or correspondence,
nor to attacks upon his honour and reputation. Everyone has the right to the protection of the law
against such interference and attacks.*

14 *Improving Access to Bank Information for Tax Purposes*, Appendix, Section 3.1.2.

data is routinely sold to criminal gangs seeking targets for kidnapping. Global sharing of information means that criminal access can occur at the weakest point of entry, multiplying the risks associated with unauthorised disclosure.[15]

The risks to personal privacy arising from the collection of financial information are disconcerting, even when apparently sophisticated governments maintain control of the information and apparatus.[16] The prospect of abuse where these vast and globally converged pools of information fall into the wrong hands en masse or through ad hoc unauthorised access is truly frightening. This is particularly so for the many families with direct experience of repressive or corrupt governments.

Compromise of the Rights of OFC States

At the outset, many of the offshore states simply insisted that the OECD had no right or authority to force changes in their domestic laws. This is true, of course, but it ignores the fact that the OECD is not dictating changes as such, but rather requesting changes with the threat of sanctions (including withholding tax and restrictions on access to onshore financial markets) for those centres which do not comply.

An offshore banking centre exists because it is able to:

♦ service clients from other jurisdictions;

---

15 A UN Report published in 1998 notes, alarmingly, that in a part of the former Soviet Union (not an OECD member), criminal gangs have bought banks in order to determine which families had bank accounts large enough to make kidnapping worthwhile. United Nations Office for Drug Control and Crime Prevention (UNODCCP), 'Financial Havens, Banking Secrecy and Money-Laundering', double issue 34/35 of the *Crime Prevention and Criminal Justice Newsletter*, and Issue 8 of *UNDCP Technical Services*, 1998, p. 68.

16 The IRS has recently been admonished by the US GAO for its failure to adequately secure access to its electronic filing systems and the electronically transmitted tax return data those systems contain. In a report dated February 2001, *Information Security: IRS Electronic Filing Systems*, the GAO states (p. 2):

We demonstrated that unauthorised individuals, both internal and external to IRS, could have gained access to IRS' electronic filing systems and viewed and modified tax payer data contained in those systems during the 2000 tax filing season. We were able to gain such access because the IRS at that time had not (1) effectively restricted external access to computers supporting the e-file programme, (2) securely configured the operating systems of its electronic filing systems, (3) implemented adequate password management and user account practices, (4) sufficiently restricted access to computer files and directories containing tax return and other system data, or (5) used encryption to protect tax return on e-file systems. Further, these weaknesses jeopardised the security of sensitive business, financial and taxpayer data on other critical IRS systems that were connected to e-file computers through its servicewide network.

♦ access international banking networks;

♦ invest in onshore securities markets.

Offshore centres rely on such access to foreign markets to conduct a local financial services industry much larger than that which could be supported by domestic demand. Accordingly, it is not practical for an OFC to isolate itself from outside pressure by unplugging from the international grid unless the centre is prepared to restrict the local financial sector to the purely domestic environment, typically tiny markets in most OFCs.

Crucially, the OECD now accepts that OFCs are free to operate income tax-free fiscal regimes.[17] High-tax OECD regimes deserve similar tolerance from OFCs. This means, at minimum, that as long as such mutual respect for different systems of taxation exists, service providers in OFCs ought not to undermine high-tax OECD regimes by inviting tax evaders to seek refuge in confidential offshore financial structures.

The opportunity to participate in the markets of other countries also implies some minimum standards of behaviour in order to justify access. Thus, onshore countries can and do take the position that they can prevent or restrict access to banking and securities markets for institutions and their clients in jurisdictions that are perceived to be poorly regulated or overly secretive.

As a general rule there are few effective limits on the right of an onshore country to restrict market access. Possible avenues include resort to the WTO for a challenge based on denial of market access pursuant to the General Agreement on Trade in Services. An alternative basis may be that such sanctions constitute an improper infringement of Article 8(2) of the IMF Agreement which limits the ability of IMF members to impose restrictions on international fund transfers.[18]

In any event, decisions to deny market access are often discretionary and as a result are difficult to attack. The banking advisories issued following the June 2000 FATF *Review to Identify Non-Co-operative Countries or Territories: Increasing the Worldwide Effectiveness of Anti-Money Laundering Measures*, for example, did not preclude market access but rather simply advised caution in dealing with institutions situated in centres deemed 'un-co-operative'. Another recent similar example of a decision which is difficult to review is the US programme designating 'qualified jurisdic-

---

17 2000 Report.

18 See Bruce Zagaris, 'OECD Harmful Tax Competition Report and Related Initiatives Leave the Caribbean Offshore "in Irons"', *Tax Notes International*, 21 August 2000; 'Caribbean Tax Havens Seek Refuge in the Arms of the WTO', *Financial Times*, Tuesday 3 October 2000.

tions' entitled to access US security markets with reduced withholding tax compliance burdens. Some response and accommodation for the demands of the onshore countries and their agencies is accordingly appropriate and desirable, as a practical matter, if an OFC wants to continue to obtain market access.

A Level Playing Field for International Financial Services?

The offshore centres are being asked to adhere to rules not universally observed by members of the club (the OECD) seeking changes. This overreaching by the OECD has blunted the force of the Harmful Tax Competition Initiative in particular, but the concern applies equally to elements of the other initiatives.

Regrettably, the OECD's high-minded commitment to a level playing field (occasionally trumpeted to garner media support for the project[19]) has not always translated into practical reality. In particular, the OECD has shown inappropriate reluctance to permit the implementation of commitments by OFCs in the context of the Harmful Tax Competition Initiative to be conditional on the implementation of equivalent commitments by all OECD member states, including Switzerland and Luxembourg.

Switzerland and Luxembourg

Switzerland and Luxembourg, both OECD members, dissented from the 1998 Report and continue to resist pressure to exchange information for tax enforcement purposes.[20] Switzerland is a decentralised federal state and even if the Federal Council were minded to negotiate on this point, there are cumbersome constitutional limitations on its ability to agree on measures to negotiate on bank secrecy.

The OECD appears to take the position that this dissenting view is *de*

---

19 In 'Towards World Tax Co-operation', *OECD Observer*, 27 June 2000, Jeffrey Owens, OECD Head of Fiscal Affairs, reviewed the OECD's demands for transparency in the Harmful Tax Competition Initiative and stated:

And let me emphasise that it is going to be the same standards for all member countries and non-member countries.

20 Swiss Economics Minister Pascal Couchepin has reiterated his country's stance on occasions saying that Swiss secrecy laws are 'not negotiable'. 'Swiss Banking Secrecy Rules Hang in the Balance as E.U. Negotiations Loom', 15 May 2001 (available on the web on www.tax-news.com).

minimus, as 27 other countries have approved the report. However, this overlooks the fact that the non-co-operating OECD states are the offshore world's principal onshore competitors, and that they account for many of the tax-neutral structures run onshore within the OECD. A common standard, universally observed by all OECD states and co-operating OFCs, must be the bedrock principle on which the initiative is based – othewise the credibility of the project suffers.

Offshore centres are concerned that if Switzerland (and Luxembourg) are not obliged to adhere to the standard sought to be imposed on offshore centres business will migrate from offshore centres to OECD member countries. If Switzerland's commitment is delayed so that it remains the 'last man standing' for clients seeking financial privacy, client structures may well come to rest there, even if Swiss laws subsequently change.

Financial Centres Outside the OECD Project

Centres such as Hong Kong, Singapore and Dubai do not appear on the OECD tax haven list (see Appendix), nor are they members of the OECD. Accordingly, their international financial services industries are effectively ignored by the project. Clearly, if the OECD's project is to move forward in a coherent fashion, it will be necessary to ensure that all international financial centres are governed by the same rules, or else business will simply move to financial centres unaffected by the project.

US State Compliance with the OECD Demands

Some OECD member countries have had difficulty in ensuring that local and state governments observe the commitments adopted by the national government. The USA, for example, comes up against constitutional constraints in supervising State governments. Thus, at the same time as the US federal government was threatening sanctions against foreign jurisdictions reluctant to compromise banking privacy, Montana and Colorado passed laws creating 'foreign capital depositories', designed as confidential accounts, and described as 'the first truly Swiss style private banking in the USA'. Advertisements for the facilities based in Colorado included representations that foreign civil and tax judgements against depositors would not be enforceable in the USA.[21]

---

21 These statements were modified after complaints by the State Bank Commissioner. See 'Offshore Bank Rethinks Image' in *Rocky Mountain News* at www.rockymountainnews.com.

Similar concerns arise from the opportunity to establish US limited liability corporations (LLCs) in Delaware (and most other US states) with
no disclosure of beneficial ownership.[22] The OECD is threatening sanctions against offshore centres which do not agree to record and exchange
information on beneficial ownership, yet US State governments would
plainly be unable to provide similar information in respect of tax-free
Limited Liability Companies established in the USA.

Clearly, the OECD has a good deal of work to do to establish the level
playing field it claims to seek in the attack on the offshore world. Without
an effective response to these concerns, the OECD will continue to be
seen, even by sympathetic observers, as an economic cartel bent on promoting the agenda of its members – and those it is prepared to accommodate – at the expense of outsiders.

As Oxfam notes in a report on tax havens:

[W]hen it comes to offering opportunities for global tax avoidance, St Kitts and
Nevis must be a marginal player compared with Switzerland or Hong Kong.[23]

Offshore Centre Agreements with the OECD

Following publication of the 1998 Report, the OECD identified 47 jurisdictions as putative tax havens. Following representations, six of these
were dropped before the 2000 Report was published. Shortly before publication of the report an additional six of the identified havens entered
into an advance commitment to make domestic changes in support of the
OECD Harmful Tax Initiative. These jurisdictions were Cayman Islands,
Bermuda, Cyprus, Malta, Mauritius and San Marino.

The OECD has announced further agreements with four other jurisdictions – Isle of Man and the Netherlands Antilles (in December 2000),
the Seychelles (in February 2001) and Aruba (in July 2001). Under the
original terms of the project, the 31 remaining jurisdictions on the list
were to be subject to the threat of co-ordinated 'defensive measures' by
OECD members if no agreement was reached with the OECD by 31 July
2001. (See list of classified jurisdictions in the Appendix.)

---

22 See the reference below to the US GAO Report, *Suspicious Banking Activities: Possible Money
Laundering by US Corporations Formed for Russian Entities.*

23 Oxfam, *Tax Havens: Releasing the Hidden Billions for Poverty Eradication*, June 2000. The
report goes on to say:

*Many developing country havens are highly distrustful of the motivations of rich countries, believing
the OECD initiative to be merely another attempt to prevent competition from developing countries
undermining their own economic interests.*

Following the US Treasury announcement, it now appears, as discussed below, that the deadline for agreement with the OECD has been pushed back to 28 February 2002, with additional delays in the threatened sanctions.[24]

Narrowed US Support for the OECD Project

The OECD project was thrown into disarray by a 10 May 2001 press release by US Treasury Secretary O'Neill. The circumstances of the announcement were confusing, as it initially appeared in an op ed article in the Washington press under the name of a junior Treasury aide, although the text was claimed within hours of publication as the statement of the Treasury Secretary.

Following the 10 May release, control of the Senate shifted to the Democrats when Senator James Jeffords left the Republican party and became an Independent on 24 May 2001. Senator Carl Levin scheduled a hearing on 18 July to review the US position on offshore tax havens. Secretary O'Neill tabled prepared remarks[25] at the hearing and provided oral testimony to clarify the position of the US Treasury. He expressed continued support for the core objective of the OECD project, which he described as 'the need for countries to be able to obtain specific information from other countries upon request in order to prevent non-compliance with their tax laws'. Secretary O'Neill also expressed his concerns about the conduct and process of the project. A summary of the current US position on the OECD Harmful Tax Competition Initiative follows.

Comments on Tax Harmonisation

In the 10 May statement the Treasury Secretary indicated that:

---

24 Progress on the initiative has also been slowed by the manner of OECD participation in the Joint Working Group on Harmful Tax Competition which arose out of the meeting in Barbados between OECD and the Caribbean offshore centres. (The offshore side of that organisation has now become the International Tax and Investment Organisation (ITIO), established in March 2001.) The offshore centre side of the Joint Working Group sought clarification of OECD views on 17 fundamental points relating to the Harmful Tax Competition Initiative at a meeting with the OECD in Paris on 28 February 2001. The OECD provided an oral response at that time and promised a subsequent written response but none has been forthcoming. (See 'Offshore Jurisdictions Push OECD to respond to Questions', 7 June 2001 (available on the web on www.tax-news.com).)

25 Statement of Paul O'Neill before the Senate Committee on Governmental Affairs, Permanent Subcommittee on Investigations, OECD Harmful Tax Practices Initiative, 18 July 2001 (available at www.senate.gov), hereafter referred to as 'O'Neill's Senate Remarks'.

The United States does not support efforts to dictate to any country what its own tax rates or tax system should be, and would not participate in any initiative to harmonise world tax systems.

Although the 1998 Report suggested that the OECD favoured tax harmonisation, this objective was abandoned by the OECD at an early stage and this abandonment has been reiterated thereafter.[26] Secretary O'Neill's lack of support for aligning tax rates attracted considerable press comment at the time although it is irrelevant to the project as it is currently conceived by the OECD.

Comments on Information Exchange

Treasury Secretary O'Neill reiterated robust support for seeking information exchange, on request, including for both 'a specific criminal tax investigation or a civil tax examination'. [27]

Exchange of information on civil tax matters (undefined by the OECD, and so susceptible to a wide interpretation) has been a particularly contentious point in OECD negotiations. Difficulties have been fuelled by the Swiss refusal to consider exchanging civil tax information. (Switzerland limits co-operation to matters involving 'tax fraud', meaning proactive and deliberate deception under a peculiarly Swiss definition for the term.) Secretary O'Neill did not comment on exchange for civil tax purposes in his 10 May statement, so his prepared remarks on this point on his 18 July statement are particularly significant.

Level Playing Field

Secretary O'Neill emphasised the crucial importance of a level playing field, indicating that 'in order for the OECD initiative to have the legitimacy it needs to succeed, jurisdictions inside the OECD must be treated no more severely than similarly situated OECD member countries'. Secretary O'Neill went on to say that 'OECD member countries should hold themselves to standards and timelines at least as rigorous as those to which they hold jurisdictions that are not part of the OECD'.[28]

---

26 Donald Johnston, Secretary-General of the OECD, restated the OECD position in his Remarks to the Joint Working Group on Harmful Tax Practices at Salle Marshall, Chateau de la Muette, France (1 March 2001) as follows:

The [Harmful Tax Practices] project is not about tax harmonisation. All countries should set whatever rates of tax they wish, with whatever they feel appropriate on the taxation of capital, income or consumption. Whether the tax rate of a particular country is zero or whether it is in excess of 50% is of no concern to the OECD in carrying out this exercise.

27 O'Neill's Senate Remarks, p. 8.

28 Ibid., p.6.

Sanctions

Following US pressure it has been agreed by the OECD that 'co-ordinated defensive measures' would not apply to 'unco-operative' tax haven jurisdictions any earlier than they would apply to similarly-situated OECD member countries. Thus, such measures would be delayed until the deadline for OECD member country compliance with demands (April 2003 at the earliest). Secretary O'Neill indicated that a deadline for offshore centres earlier than the one set for OECD countries would not be fair, noting that 'it is not surprising there was unanimous support among G7 countries to address this inequity'.[29]

Secretary O'Neill also noted that defensive measures are by their nature 'highly coercive' and should be reserved only for jurisdictions acting in bad faith. The Secretary indicated that the USA would 'strongly prefer working co-operatively with jurisdictions rather than contemplating the imposition of co-ordinated defensive measures' which he suggested 'must be truly measures of last resort'.[30]

Ring-fencing

The OECD proposed to treat an offshore jurisdiction as 'unco-operative' if it maintained a regime that facilitates the establishment of entities with 'no substantial activities'. A closely related criterion provided that countries which 'ring-fenced' aspects of their tax regime to make them available only to non-residents would be similarly treated. Such concessions are commonplace in OECD member countries and so, not surprisingly, the US regards these criteria as problematic and difficult to apply. Secretary O'Neill noted that the OECD has now agreed to abandon such criteria for determining whether a jurisdiction is unco-operative.

Deadline for OECD Commitments

Secretary O'Neill noted that the OECD has agreed to extend the deadline for offshore centres providing commitments to the OECD. The offshore centre discussions with the OECD have been largely discontinued while the OECD has failed to communicate its position in response to US comments, so this extension is necessary and appropriate.

---

29 Ibid., p. 6.

30 Ibid., p. 9.

US Plans for the Future

Secretary O'Neill's remarks showed considerable sensitivity to fairness of process and the need to refocus the project in order to ensure a constructive result. Oral remarks of the Treasury Secretary at the hearing show an ambitious timetable for continuing US efforts on information exchange, as Secretary O'Neill indicated that the USA would seek to conclude tax information exchange agreements with at least half of the tax havens on the OECD list within 12 months. Senator Levin extended an invitation to the Secretary to return to the Senate to review progress at the expiration of that period.

Implications of the Treasury Statement

The drive for transparency has considerable momentum now and is unlikely to disappear. The USA and other OECD member countries and many offshore centres have articulated broad support for information exchange, on request, for criminal tax matters. Switzerland and Luxembourg excepted, there is also support in principle for information exchange on civil tax matters, though there is no international consensus on what is meant by that term.

Offshore centres may be better positioned to negotiate information exchange agreements through reliance on a universal standard acceptable to all (i.e. including Switzerland) so that any negotiations over information exchange are conducted within broadly agreed parameters. Without some external standard, OFCs could find themselves under pressure to agree to information exchange with no reference points to restrain the demands of aggressive high-tax countries. Accordingly, OFCs may now perceive that there is some advantage in participating in the OECD initiative, particularly if the standard to be set for a template information exchange agreement results from truly inclusive dialogue with the OFCs.

OECD Reaction to the Shift in the US Position

Official OECD reaction to the US Treasury Secretary's remarks has been conspicuously muted. Details of an agreement by OECD member states in response to the shift in the US position were leaked to the press in late June 2001,[31] apparently directly from the OECD press office. A formal response was delayed by a Spanish threat to veto an agreement on the

---

31 'OECD May Have Deal to Fight Tax Evasion', *Financial Times*, 28 June 2001.

project unless the United Kingdom agreed to ensure that Gibraltar will respect the agreement.[32]

The current position was officially stated by the OECD only in a cryptic press release dated 31 July 2001 confirming a delay in the deadline previously set for that day. Curiously, the information gap was filled by the G7 Finance Ministers in the communiqué tabled following their 7 July 2001 meeting in Rome[33] which confirmed that the OECD intended to:

◆ Extend the existing 31 July 2001 deadline for offshore centre commitments on transparency and effective information exchange;

◆ Delay possible sanctions on offshore centres deemed non-co-operative until mid-2003;

◆ Eliminate the 'no substantial activities' and 'ring-fencing' criteria.

Agreements are now sought by 28 February 2002 with the putative tax havens on the following issues.

Criminal information exchange: The OECD seeks procedures for efficient administrative exchange of reliable financial data by 2004, achieved through tax information agreements with OECD member countries.

Comment: The 'level playing field' principle indicates that the appropriate standard is the one unanimously agreed by OECD members in paragraph 21[34] of the OECD's April 2000 *Report on Improving Access to Bank*

---

32 The UK takes the position, at least formally, that it will not interfere in the domestic affairs of its overseas territories. Spain is reluctant to see this practice extended to Gibraltar, taking the view that independent action taken by Gibraltar in the international field effectively recognises Gibraltar's international status at a time when Spain claims sovereignty over it.

33 *Fighting the Abuses of the Global Financial System*, Report of G7 Finance Ministers and Central Bank Governors, 7 July 2001, Rome, Italy.

34 Paragraph 21 of the OECD *Report on Improving Access to Bank Information for Tax Purposes* reads as follows:

The Committee on Fiscal Affairs encourages Member countries to:

(a) undertake the necessary measures to prevent financial institutions from maintaining anonymous accounts and to require the identification of their usual or occasional customers, as well as those persons to whose benefit a bank account is opened or a transaction is carried out. The committee will rely on the work of the Financial Action Task Force in ensuring the implementation of these measures by Member countries;

(b) re-examine any domestic tax interest requirement that prevents their tax authorities from obtaining and providing to a treaty partner, in the context of a specific request, information they are otherwise able to obtain for domestic tax purposes with a view to ensuring that such information can be exchanged by making changes, if necessary, to their laws, regulations and administrative practices.

Information for Tax Purposes. Given the parameters of paragraph 21, this obligation should be limited to exchanging information in circumstances involving the following:

♦ a specific request

♦ in respect of deliberate conduct

♦ which is subject to criminal tax prosecution.

Civil tax information exchange: The OECD seeks procedures in place for efficient administrative exchange of 'civil' tax data by 2006. Once again, this would be limited to circumstances where there is a specific request.

Comment: Some OECD member states (i.e. Switzerland and Luxembourg) have refused to provide civil tax information, so the OECD request for this does not observe the 'level playing field' principle. Further, Secretary O'Neill notes that:

Any jurisdiction that makes a commitment to meet international standards of transparency and effective exchange of information will not be listed as 'uncooperative' ...[35]

As the international standard for exchange of civil tax information is neither settled nor agreed, any OFC commitment on this point should be limited to indicating a willingness to engage in multilateral discussions with OECD member countries and co-operating OFCs to establish the appropriate standard.

Access to ownership and financial data: The OECD seeks effective government access to locally maintained information regarding beneficial

---

The Committee suggests that countries take action to implement these measures within three years of the date of approval of this Report;

(c) re-examine policies and practices that do not permit tax authorities to have access to bank information, directly or indirectly, for purposes of exchanging such information in tax cases involving intentional conduct which is subject to criminal tax prosecution, with a view to making changes, if necessary, to their laws, regulations and administrative practices. The Committee acknowledges that implementation of these measures could raise fundamental issues in some countries and suggest that countries initiate a review of their practices with the aim of identifying appropriate measures for implementation. The Committee will initially review progress in this area at the end of 2002 and thereafter periodically.

The Committee notes the international trend to increase access to bank information for tax purposes. In the light of this trend, the Committee encourages countries to take appropriate initiatives to achieve access for the verification of tax liabilities and other tax administration purposes, with a view to making changes, if necessary, to their laws, regulations and administrative practices. The Committee intends to engage in an ongoing discussion, within the constraints set out in the preface, to promote this trend.

35 O'Neill's Senate Remarks.

ownership and financial statements for companies and trusts to facilitate the requested exchange of tax data.

Comment: Local service providers should be required to know beneficial ownership and hold financial statements for structures established in the jurisdiction. (Incongruously, the records of US corporations established in Delaware for foreigners do not contain this information[36] so offshore centres should insist on changes in the USA to ensure a level playing field.) Such information should be accessible to local authorities, on specific request, when required.

OECD Report on the Misuse of Corporate Vehicles

The OECD has recently tabled a *Report on the Misuse of Corporate Vehicles for Illicit Purposes.*[37] The Report details concerns and criticisms regarding corporate and non-corporate vehicles (including trusts) and is no doubt designed to contribute to the ongoing conversation between the OECD and the offshore centres on the form of information exchange agreements. Once again, the report shows the skewed perspective resulting from preparation by a body like the OECD which represents a narrow interest group. The report proceeds from the premise that offshore centres are the problem,[38] with only passing mention of the issues posed by vehicles established in OECD member states and used in the offshore world.

As anyone familiar with the offshore world today knows, the US limited liability corporation, widely available now under the laws of most US states, is a ubiquitous offshore vehicle. Where established by a non-US person, a US LLC is generally tax free from a US perspective. LLCs can be formed by fax with no due diligence requirements and no requirement to track or disclose beneficial ownership.

A report by the US GAO dated 31 October 2000, *Suspicious Banking Activities: Possible Money Laundering by US Corporations Formed for Russian Entities,*[39] prepared for US Senator Carl Levin's Committee on correspondent banking details the activities of one service provider which formed approximately 2,000 Delaware companies exclusively for

---

36 As noted above. See the reference to the US GAO *Report on Suspicious Banking Activities: Possible Money Laundering by US Corporations Formed for Russian Entities* below.

37 The report was adopted by the OECD Steering Group on Corporate Governance and declassified on 29 May, 2001. It is available on the OECD website at www.oecd.org.

38 *Report on Misuse of Corporate Vehicles for Illicit Purposes,* para. 28.

39 www.gao.gov.

brokers in Moscow, Russia. Many US LLCs opened bank accounts with major US institutions without, apparently, identification of beneficial owners. Senator Levin's *Report on Correspondent Banking*[40] was silent on the absence of Delaware records on beneficial ownership for structures established in the State despite evident dangers noted in the Report:

The records of the registered agents we reviewed generally contain the name of the person or entity requesting the formation of the [Delaware] *corporation but do not contain the names of the corporation's principals. Thus, neither state records nor the records of the registered agents contain the names of the principals of the incorporated companies.* (pp. 5–6)

Two registered agents informed us that they often form corporations in blocks of 10 to 20 at a time to accommodate single requests from foreign brokers. A registered agent also disclosed that these corporations are sometimes sold by the brokers to others who may, in turn, sell them again.

Why was the US LLC vehicle, widely used in the offshore world, not properly considered in the OECD *Report on Misuse of Corporate Vehicles*?

The Financial Action Task Force – Countering Money Laundering

Former IMF Managing Director Michael Camdessus has estimated that the volume of cross-border money laundering is between 2 and 5 per cent of the world's gross domestic product.[41] Although money laundering by its nature defies detection, this suggests that US$600billion is laundered annually through the world's financial system.

The Financial Action Task Force was established by the G7 summit held in Paris in 1989. The FATF examines money laundering techniques and trends and sets and communicates standards for combating such activity. The FATF was established with 16 member countries, and now has 29 members.[42] Like the OECD, the FATF has elite (as opposed to universal)

---

40 Minority Staff of the Permanent Subcommittee on Investigations, *Report on Correspondent Banking: A Gateway for Money Laundering*, 5 February 2001.

41 *US National Money Laundering Strategy for 2000*, pp. 6–7.

42 The 29 FATF member countries and governments are: Argentina, Australia, Austria, Belgium, Brazil, Canada, Denmark, Finland, France, Germany, Greece, Hong Kong, China, Ireland, Italy, Japan, Luxembourg, Mexico, the Kingdom of the Netherlands, New Zealand, Norway, Portugal, Singapore, Spain, Sweden, Switzerland, Turkey, the UK and the USA.

membership and membership is not open to the offshore states. Regional bodies such as the Caribbean Financial Action Task Force support the work of the FATF.

The FATF published a report on 22 June 2000 entitled *Review to Identify Non-Co-operative Countries or Territories*. The report was preceded by a review of 29 jurisdictions over a four-month period to analyse anti-money-laundering regimes. This report relates exclusively to the regimes of non-member countries (the FATF does not publish its reviews of compliance by member states). A number of other jurisdictions have not been reviewed or rated. More than half of the reviewed jurisdictions were identified as non-co-operative. Assessments of additional jurisdictions were considered at the recent FATF plenary which took place on 20–22 June 2001.

The FATF labels the non-member jurisdictions that it sees as requiring improvement as 'non-co-operative'. This description is inappropriate in many cases, as it suggests that the jurisdiction is being deliberately obstructive. While there are issues of adequacy in the regimes of a number of offshore centres (as there are in many onshore centres[43]), there is little doubt about the desire of most offshore centres to co-operate to eradicate money laundering.[44]

The FATF did not articulate standards for removal of jurisdictions from the non-co-operative list at the time of their review. However, the FATF took the position that only legislation which is passed and currently in force will be taken into account. The FATF has advised that while technical help is available, such help is provided only after legislation has been adopted. This is curious, of course, since one would expect that the FATF would value consistent, quality legislation to address issues in a comprehensive fashion

---

43 The UK Financial Services Authority investigated anti-money-laundering controls at 23 banks in the UK which maintained accounts linked to General Sani Abacha, the former President of Nigeria. The investigation found that 15 of the banks had significant control weaknesses. Phillip Thorpe, Managing Director of the FSA, called the extent of the weaknesses identified 'frankly disappointing'. Seven banks with significant control weaknesses was ordered to rectify problems within strict deadlines and potential breaches of the Money Laundering Regulations were reported to law enforcement authorities (Financial Services Authority press release, 8 March 2001).

44 The Intergovernmental Group of Twenty-Four on International Monetary Affairs, meeting at the time of the G7 conference in late April 2001, noted on page 4 of their 28 April 2001 Communiqué as follows:

Ministers caution against the non-voluntary and non-co-operative manner in which the Financial Action Task Force (FATF) 40 recommendations are currently applied to non-FATF members.

The FATF plenary in June 2001 concluded with a decision to remove four jurisdictions from the non-co-operative list – the Bahamas, the Cayman Islands, Panama and Liechtenstein. Six countries were added at that time, though none of the additions are significant financial centres. The updated list of non-co-operative countries and territories is as follows (new additions are shown in italics):[45] Cook Islands; Dominica; *Egypt*; *Guatemala*; *Hungary*; *Indonesia*; Israel; Lebanon; Marshall Islands; *Myanmar*; Nauru; *Nigeria*; Niue; Phillipines; Russia; St Kitts and Nevis; and St Vincent and the Grenadines.

Striking a reasonable balance between regulation to counter money laundering and the demands of efficient commerce is difficult for all financial centres, offshore and onshore. The US Treasury has, for example, recently indicated plans to review 'burdensome' rules to combat money laundering, following pressure from banks to ease reporting requirements seen as 'intrusive and costly'.[46] By contrast, non-FATF member states proceed in a climate of threats and coercion and are, of course, denied a similar opportunity to take domestic policy considerations into account when designing anti-money-laundering regimes.

New developments in the FATF programme appear in the *Report on Money Laundering Typologies 2000–2001* tabled at the FATF plenary in February 2001. That report proposes a major new initiative on trusts and other non-corporate vehicles, even suggesting that standardised documentation for offshore trusts be imposed. The Typologies report also proposes further pressure on 'gatekeepers', including lawyers, accountants and other professionals offering financial advice.[47]

Financial Stability Forum

The Financial Stability Forum was established pursuant to a G7 initiative in early 1999. At its inaugural meeting on 14 April 1999 the Forum established an OFC working group chaired by John Palmer, Superintendent of Financial Institutions, Canada. The purpose of the group was to consider the role of OFC banks in the stability of the world's financial system. The mandate of the working group was as follows:[48]

---

45 FATF Review to Identify Non-Co-operative Countries and Territories, 22 June 2001.

46 'U.S. Treasury Hopes to Ease Burden of Anti-Laundering Effects on Banks', *Wall Street Journal*, 7 June 2001.

47 For secondary commentary, see 'The Gatekeeper's Initiative: an Emerging Challenge for International Financial Advisors', 22 *Tax Notes International*, 2293–98, 7 May 2001 (Bruce Zagaris).

48 See *Financial Stability Forum Report*, p. 6, supra note 1.

♦ to consider the uses of OFCs and the possible role they have had or could play in posing threats to the stability of the financial system;

♦ to evaluate the adherence of OFCs to internationally accepted standards and good practices;

♦ to make recommendations, including to enhance problematic OFCs' observance of international standards.

In carrying out its mandate the FSF was primarily concerned with the activities of the OFC banks in two areas as follows:

♦ *prudential concerns*, relating to the scope for effective supervision of internationally active financial intermediaries; and

♦ *market integrity*, relating to the effectiveness of international enforcement efforts in respect of illicit activity and abusive market behaviour.

A report was tabled by the working group on 5 April 2000. The report contained a number of observations on the role and workings of the offshore world and concluded with an evaluation of the existing calibre of regulation in a number of OFC jurisdictions. (See Appendix.) Not surprisingly, the report concluded that the enhanced acceptance and implementation of international standards by OFCs would address many of the concerns raised about OFC regulation.

The FSF classified OFCs into three groups as follows:[49]

♦ The first group are jurisdictions generally viewed as co-operative jurisdictions with a high quality of supervision, which largely adhere to international standards.

♦ The second group of OFCs are jurisdictions generally seen as having procedures for supervision and co-operation in place, though actual performance falls below international standards and there is substantial room for improvement.

♦ A third group of OFCs are jurisdictions generally seen as having a low quality of supervision, and/or being non-co-operative with onshore supervisors, with little or no attempt being made to adhere to international standards.

The majority of OFCs (25 jurisdictions) were placed into category three, with nine and eight, respectively being placed in categories two and one.

---

49 See *Financial Stability Forum Report*, p. 46, supra note 1.

FSF work is now being continued by the IMF which will be conducting assessments of a number of OFCs over the next year.

Conclusion

The remarkable success of the world's offshore centres has invited scrutiny from onshore governments and their agencies. A chorus of overlapping demands for change has followed, so much so that the offshore centres now suffer from 'initiative fatigue'. However, in all of this change, OFCs will retain the great advantage of being able to transact business in a tax-neutral fashion while client demand for such services remains unabated, despite supranational pressures.

Offshore centres rely on access to onshore clients, banking and securities markets for their success. Countries which provide such facilities are in a position to restrict access for jurisdictions perceived to be unruly customers. Such decisions are open to challenge, but the prospects for that are cumbersome and uncertain, particularly where the decisions involve discretionary elements determined behind closed doors.

A constructive response to the reasonable concerns of onshore countries is essential for any OFC, unless it is prepared to unplug from the international grid. Responsible OFCs will take steps to ensure that their service providers refrain from disrupting the fiscal systems of high-tax countries by inviting tax evaders to alight in the jurisdiction. OFCs must also be prepared to devote resources and provide active assistance in the international fight against money laundering.

Onshore countries and their agencies should, in turn, recognise that they will be judged by the fairness of their demands and process. At minimum, this means that standards should be set by bodies with *universal* (as opposed to *elite*) membership. Crucially, there must also be *a level playing field for all parties*. OFCs need to know that the same rules will be applicable to all. It is not sufficient to say that *most* members of the club (i.e the OECD) adhere to the rules demanded. This is particularly so where the dissenting voices emanate from those jurisdictions which compete most effectively with the offshore world.

The recent statements by the US Treasury Secretary demonstrate long overdue concern for the heavy-handed tactics adopted by the OECD in conducting its project. In the wake of the US shift in position, the OECD and its supranational brethren should pause and reflect on the need to constructively engage the offshore centres in their projects, and show that they are willing to translate the rhetoric regarding level playing fields into reality. The combative postures adopted by both sides to date may yet yield to cohabitation rather than continuing collision, provided offshore centres are given a genuine and substantial part to play in the design of the changes to come.

Annex

Supranational Classifications of Offshore Financial Centres

	OECD		FATF		FSF		
	Classified As Tax Havens		Anti-Money Laundering Review		Standards of Financial Regulation		
	Commitment Agreed	No Agreement with OECD	Rated Not Censured	Deemed Non-co-operative	I High	II Medium	III Low
Andorra		X				X	
Anguilla		X					X
Antigua and Barbuda		X	X				X
Aruba	X						X
The Bahamas		X	X				X
Bahrain		X				X	
Barbados		X				X	
Belize		X	X				X
Bermuda	X		X			X	
British Virgin Islands		X	X				X
Cayman Islands	X		X				X
Cook Islands		X		X			X
Costa Rica							X
Cyprus	X		X				X
Dominica		X		X			
Dublin (Ireland)					X		

OECD	FATF Classified As Tax Havens		FSF Anti-Money Laundering Review		FSF Standards of Financial Regulation		
	Commitment Agreed	No Agreement with OECD	Rated Not Censured	Deemed Non-co-operative	I High	II Medium	III Low
Gibraltar		X	X			X	
Grenada		X					
Guernsey		X	X		X		
Hong Kong SAR					X		
Isle of Man	X		X		X		
Jersey		X	X		X		
Labuan (Malaysia)						X	
Lebanon				X			X
Liberia		X					
Liechtenstein		X	X				X
Luxembourg					X		
Macau SAR						X	
Maldives		X					
Malta	X		X			X	
Marshall Islands		X		X			X
Mauritius	X		X				X
Monaco		X	X			X	
Montserrat		X					
Nauru		X		X			X

| OECD | FATF | | FSF | | | | |
| | Classified As Tax Havens | | Anti-Money Laundering Review | | Standards of Financial Regulation | | |
	Commitment Agreed	No Agreement with OECD	Rated Not Censured	Deemed Non-co-operative	I High	II Medium	III Low
Netherlands Antilles	X						X
Niue		X		X			X
Panama		X	X				X
St Kitts and Nevis		X		X			X
St Lucia		X	X				X
St Vincent & the Grenadines		X		X			X
Samoa		X	X				X
San Marino	X						
Seychelles		X	X				X
Singapore					X		
Switzerland					X		
Turks & Caicos		X	X				X
US Virgin Islands		X			X		
Vanuatu		X	X				X

Additional countries reviewed by the FATF but not classified as offshore centres by the OECD: Rated but not censured – Czech Republic, Poland, Slovak Republic, Uruguay; Deemed non-cooperative – Egypt, Guatemala, Hungary, Indonesia, Israel, Myanmar, Nigeria, Philippines, Russia

Reports: OECD, *Towards Global Tax Co-operation*, 26 June 2000 (July 2001 deadline for agreement with OECD to avoid proposed sanctions)

FATF, *Reviews to Identify Non-Cooperative Countries or Territories*, 22 June 2000 and 22 June 2001

FSF, *Report of the Working Group on Offshore Centres*, 5 April 2000 MF now undertaking OFC assessment and assistance programme)

Source: Stikeman Elliott, 23 August 2001

Transparency versus Privacy: Reflections on OECD Concepts of Harmful Tax Competition

Terence Dwyer and Deborah Dwyer[1]

The formal models for a small open economy forecast that the optimal tax rate on capital income is simply zero.
Taxation of Capital Income vs. Labour Income: An Overview, Gordon, 2000

Background: The OECD Attack on Tax Haven Financial Privacy

High-taxing European Treasuries face grave problems as they try to finance redistributive welfare states in societies with low birth rates and declining labour tax bases in an age of globalising investment. Their problem is not much different to the problem faced by the Roman Emperors[2] (though Constantine humanely disclaimed the previous use of the scourge and the rack and contented himself with incarceration of insolvent taxpayers). In those days wealth was buried as gold in the grounds of the villa; in our day it may be buried in overseas parent or subsidiary companies. The reality remains that capital and business income can be made less visible to the tax collector than landed property. The solution of the late Roman Empire was to visit corporal punishment on the taxpayer. The solution now being urged by the OECD in Paris is that small or developing countries with offshore financial centres be pressed into service as subsidiary tax enforcers to boost OECD coffers. The OECD approach is multifarious, involving the criminalisation of tax avoidance and the elimination of various forms of tax competition from these centres in all geographically mobile service industries, including not

---

1 The authors are Visiting Fellows at the Asia-Pacific School of Economics and Management, Australian National University; e-mail Terry.Dwyer@anu.edu.au

2 'The secret wealth of commerce, and the precarious profits of art or labour, are susceptible only of a discretionary valuation, which is seldom disadvantageous to the interest of the treasury; and, as the person of the trader supplies the want of a visible and permanent security, the payment of the imposition, which, in the case of a land-tax, may be obtained by the seizure of property, can rarely be extorted by any other means than those of corporal punishments.' Edward Gibbon (1776–1781), *The Decline and Fall of the Roman Empire*, Vol. II, Chapter xvii, p. 211. Bury ed., 1909.

only financial, but also distribution services, shipping, service industries and company headquartering. The OECD Initiative is already drafting similar action on competition in e-commerce, with manufacturing industry having been flagged up for future action in the 1998 OECD report.[3]

What could be more reasonable? That, in the interests of comity between nations and the protection of their mutual sovereignty, nations should help each other catch 'tax cheats' by insisting on transparent legal structures and exchange of tax information on request or even spontaneously? Is this not a self-evident case of collective interest in effective law enforcement? And if nations are successful in increasing revenue by deterring or catching tax cheats, won't they be able to lower tax rates, improve economic efficiency, expand output and deliver rising living standards? So stated, the current OECD campaign to eliminate tax havens seems to make both legal and economic sense. But, as with many apparently self-evident truths propounded in the popular press, such propositions may not withstand closer examination.

Indeed, there is a remarkable parallel between the OECD campaign to end tax haven privacy and the US law enforcement agencies' push for the Clipper Chip. The Clipper Chip was put forward in 1993 as the answer to the public and commercial demand for privacy through computer file and e-mail encryption while allowing governments to eavesdrop for law enforcement purposes.

In the case of the Clipper Chip

♦ The initiative was urged strongly at the bureaucratic level;

♦ The initiative was adopted at the highest governmental level;

♦ Public reaction domestically was initially not unfavourable;

♦ Overseas commercial interests and governments became sceptical;

♦ Later domestic public reaction to loss of privacy and commercial secrecy became unfavourable.

In the case of the Clipper Chip, US public opinion, from computer nerds

---

3 Indeed, the OECD seems to be intent on eliminating what they regard as 'harmful' fiscal competition in vast swathes of key global industries. However, on closer inspection, their efforts seem to be focused on industries in which OECD countries are more competitive. Hence the rather telling omission of agriculture, which has 'harmful' fiscal competition amounting to US$360 billion provided by OECD countries to their farmers at the expense of farmers in many poor developing countries as well as countries such as Australia and New Zealand. The agricultural sector is never mentioned in all the OECD exhortations for other countries to eliminate harmful fiscal practices.

to powerful corporations, became so violently hostile that the best laid plans of powerful security and law enforcement agencies were swept away by a public deeply suspicious of letting governments have the keys to their private information.[4]

It remains to be seen whether there will be a similar hostile public reaction against the OECD proposal to eliminate financial privacy in tax havens and whether this OECD initiative will go the way of the proposed OECD Multilateral Agreement on Investment (MAI). But surprises do happen and public opinion often overthrows propositions which seem eminently sensible to the particular agency interests of bureaucrats. Sometimes bureaucratic initiatives can even be dangerous for their instigators, as well as for the Ministers they advise.[5]

Intra-OECD Tensions between Capital-Importing and Capital-Exporting Countries

Just as the data security debate highlighted differences between American and European interests, there are latent differences of interest between capital-exporting and capital-importing OECD nations. Capital-importing OECD countries, such as Australia and the USA which rely on capital inflow to run large structural current account deficits, must come to question support for OECD 'pseudo-residence' tax norms which create disincentives to global capital mobility. In particular, Australia can hardly afford to deter foreign investment, while new US Internal Revenue reporting regulations are likely to affect US capital markets adversely. As 'source-of-income' countries, their national interests do not lie in helping 'residence of recipient' countries negate their attractiveness as investment destinations. This latent clash of interests within the OECD has not yet to surface fully.

The purpose of this paper is not to predict all the twists and turns or final outcome of the current tax haven financial privacy debate, nor to deny that there are gains to be had from international co-operation against common criminals (indeed, most offshore financial centres already provide full co-operation with OECD countries on criminal matters[6]), but

---

4 See Levy, 2001, pp. 226–312.

5 Hayek (1960, p. 308) recalls the acid remark of the great French Physiocrat, Turgot, who commented 'One ought to execute the author and not the project', in relation to graduated income taxation.

6 The OECD wants them to go further and, in effect, assist in enforcing expanded OECD concepts of fiscal criminality. Such demands for the extra-territorial enforcement of other countries' expanded concepts of criminal law raise basic issues of the independence and sovereignty of offshore financial centres.

rather to suggest that tax haven financial privacy is not a simple issue of stamping out fraud. Indeed, the OECD initiative raises many questions about optimal tax policies, about the legal ground norms for protection of privacy and property in liberal democratic (as opposed to collectivist or socialist) countries and about extra-territorial enforcement of domestic laws. The purpose of this paper is not to answer definitively such questions nor even to express concluded views: its purpose is to promote a more incisive debate.

A Little History

Interest in tax competition is not new. Adam Smith wrote:

The interest of money seems at first sight a subject equally capable of being taxed directly as the rent of land. Like the rent of land, it is a net produce which remains after completely compensating the whole risk and trouble of employing the stock. As a tax upon the rent of land cannot raise rents; because the net produce which remains after replacing the stock of the farmer, together with his reasonable profit, cannot be greater after the tax than before it, so, for the same reason, a tax upon the interest of money could not raise the rate of interest; the quantity of stock or money in the country, like the quantity of land, being supposed to remain the same after the tax as before it. The ordinary rate of profit ... is everywhere regulated by the quantity of stock to be employed in proportion to the quantity of the employment, or of the business which must be done by it. But the quantity of the employment, or of the business to be done by stock, could neither be increased nor diminished by any tax upon the interest of money. If the quantity of the stock to be employed, therefore, was neither increased nor diminished by it, the ordinary rate of profit would necessarily remain the same. But the portion of this profit necessary for compensating the risk and trouble of the employer would likewise remain the same, that risk and trouble being in no respect altered. The residue, therefore, that portion which belongs to the owner of the stock, and which pays the interest of money, would necessarily remain the same too. At first sight, therefore, the interest of money seems to be a subject as fit to be taxed directly as the rent of land.

There are, however, two different circumstances which render the interest of money a much less proper subject of direct taxation than the rent of land.

First, the quantity and value of the land which any man possesses can never be a secret, and can always be ascertained with great exactness. But the whole amount of the capital stock which he possesses is almost always a secret, and can scarce ever be ascertained with tolerable exactness. It is liable, besides, to almost continual variations. A year seldom passes away, frequently not a month, sometimes scarce a single day, in which it does not rise or fall more or less. An inquisition into every man's private circumstances, and an inquisition which, in order to accommodate the tax to them, watched over all the fluctuations of his fortunes, would be a source of such continual and endless vexation as no people could support.

Secondly, land is a subject which cannot be removed; whereas stock easily may. The proprietor of land is necessarily a citizen of the particular country in which his estate lies. The proprietor of stock is properly a citizen of the world, and is not necessarily attached to any particular country. He would be apt to abandon the country in which he was exposed to a vexatious inquisition, in order to be assessed to a burdensome tax, and would remove his stock to some other country where he could either carry on his business, or enjoy his fortune more at his ease. By removing his stock he would put an end to all the industry which it had maintained in the country which he left. Stock cultivates land; stock employs labour. A tax which tended to drive away stock from any particular country would so far tend to dry up every source of revenue both to the sovereign and to the society. Not only the profits of stock, but the rent of land and the wages of labour would necessarily be more or less diminished by its removal.

An Inquiry into the Nature and Causes of the Wealth of Nations, Book V, ii, f, pp. 847–849, 1776

It is some 225 years since publication of the *Wealth of Nations* and the American Revolution. The American Revolution had its genesis in the refusal of American colonists to aid the King's excise officers in clamping down on some 'harmful tax practices' – such as smuggling. Adam Smith's observations show why, after two centuries, he commands perennial respect from economists as the master of his subject, for he anticipated both the economic and legal issues raised by the OECD campaign to eliminate harmful tax practices through cartel-like co-operation.

Economic Arguments

Adam Smith correctly observes that a tax-induced emigration of capital (a mobile factor of production) will lower the returns to labour (much less mobile) and land (totally immobile). He therefore prefers taxation of the immobile factor, land. In pointing out that a country can protect itself from tax competition by taxing immobile factors, Adam Smith anticipates, by over 200 years, Gordon's conclusion (Gordon, 2000, p. 26) that 'The formal models for a small open economy forecast that the optimal tax rate on capital income is simply zero'.

It is a salient weakness of the OECD arguments on 'harmful' or 'unfair' tax competition that it is implicitly taken for granted that a graduated individual residence (or pseudo-residence) income taxation system is optimal (and that public spending must be taken as given). Yet these assumptions are not correct. For example, OECD countries have often created a 'win-win' situation for themselves by privatising to some extent future public pension payouts through domestic tax havens (such as tax-deductible and tax-exempt pension fund arrangements).

If it be argued that the problem pointed out by Adam Smith of capital emigration can be avoided by governments organizing a global tax cartel to enforce each others' revenue laws, we are back in the familiar closed economy arguments on whether capital income should be taxed. The short answer is that it is not optimal to tax capital income even in a closed economy as savings and investment are adversely affected, feeding into a lower productivity of land and labour and a lower wage tax base.[7]

The 'Broad Base Low Rate' Anti-Avoidance Thesis

A popular academic argument for action to stop offshore tax avoidance or evasion is that by broadening the tax base, it becomes possible for governments to lower overall tax rates and reduce tax distortions.

For example, Brooks and Head (1997, p. 55) argue that 'following the well known work of Henry Simon, it has been generally accepted among economists that income taxation should be based on the most comprehensive feasible economic income concept. On this view, as far as possible all the different types and sources of income should be taxed uniformly and consistently'. The received dogma is that 'a broad tax base with a low rate is more efficient' and therefore all forms of tax avoidance (whether through changed behaviour or legal form) or evasion are distorting. Even where there is no immediate excess burden because avoidance is legally easy, a common view is that tax revenue losses must 'be made up by rate increases on a narrower base, thus increasing welfare cost, or public expenditure benefits must be reduced'.[8] However, this is really an economic heresy.

Like all dogmas, the 'broad base with low rate is more efficient' dogma is only true on certain assumptions. It is only true if the tax base you are talking about is all of the same kind.

The key question is whether all forms of income should be taxed equally. The answer depends on how responsive different parts of the tax base are. Income is not a homogeneous tax base. It is not sensible to tax all forms of income at the same rate if the factors of production generating the

---

7 These arguments are set out in more detail in Dwyer, 2000.

8 Brooks and Head, 1997, p. 71.

income are not all equally mobile. In particular, it does not make sense to tax mobile capital, especially capital supplied by foreigners, at the same tax rate as income arising from land or immobile labour tied to the jurisdiction.[9]

In reality, there is no such thing as an income tax. As Adam Smith recognised, a tax on income is three taxes – a tax on the wages of labour, a tax on the rent of land and a tax on the profits of capital.

The OECD (1998, p. 14, para. 23) argues that tax competition 'may alter the structure of taxation (by shifting part of the tax burden from mobile to relatively immobile factors and from income to consumption) and may hamper the application of progressive tax rates and the achievement of redistributive goals'.

But is the OECD correct to see tax competition as a problem to be solved by enforcing residence (or pseudo-residence[10]) taxation of mobile capital income?

If tax competition shifts the tax burden from mobile to relatively immobile factors, it is doing the world a service. Economic theory has always held that, from an efficiency point of view, taxes should be laid on things which are inelastic in supply (of which the prime example is land rents). As for progressive marginal income tax rates and income redistribution, there are many economists who would argue that both are economically inefficient. It is also odd that a report which complains (1998, p. 15, para. 25) that tax havens are 'free riders' accepts as given the 'free riding'

---

9 Brooks and Head (1997, p. 60) try to deny this, baldly asserting that the 'information necessary for the design of such a system [of differentiated taxes] is not available, and the administrative requirements and political acceptability features must anyway render such an approach totally impractical'. They appear to be unaware of the fact that land in Australia has been valued and taxed for over a century. Scott's (1969) and (1986) figures computed within the Research Department of the Reserve Bank of Australia demonstrate land values rising since World War II as a potential tax base in line with personal income or corporate taxes, with most of the value being concentrated in the large cities. As for political acceptability, that is not the function of economic advice. But if European countries choose not to tax their potential and territorially immobile land value tax bases in cities such as London, Paris or Berlin, they can hardly cry foul against small island offshore financial centres willing to offer low taxes on mobile capital.

10 In fact the operation of controlled foreign company or trust income attribution rules often means that OECD countries are asserting the right to tax foreign income of a foreign company or foreign trust (even several times removed), even if their residents have no legal or equitable right to that income. The residence 'principle' is really becoming in reality a mercantilist export tax on capital in the form of perpetual taxation by the country of residence of the original source of the mobile capital.

implicit in redistributive taxation (1998, p. 14, para. 23). Some 'free riders' are more equal than others, it seems.[11]

Territorial Revenues from Land Rents

A fundamental defect of the harmful tax competition thesis is that it ignores territorially fixed and stable sources of revenue such as land rents. There are three economic factors of production, not just two: land, as well as labour and capital, is a factor of production. Economic theory since the Physiocrats and Adam Smith has always said it is better to tax what is inelastic in supply (for example land) in preference to what is mobile (for example capital). Modern optimal tax theory is just another rediscovery of that principle.

Economic theory declares that the most desirable tax base is a tax on unimproved land and resource values because it cannot be shifted and has no distorting effects on investment in physical capital or labour supply. As Kopits (1992, p. 5) notes, a country can use its resource rents to respond successfully to tax competition for mobile capital. Professor Martin Feldstein, former Chairman of the US Council of Economic Advisers, acknowledges a tax on unimproved land values 'involves no distortion' and is clearly efficient.[12] A beauty of such territorial-based taxation is that it also solves the tax treaty issue – international double taxation becomes a non-issue and the OECD tax treaty network becomes unnecessary.

There is no reason why reduced taxes on mobile capital could not be financed by increased land taxes within the OECD countries. If they

---

11 The OECD report (1998, p. 15, para. 25) argues: 'governments and residents of tax havens can be 'free riders' of general public goods created by the non-haven country'. The report does not specify what these public goods are. One might observe that, typically, public goods or income redistribution benefits are only available to residents of a country. If a country such as the UK chooses to allow residents of its offshore islands free migration access to the UK or access to social security or public health care or chooses to defend dependent territories then one must presume such a decision is taken in the interests of the UK as much as any dependent territory. As for domestic free riders, it is nonsense to argue that domestic tax avoiders or evaders are 'free riders' without looking at the 'free rider' beneficiaries of tax-financed redistribution. Who is the free rider – the man who wants to keep his hard-earned money from the tax collector or the welfare recipient waiting for the cheque from the government treasury? The answer often seems to depend on political or ideological proclivity. Taxpayers often argue that they do not mind financing genuine common public needs but they do resent paying for welfare state beneficiaries who have contributed little or nothing themselves. This is not the place to settle such arguments but it is foolish to ignore their existence if one is trying to understand tax avoidance or evasion as social phenomena.

12 Feldstein, 1976, p. 96. See also Musgrave, 1959, p. 158.

choose to tax their workers more, rather than land, that is their domestic political decision, just as it was a domestic political decision for many OECD countries, notably in Europe, to embark on high welfare spending programmes which necessitated high taxes on labour and made them internationally uncompetitive. Having made those decisions, they should not blame the rest of the world for the logical economic consequences.

The implicit assumption of the OECD model is quite wrong. The world supply of capital is not fixed and depends on the net rate of return. If all governments successfully co-operated to increase the tax burden on capital income, world capital accumulation would slow down and world living standards would stagnate. Once this fundamental error of the harmful tax competition model is grasped, the concept collapses – it is really a new mercantilist error of the kind excoriated by Adam Smith – and damaging to OECD countries themselves as well as to offshore financial centres. Indeed it is perplexing that the OECD paper has no theoretical discussion at all on why tax competition is harmful in a *worldwide* sense as opposed to the narrow interests of OECD national tax collecting agencies. Nor does the OECD acknowledge that OECD citizens may have different interests to those of OECD tax bureaucrats.

The Zero Optimal Tax Rate on Capital even in a Closed Economy

The fundamental Ramsey principle of taxation is that taxes should be levied on those activities which are least responsive. One would not tax a factor of production which was in perfectly elastic supply. This has profound implications for internationally mobile capital. Theoretical models of optimal taxation in an open economy produce two broadbrush results (Frenkel and Razin, 1996, Chapter 14).

1. The optimal principle of international taxation is the residence principle, that is non-residents should not be taxed on their capital income by the source country.

2. The optimal tax rule for a country that cannot enforce taxes on foreign source capital income is to abstain entirely from taxation of domestic source capital income as well.

Even in a closed economy, it may be efficient to exempt capital income from tax in the long run (Chamley, 1986; Correia, 1996). The optimal tax rate on capital income from all sources is thus zero. The intuition behind these conclusions is not that difficult to understand, even though the policy implications are dramatic. One would not tax non-residents on their capital income because that drives up the cost of capital to the local economy – non-residents can take their mobile capital and invest it elsewhere. By driving away mobile capital, the tax becomes an inefficient tax on immobile factors of production, such as immobile labour or land (Kopits, 1992, pp. 5, 15; Head, 1997, p. 86). One should not tax the capital income of non-residents just as one does not outlaw foreign investment. One wants foreign capital to increase the productivity and wages of the local population.

The crucial principle of open economy tax policy is that one should always tax an immobile factor in preference to a mobile factor. The reason for this is that, if taxed, the mobile factor will in the long run start to exit and shift the burden back to the immobile factor *but with a greater economic loss* than if the tax had been placed on the immobile factor in the first place.

Just as capital can flow across borders, so capital can evaporate over time. Hence, in the long run, the optimal tax rule is not to tax capital income at all. Taxing the return on capital lowers the capital intensity of the economy and reduces the productivity and wages of labour. This is one of the major arguments for shifting from an income to a consumption tax base (although that can be done just as – or more – easily by exempting capital income from tax).

The second principle states that if capital income is to be taxed without distorting the allocation of investment then, other things being equal, it is desirable to tax income from domestic and foreign investments equally. But if one cannot tax foreign income equally – and even with the most sophisticated legislation that is likely – then one should cut the rate of tax on domestic capital income.

So, economic freedom and international tax competition are *world* welfare enhancing. Far from hurting the OECD, it is nudging OECD countries towards optimal tax policies which are in the best interests of their citizens.

If the optimal tax rate on capital income is zero, and capital is mobile in any case, the attempt of OECD officials to promote worldwide enforcement of 'residence' capital taxes is as pointless and futile as Xerxes flogging the waters of the Hellespont or Canute commanding the tide to retire.

Legal Arguments

Leaving aside the economic arguments, it is noteworthy that Adam Smith bases his first objection on the intolerable vexation an inquisition into every man's affairs would involve. This objection comes naturally to English-speaking peoples. Since before Magna Carta of 1215 through the Bill of Rights of 1688 to the present day, the sentiment of common law jurisprudence has always been that the subject is free and that the common law exists to protect his property and his privacy. The common law is not the code of a sovereign such as Justinian but the protecting law of the people.

Among the common law rights of the people which have been protected over the centuries are:

- The right to trial by jury;

- The presumption of innocence;

- The right not to be forced to incriminate oneself;

- The right not to be arrested or invaded in one's privacy other than by judicially-supervised warrants based on cause;

- The right not to be deprived of life, liberty or property other than in accordance with due process of law;

- The right to ensure confidential communications with spouses or lawyers are not used as evidence against oneself.

Thus it is hardly surprising that Article IV of the Bill of Rights to the United States Constitution entrenches the common law. 'The right of the people to be secure in their persons, houses, papers, and effects, against unreasonable searches and seizures, shall not be violated, and no Warrants shall issue, but upon probable cause, supported by Oath or affirmation, and particularly describing the place to be searched, and the persons or things to be seized.' Article V goes on to protect the right not to be forced to incriminate oneself and to protect life, liberty and property against unlawful deprivation.

Economists and business people usually take the legal foundations of a free society and a free market economy for granted. But the declaration of the rights of individuals evolved as concrete responses to abuse of state power. An example of their value is seen in one of the earliest US Fourth Amendment cases. Decided in 1886, *Boyd v. United States* involved a federal customs statute that required businessmen (involved in importing goods) to choose between producing invoices and record books during a government inspection or having the imported goods confiscated by custom officials. Justice Joseph P. Bradley, delivering the opinion of the Court, struck down the customs statute. He declared, 'It is not the breaking of a man's doors and the rummaging of his drawers that constitutes the essence of the offense; but it is the invasion of his indefeasible right of personal security, personal liberty and private property, where that right has never been forfeited by his conviction of some public offense'.

English-speaking peoples have tended to be wary of the dangers of majoritarian collectivistism crushing individual rights. As Hayek (1960, p.195) observed:

The decisive factor which made the efforts of the [French] Revolution toward the enhancement of individual liberty so abortive was that it created the belief that, since at last all power had been placed in the hands of the people, all safeguards against the abuse of this power had become unnecessary. It was thought that the arrival of democracy would automatically prevent the arbitrary use of power. The elected representatives of the people, however, soon proved much more anxious that the executive organs should fully serve their aims than that the individual should be protected against the power of the executive. Though in many respects the French Revolution was inspired by the American, it never achieved what had been the chief result of the other – a constitution which puts limits to the powers of legislation.[13]

For many years, taxation in common law countries was essentially a civil matter. With none of the serious consequences of criminal penalties to consider, legislatures felt few reservations when granting privileged litigant status on the officers of the Revenue. For example, the taxpayer was required to furnish the information necessary to expose himself to a tax liability and the Revenue was allowed free and full access to private papers by way of audit and might be able to make an arbitrary assessment and the onus would then lie on the taxpayer to disprove it. However, in recent years, there has been a tendency to treat tax defaults as a criminal matter, without removing the privileged position of the Revenue as a civil litigant. The inevitable result is that many of the common law rights enunciated above are becoming non-existent or tenuous in not only civil but criminal tax matters: there is no bar to using information acquired for civil disputes in criminal prosecutions. In particular, while common law countries have never formally subscribed to the legal self-contradiction known as 'abuse of law' in fiscal matters, the advancing tide of obscure and subjective anti-avoidance legislation, aided by occasional judicial *realpolitik*, has created a situation where unsuccessful tax planning or tax avoidance may be re-characterized as attempted criminal tax evasion.[14]

---

13 Rights in European Constitutions or the European Declaration on Human Rights have tended to be hypothetical when it comes to taxpayer rights, see Cooper (1997).

14 Once tax matters are characterised as criminal, not only taxpayers but also professional advisers, banks and financial institutions are exposed to penalties. Brandon (2000, p.43)

In these circumstances, not only taxpayers but their lawyers and accountants may be prosecuted and incarcerated as criminals for the offence of unsuccessfully trying to protect taxpayer's money from the possible ambit claims of the Revenue. Such prosecutions are immensely aided by information obtained without any of the normal protections for the accused in a criminal trial.

Anti-Avoidance Legislation and Corruption of the Rule of Law in OECD Countries

These considerations partly explain why the OECD's arguments for exchange of information from offshore financial centres are arousing strong passions from lawyers and their international business and personal clients. They argue that 'tax evasion' is not a simple concept, that to characterise failed tax planning as fraudulent tax evasion is to criminalise the natural human instinct to hold on to what one has worked for and that 'tax evasion' in modern revenue legislation becomes an exceedingly subjective concept as most anti-avoidance legislation is predicated on deemed mental states.

Indeed, many lawyers would argue that modern OECD income tax systems in their anti-avoidance legislation often tax, not on the basis of facts, but on the basis of hypotheses as to what the taxpayer thought or intended – a modern form of Orwellian 'thought crime'.[15] They would argue that the enormous fiscal discretions invariably given to tax officials

---

notes 'If the professional adviser suspects that his client is engaged in tax evasion, *whether in his own jurisdiction or outside it,* he should consider disclosing his suspicion ... he is at risk of prosecution if he does not disclose.' (Emphasis added.) What is going to be the long-run economic cost to international financial markets of trying to turn every officer of every financial institution worldwide into some sort of global tax policeman? Do ordinary police officers face the risk of prosecution for failing to arrest where they 'should' have suspected criminal activity? Why should higher burdens be placed on persons or institutions conducting commercial dealings?

15 The situation has not improved since Tipke (1984) outlined some basic rules for tax justice such as objective rules and ethics in the tax laws and government themselves. On the question of being punished for presumed 'thought crimes', it is a crime under UK money laundering legislation, not to report a suspicion (as opposed to knowledge) relating to financial dealings with criminal proceeds. Leaving aside the philosophical question of whether it is wise for a legal system to inculcate distrust between subjects in their commercial dealings rather then the reverse, how does a legal system look into a man's head? The tactic used has been to reverse the onus of proof, so that an accused banker, for example, must prove h not suspect. This, in turn, conflicts with the presumption of innocence and in *McIntosh v Her Majesty's Advocate*, the Scottish Appeals Court has struck down such a reversal of the onus of proof as being in conflict with the now-binding European Convention on Human Rights.

under anti-abuse or anti-avoidance legislation are a corruption of the rule of law, under which every taxpayer should be entitled to hold on to and dispose of property without being taxed on other than objective and verifiable criteria. More ominously, they would argue that wide discretions in the hands of tax collectors are an invitation to corruption and abuse, just as the wide discretions given to officials in the Soviet era led to entrenched corruption in the post-Soviet pseudo-market economies.[16]

Given this background, many lawyers would argue that it is hardly surprising that taxpayers want financial privacy offshore to avoid exposure to harassment by vindictive or ideological revenue officials. They would have us remember Adam Smith's words

The tax which each individual is bound to pay ought to be certain, and not arbitrary. … Where it is otherwise, every person subject to the tax is put more or less in the power of the tax-gatherer, who can either aggravate the tax upon any obnoxious contributor, or extort, by the terror of such aggravation, some present or perquisite to himself. The uncertainty of taxation encourages the insolence and favours the corruption of an order of men who are naturally unpopular, even where they are neither insolent nor corrupt.

An Inquiry into the Nature and Causes of the Wealth of Nations, Book V, ii, b, pp. 825–26, 1776

On the other side, the OECD view is that, unless Revenue authorities have free and full access to information, there is an incentive to cheat; effective enforcement of modern 'residence-based' income tax legislation requires access to information in foreign countries. Offshore financial centres which guarantee privacy are seen as virtually inciting domestic taxpayers to evasion.

Transparency versus Privacy

It is not surprising that 'transparency' has become almost a mantra for the OECD in pressing the case against 'unfair tax practices'. The word sounds a positive good – and it is, when one is speaking of the accountability of taxpayer-funded bureaucracies, domestic or international, to those who pay for them. For example, when billions of dollars of funds provided to Russia go missing, a little transparency and accountability to taxpayers is a good thing.

But it is an inversion of the roles of master and servant to suggest that the private affairs of the subject should be transparent to an all-powerful

---

16 The IMF has pointed to the dangers of discretionary, non-transparent tax laws in fostering corruption (see Wolf and Gurgen, 2000, p.6).

state. Privacy is a basic human right and civilized society – as well as commerce – would be rendered impossible without it. The word 'privacy', like 'property', connotes what is peculiarly one's own. The common law utterly rejects the idea that the citizen belongs to the state. No clearer expression of that rejection was ever seen than when Britain and the Commonwealth stood alone against what Winston Churchill described as a 'monstrous tyranny' founded upon the opposite principle. The German National Socialist dictatorship completely subordinated the individual and the private to the demands of the state and its state police had neither restraint from warrants nor any respect for business, bankers', lawyers' or family confidences.

Seen from this legal and historical perspective, demands that foreign governments should be able to invade the privacy of the subject in Commonwealth countries become troublesome indeed. It is a serious concern that basic legal protections and rights have been already eroded by tax collection imperatives in OECD countries. It is a troubling notion to both offshore financial centres and their investors that foreign government officials should be able to extract information concerning the private financial affairs of families or companies without a local warrant showing good cause and without notice to persons affected.

A Convergence of Legal and Economic Arguments for Privacy?

There are many reasons for these concerns. Why *should* offshore financial centres degrade the protections of their own legal systems or the rights of their own citizens by co-operating with OECD demands? OECD countries do not, for example, enforce against any resident Afghan citizens the laws made by the Taliban government of Afghanistan prohibiting women from certain occupations: the law they apply to the actions of resident Afghans is their own law. When the Taliban government issued a new law in 2001 that its minority Hindu citizens were required to wear a yellow badge stating that they were Hindus, the US Congress did not decide to go along with it and enforce this law against Afghan Hindus in the US, but rather voted 420–0 to strongly condemn the Taliban law and helped the momentum of international outrage that forced the Taliban government to withdraw this decree. Summing up the outrage of the US Congress, Representative Tom Lantos, California Democrat and Holocaust survivor, and the ranking minority member of the US House International Relations Committee, said: '*We cannot allow the Taliban to systematically repress its Hindus in such an eerily similar manner* [to the Holocaust]'.

Nor, for example, did Australia assist Serbia to call up Serbian-Australian dual nationals for military service. Why, then, should offshore financial centres be expected to assist in applying the tax laws of OECD countries against their own citizens or companies or against income arising or received within their borders? Are they not entitled to say that they, too, are sovereign and *their* tax laws apply to acts done in *their* territory?

This is particularly important when it comes to invading personal privacy, commercial confidentiality or attorney-client privilege. Respect for privacy is not merely an old-fashioned nineteenth-century virtue demonstrating good breeding – it is vital for modern commerce. The US Government sought long and hard to prevent the spread of computer encryption technology on national security grounds. Yet it had to abandon that fight, not simply because of the resistance of outraged libertarians, jurists, academics and computer enthusiasts, but because America's largest corporations demanded and needed bullet-proof encryption technology to carry on their worldwide businesses. Indeed, the subject of commercial privacy has become a controversial issue in the EU with allegations that European companies have lost contracts due to lack of data security against American competitors.

It is therefore hardly surprising that, for reasons not necessarily connected with taxation, individual and corporate clients of offshore financial centres may view OECD demands for transparency and exchange of information with alarm. Where, for example, are the safeguards to prevent a foreign tax official passing on the data provided to a rival in a tender bid for a defence technology contract, especially if the rival bidder is from that official's country? (For a recent example of this type of concern, see 'Euro Police HQ Raided in Fraud Inquiry', *Daily Telegraph*, 2 June 2001: 'Three years ago, it was discovered that an official in the EU's Schengen Information System, a separate body, was selling computer data to organised crime groups'.)

What the critics of the OECD are urging is that access to information about the subject is a form of political power and that, in Lord Acton's (and Pitt's) dictum, power is apt to corrupt the minds of those who possess it. Once tax bureaucrats have privileged access to information about the direct or indirect affairs of billionaires and famous persons, there is an incentive to bribe and corrupt them; those interested may include rival corporations, jilted lovers, political opponents, extortionists or foreign power seeking influence via blackmail.[17] Far from improving *government*

---

17 Even in a relatively non-corrupt country such as Australia, there have been disturbing cases of abuse of information by persons in the employ of government authorities.

transparency, unchecked official access to *private* information[18] is seen by critics as likely to create a new privileged class of bureaucrats with every opportunity and incentive for corruption or other abuses of power.

The issue of the legitimacy or otherwise of personal and commercial privacy brings us to another interesting issue – the role of the market in eliciting information. As Friedrich von Hayek and his fellow Austrian economists were fond of pointing out, a free market economy is an information processing mechanism. Private information is only made available to the market by a system of rewards, a reality recognised by the World Trade Organization and Trade Related Aspects of Intellectual Property (TRIPs) agreements expanding intellectual property protection for patents (whether appropriately or not is beyond the scope of this paper). Thus some countries, while enforcing fiduciary and contractual duties of employees, directors and contractors do not outlaw 'insider' trading *per se*. They, like many economists, take the view that, provided there is no breach of duty or contract, the prospect of profits from acting on inside knowledge serve the useful purpose of embedding that information as rapidly as possible in the share price. To put it another way, transparency is a surrender of privacy and the price of that surrender is a profit to he who provides the information. What corporation does not keep as closely guarded a secret as it can, its plans for merger or takeover with another company or for launch of a new business?

Once one begins to think about the positive role of privacy in inducing quiet labour and planning towards socially useful economic activity, demands for abolition of offshore financial privacy are no longer seen as an unambiguously 'good thing'. The world is more subtle than that and the efficient operation of financial markets is seen to demand respect for financial and business privacy, just as much as the proper accountability of public moneys is seen to demand transparency.

Conclusion

There seems reason to question the OECD assumption that transparency and exchange of information to foreign tax officials should be accepted as self-evident truths in the quest for a better world economic order. This is

---

18 In John Locke's and American classical political philosophy, governments are created to protect life and property, not to take them. There is no inconsistency, on this view of the world, between accepting, on the one hand, warrants for officials to gain information about suspected terrorists or drug traffickers while rejecting, on the other hand, any invasion of privacy by tax collectors.

not to say that it is desirable that malefactors hide their misdeeds, but rather to urge re-consideration of OECD arguments against the centuries-old wisdom – in both legal and economic terms – of fundamental principles of the common law protecting privacy. Almost all offshore centres do co-operate against common criminality, but it is quite another matter to expect them to damage both their own citizens' rights and their own economic prospects by attacking the legitimate privacy of their financial sectors at the behest of foreign tax collectors. Privacy of private sector information has social and economic benefits, just as transparency of public affairs has benefits.

But, at the end of the day, perhaps the tax haven debate will be resolved not by OECD governments or their bureaucrats, or by academic debate, but by the answer businesses and citizens of both OECD and offshore financial centres give to the privacy question which decided the outcome of the American cryptography debate – 'Do you trust your own or foreign government officials with free, unmonitored and unchallengeable access to your private information or private information about you?' We suspect the answer may be be a very loud 'No'.

Postscript

This article was originally written prior to the terrorist attacks of 11 September 2001 against the USA. Like millions of others around the world, we watched with horrified disbelief when television made us unwilling witnesses to the deaths of thousands of human beings as the second World Trade tower was hit and both towers later collapsed. Given the shock, psychic depression and insecurity which now afflicts so many people, it is perhaps inevitable that governments will seek extraordinary powers to prevent and punish such evil acts.

Yet we still think the distinction needs to be made – and that it is vital that it is made – between acts which are, or ought to be, criminal in anyone's language or culture and the routine administrative fiscal matters that the OECD is trying to address, including through measures which many regard as anti-competitive. Nor does every command of an earthly sovereign or majority stand as one of the ten commandments – *vox populi* is not *vox Dei*. Moral distinctions lie at the heart of the rule of international law requiring common criminality as a precondition for legal assistance.

It is right and proper for countries to seek and expect international co-operation to suppress inherently immoral things such as terrorism, piracy, and murder which are universally condemned. In these matters, as Edmund

Burke put it on 28 May 1794: 'There is but one law for all, namely, that law which governs all law, the law of our Creator, the law of humanity, justice, equity – the law of nature, and of nations'.

It is quite another matter for any country to expect others to enforce its merely regulatory or positive laws, be they taxation, traffic, religious or liquor laws. From the times when England gave protection to the Jews and Huguenots to the Canadian supply of liquor to the USA in the 1920s, governments have often wisely chosen not to enforce their neighbours' more repressive laws.

Equally, however, governments have often been willing to co-operate against internationally condemned acts of criminality, such as piracy or the slave trade. On current limited public information, it appears that most offshore financial centres are rightly extending the fullest co-operation and assistance to the US authorities, and that most of the terrorist networks used onshore banking systems in Europe, the USA and the Middle East extensively. From the little that has been publicly reported, it seems money may have been raised from ostensibly legitimate sources within the USA, UK, Europe and the Middle East for terrorist ends. Any attempt to use terrorism as an international G8/OECD bureaucratic springboard to fiscal or financial protectionism against offshore financial centres which respect normal client financial privacy would therefore appear to be both unjustified and unwise. It would be unjustified because these small countries are co-operating with anti-terrorist measures and unwise because coercion on unrelated, merely regulatory, matters may prejudice otherwise willing future co-operation towards the global common good in preventing and punishing truly awful criminal acts. This appears to be the view of the US Administration which recognises that international co-operation through consensus and coalition is essential to eliminating terrorism.

References

Brooks, Michael and John Head (1997). *Tax Avoidance: in Economics, Law and Public Choice*, in Cooper (ed.), pp. 53–91.

Brandon, Ben (2000). 'Tax Crimes Money Laundering and the Professional Adviser', *Journal of Money Laundering Control*, Vol. 4 No. 1, Summer.

Chamley, C. (1986). 'Optimal taxation of capital income in general equilibrium with infinite lives', *Econometrica*, Vol. 54, pp. 607–622.

Cnossen, Sijbren (ed.) (2000). *Taxing Capital Income in the European Union: Issues and Options for Reform*, Oxford University Press.

Cooper, Graeme S. (ed.) (1997). *Tax Avoidance and the Rule of Law*, International Bureau of Fiscal Documentation, Amsterdam.

Correia, Isabel H. (1996). 'Should capital income be taxed in the steady state?', *Journal of Public Economics*, Vol. 60, pp. 147–151.

Dwyer, T. (2000). '"Harmful" tax competition and the future of offshore financial centres, such as Vanuatu', *Pacific Economic Bulletin*, Vol. 15, no 1. pp. 48–69.

Feldstein, Martin (1976). 'On the theory of tax reform', *Journal of Public Economics*, v 6, July–August, pp. 77–104.

Frenkel, Jacob A., Razin, Assaf and Sadka, Efraim (1991). *International Taxation in an Integrated World*. Cambridge, Massachusetts: MIT Press.

Frenkel, Jacob A. and Razin, Assaf (1996). *Fiscal Policies and Growth in the World Economy*, third ed., Cambridge, Massachusetts: MIT Press.

Gibbon, Edward (1776–1781). *The Decline and Fall of the Roman Empire*, Bury (ed.) 1909, Methuen, London.

Gordon, Roger H. (2000). 'Taxation of capital income vs labour income: an overview', in Cnossen (ed.). *Taxing Capital Income in the European Union: Issues and Options for Reform*, Oxford University Press, pp. 15–45.

Hayek, Friedrich A. (1960). *The Constitution of Liberty*, University of Chicago Press.

Head, John G. (1997). 'Company Tax Structure and Company Tax Incidence', *International Tax and Public Finance*, Vol. 4, pp. 61–100.

Kopits, George (ed.) (1992). 'Tax Harmonization in the European Community: Policy Issues and Analysis', International Monetary Fund, occasional paper 94, Washington DC.

Levy, Stephen (2001). *Crypto: How the Code Rebels Beat the Government – Saving Privacy in the Digital Age*, New York: Viking.

Musgrave, R. A. (1959). *The Theory of Public Finance: A Study in Public Economy*, New York: McGraw Hill.

OECD (1998). *Harmful Tax Competition: An Emerging Global Issue*, Paris.

Scott, R. H. (1986). *The Value of Land in Australia*, Centre for Research on Federal Financial Relations, Research Monograph No. 47, Canberra: Australian National University.

Scott, R. H. (1969). 'The Value of Land in Australia', paper presented to Australian and New Zealand Association for the Advancement of Science (ANZAAS), 41st Congress, Section 24, Adelaide, 18–22 August.

Smith, Adam (1776). *An Inquiry into the Nature and Causes of the Wealth of Nations*, Glasgow ed., Oxford, 1976.

Tipke, Klaus (1984). 'Justice in Taxation', *Bulletin of the International Bureau of Fiscal Documentation*, pp. 531–535.

Wolf, Thomas and Emine Gurgen (2000). *Improving Governance and Fighting Corruption in the Baltic and CIS Countries: The Role of the IMF*, Washington DC: IMF.

International Legal and
Constitutional Issues

Some Legal Issues Arising out of the OECD Reports on Harmful Tax Competition[1]

David Simmons QC, BCH

The Government of Barbados has a number of concerns about the legal implications of the OECD initiative in fighting alleged 'harmful tax practices'. I merely wish to highlight some of those concerns in the hope that discussion may be stimulated and responses offered by delegates of the OECD.

The Issue of Sovereignty

The Government of Barbados does not accept that the OECD has any lawful authority to seek to cause any sovereign government to so order its taxation regime in a way that fetters the supremacy of that government's parliament. Taxation policy is essentially a matter within the sovereign authority of a parliament. Only the government or state in a jurisdiction has the authority to tax. It is a sovereign power and under public international law the sovereignty of a state is recognised as being territorial in scope.

OECD countries have chosen particular ways of establishing their tax bases, whereas countries described as 'tax havens' or those offering 'preferential tax regimes' have chosen different modes of taxation as is their sovereign right. That is the essence of tax competition between states and a characterisation of such competition as harmful is really the imposition of a subjective opinion. Essentially, what is at issue between the OECD countries and ourselves is a difference in approach, policy and philosophy to taxation and fiscal engineering.

We would thus be concerned with the implications of that part of the OECD's Memorandum of Understanding headed '(E) Stand-Still', requiring a State 'to refrain from introducing any new regime that would

---

1 This paper is based on a speech given by David Simmons, former Attorney-General of Barbados, at the High Level Consultations on the OECD Harmful Tax Competition Initiative, Barbados, 8–9 January 2001.

constitute a harmful tax practice under the OECD 1998 *Report on Harmful Tax Competition*', and indeed modifying existing regimes.

From this premise springs the second major concern of Barbados.

The Principle of Non-Intervention

This principle of international law has developed to go beyond practices involving the threat or use of armed force.

Thirty years ago the United Nations issued its 'Declaration on Principles of International Law concerning Friendly Relations and Co-operation among States in accordance with the Charter of the UN'.

The Declaration provides that:

No State or group of States has the right to intervene, directly or indirectly, for any reason whatever, in the internal or external affairs of any other State. Consequently, armed intervention and all other forms of interference or attempted threats against the personality of the State or against its political, economic and cultural elements, are in violation of international law.

It continued:

Every State has an inalienable right to choose its political, economic, social and cultural systems, without interference in any form by another State.

Those general principles have been enacted in the Charter of the Organisation of American States (OAS). Barbados, like the USA, is a member of the OAS and both are equally governed by the law as expounded in Articles 18 and 19 of the Charter. Article 18, for example, states:

No State or group of States has the right to intervene, directly or indirectly, for any reason whatever, in the internal or external affairs of any other State. The foregoing principle prohibits not only armed force but also any other form of interference or attempted threat against the personality of the State or against its political, economic, and cultural elements.

In Article 19 it is provided that:

No State may use or encourage the use of coercive measures of an economic or political character in order to force the sovereign will of another State and obtain from it advantages of any kind.

Most recently, in 1984, the British Foreign and Commonwealth Office commented that 'apart from force, there are other means, of which economic coercion and propaganda are two examples, of violating a state's absolute sovereignty over its domestic affairs'.

There is little doubt that the principle of non-intervention forms part of customary international law.

The issues which arise, therefore, are these:

◆ Is it legitimate, under public international law, for states within the OECD to seek to violate the absolute sovereignty of blacklisted states over their domestic fiscal affairs by the propaganda and threatened sanctions contained in the 1998 and 2000 Reports?

◆ Do the threats of sanctions and propaganda breach the principle of non-intervention?

◆ Have any OECD member states considered that in threatening sanctions and giving bad publicity to countries, they may well be about to act in breach of international law?

The Nature and Extent of Sanctions

The language of the OECD reports is imprecise. The reports speak of 'co-ordinated defensive measures', 'counter measures', 'enforcement measures', 'defensive measures' and 'counteracting measures'. What precisely is intended? The OECD needs to take this opportunity to clarify its terms and intentions.

This is not simply an issue of vocabulary. It is a matter of substance because the International Law Commission has identified at least four attributes of a countermeasure. Most importantly, countermeasures can only be taken in response to an unlawful act in international law.

It will thus be particularly relevant for the OECD to identify what rule of international law has been broken by, say, Barbados. One may go further and ask: What is the international standard, established by law, that Barbados has not attained?

In other words, to what extent are the tax practices of Barbados in violation of international legal obligations?

The OECD and the WTO

We appreciate that the OECD only enjoys observer status in the WTO but each of its members is a member of the WTO and, to that extent, if there were a challenge to the actions of the WTO, cases would have to be brought against individual states parties.

We see great difficulties in the threats. Under GATS, it seems that any measures taken by an OECD member that limit consumption of services in third countries will, in principle, infringe any concessions offered by that WTO member under the GATS.

For example, any direction by a national bank of a member not to deal with banks or financial institutions in a third country may well be in breach of the GATS.

Similarly, we think that if an OECD country were to enforce its recommendations by restricting access to the services market of a WTO member, it would be in violation of the GATS. Threats to close down certain jurisdictions fly in the face of the principle of reciprocity which runs through much of the content of the GATS and the WTO agreements.

Over and above all that, it is our understanding that, under the WTO, special permission of the WTO has to be sought for retaliatory measures.

I have dwelt on potential sanctions because the 2000 Report indicates that OECD members 'reserve the *right* to apply defensive measures on a unilateral basis'.

Transparency and the Need for Reciprocity

In the 1998 OECD report it is argued that lack of transparency is a harmful practice. There can be no doubt that, in the larger context of controlling international crime, including tax crime, all jurisdictions need on a collective basis to discuss a series of legal mechanisms aimed at increasing transparency to determine the true ownership of assets.

But at present the playing field, as they say, is 'not level'. US law, for example, does not have simple procedures for exchange of tax information and much of the reciprocity in the exchange of information with the USA rests upon special treaties or agreements such as the one negotiated with Barbados in 1983.

We believe that the blacklist has been compiled on an arbitrary basis with small countries targeted for naming and shaming. On the contrary, countries within the OECD and some outside with harmful practices have escaped black listing. France, Canada, Ireland, Portugal have tax schemes which could reasonably cause them to be listed as tax havens.

Barbados believes that there should be a new approach to identify the principles which could lead to greater transparency but to which all countries will be subject to evaluation.

In Section B of the Memorandum of Understanding dealing with

Beneficial Ownership information, it is proposed that regulatory or tax authorities should have access to information regarding the beneficial ownership of companies and trusts.

As I conceive it, we are on the way to creating the demise of the legal phenomenon of the trust.

Take this example:

'B', an Englishman living in England, wishes to invest £300 000 in a company in England by way of a trust arrangement. He appoints 'T' as his trustee of the shares.

What appears on the Register of Companies in England is that the shares are owned by 'T'. The share certificate is issued in his name. However, the fact of the trust is not disclosed on the register and a third party dealing with the company will have no means of knowing that the beneficial owner of these substantial shares is 'B' who may, in fact, be a money launderer. Why? Because under Section 360 of English Companies Act 1985 'no notice of any trust, express, implied or constructive, must be entered on the Registrar or be receivable by the Registrar ...'

So, how is there transparency in that scenario? Will the UK now repeal Section 360 and require all companies to unfrock their shareholders and disclose who are the trustees and who are the beneficiaries?

In Barbados we have a similar provision (S. 171) to the English provision. Barbados should not be asked to lift the veil of the trust to increase transparency unless the UK is required to do the same.

In other words, we must be firm that the principle of reciprocity guides our desires for transparency.

Towards a Shared Perspective

In the new global architecture it is almost axiomatic that new mechanisms will have to be developed to preserve the integrity of financial services. The 1998 OECD report refers to 'internationally accepted standards'. But the international community has not developed standards. One section of the international community has purported to impose a set of rules on others. It is more like dictation than consultation. The development of a set of international standards requires a multilateral environment in which all countries can contribute. Thereafter, those internationally agreed standards may be raised to the level of positive international law through an appropriate international instrument. After that, talk of sanctions can be entertained.

We should seek first to develop a set of agreed principles applicable to all nations in the business. The development of these principles can fairly and properly take place only in a consultative environment across regions of the world in a context of multilateralism.

An Instrument to which OECD countries and other individual states will subscribe to the negotiated document may be an International Instrument in the nature of a Convention relevant to those countries offering offshore services.

The OECD, Harmful Tax Competition and Tax Havens: Towards an Understanding of the International Legal Context

William Gilmore[1]

Introduction

The primary purpose of this paper is to provide an initial and necessarily partial contribution to an understanding of the general international legal aspects which arise from that part of the OECD initiative on harmful tax competition which relates to so-called tax havens. In this regard the OECD initiative has been taken to be that represented by the reports entitled *Harmful Tax Competition: An Emerging Global Issue*[2] and *Towards Global Tax Co-operation: Report to the 2000 Ministerial Council Meeting and Recommendations by the Committee on Fiscal Affairs*.[3] Account has also been taken of associated governmental and intergovernmental documents (the majority of which are in the public domain) including the 'Framework for a Collective Memorandum of Understanding on Eliminating Harmful Tax Practices'.[4]

The practical need for analysis in this area is evident from the fact that while the central OECD reports which give expression to the initiative on harmful tax competition are not couched in legal terms, certain members of the international community whose interests are affected by it have specifically invoked legal arguments in response. For example, the 'Statement on OECD Harmful Tax Policy' that formed part of the communiqué issued by CARICOM Heads of Government on 6 July 2000 reiterated the view 'that the proposed OECD actions have no basis in international law and are alien to the practice of inter-state relations'.

A range of complex and in some instances controversial legal issues arise

---

1 Professor William Gilmore is Professor in the Faculty of Law, University of Edinburgh. He was formerly Assistant Director, Legal Division, Commonwealth Secretariat.

2 OECD, 1998, Paris. Hereafter referred to as the 1998 Report.

3 OECD, 2000, Paris. Hereafter referred to as the 2000 Report.

4 B. Zagaris, 'OECD Releases MOU on Harmful Tax Practices', *International Enforcement Law Reporter*, 2001, 17, pp. 13–15. The text can be consulted at www.oecd.org.

in an examination of the international legal context in which the OECD initiative operates and of the matters to which it gives rise. What follows is not intended to be comprehensive in its coverage. Its focus is on general international law matters. The examination of the compatibility of what is contemplated with specific treaty obligations which may subsist between affected jurisdictions (such as with the Charter of the OAS for members of that regional body or those which arise in the WTO context) lie beyond its scope. In addition, it deals exclusively with issues which are relevant for jurisdictions which are states for the purposes of international law. Additional factors which relate to the legal position of entities which enjoy an international legal status other than that of full statehood have not been addressed.

The Context

The adoption by the Committee on Fiscal Affairs of the OECD of the 1998 Report represented a significant milestone in what has been a lengthy engagement with the range of issues addressed therein. Tax matters and international co-operation are central to the OECD's mandate.[5] Similarly, the issues of tax avoidance and evasion and the subject of 'tax havens' have commanded considerable attention over the years. For example, in 1987 the OECD published the influential monograph *International Tax Avoidance and Evasion: Four Related Studies.*[6]

In subsequent years, concern over these issues gradually intensified as OECD member governments came to focus on the perceived drawbacks, as well as the manifest advantages, which flow from economic globalisation.[7] As Jeffrey Owens, a senior OECD official, has remarked:

Similarly, increased liberalization of financial markets has improved the international allocation of savings and capital and reduced the cost of capital to enterprises. But it has also widened opportunities for tax evasion and avoidance. In this new environment, tax havens have thrived and some governments have adopted preferential tax regimes specifically targeted at attracting mobile activities.

---

5 See, for example, H. Hahn, Organisation for Economic Co-operation and Development, 1997, III *Encyclopedia of Public International Law*, pp. 790–799 and the literature cited therein.

6 OECD, 1987, Paris.

7 See, for example, R. Avi-Yonah, 'Globalization, Tax Competition, and the Fiscal Crisis of the Welfare State', *Harvard Law Review*, 2000, 113, pp. 1573 *et seq*. See also 'A Survey of Globalisation and Tax', *The Economist*, London, 29 January 2000 and 'Who will collect taxes in a global village?' *The Times*, London, 10 April 2000.

If nothing is done, governments may increasingly be forced to engage in competitive tax bidding to attract or retain mobile activities. That 'race to the bottom', where location and financing decisions become primarily tax driven, will mean that capital and financial flows will be distorted and it will become more difficult to achieve fair competition for real economic activities.[8]

Eventually, in May 1996, OECD Ministers called upon the organisation to 'develop measures to counter the distorting effects of harmful tax competition on investment and financing decisions and the consequences for national tax bases, and to report back in 1998'.[9] At their summit meeting in Lyon, France, later the same year Heads of State and Government of the G7 countries offered their support and encouragement to this initiative.[10]

The Committee on Fiscal Affairs established the 'Special Sessions on Tax Competition', under the joint Chairmanship of France and Japan, to carry forward the mandate in this area. The resulting report was adopted by the Committee on 20 January 1998 and approved by the OECD Council on 9 April. In its Recommendation on Counteracting Harmful Tax Competition, the Council took note of the report and recommended, *inter alia*, that member countries implement its recommendations. In order to facilitate this process it instructed the Committee on Fiscal Affairs to establish a Forum on Harmful Tax Practices.[11] Luxembourg and Switzerland abstained.[12] In May of 1998 G7 Finance Ministers warmly welcomed the above developments and strongly endorsed the OECD recommendations, including the establishment of the Forum.[13]

At a general level the report 'is intended to develop a better understanding of how tax havens and harmful preferential tax regimes, collectively referred to as harmful tax practices, affect the location of financial and other service activities, erode the tax bases of other countries, distort trade and investment patterns and undermine the fairness, neutrality and broad social acceptance of tax systems generally'.[14] The underlying perspective is that 'such harmful tax competition diminishes global welfare

---

8 J. Owens, 'Curbing Harmful Tax Competition – Recommendations by the Committee on Fiscal Affairs', *Intertax*, 1998, 26, pp.230–231.

9 1998 Report, p. 1.

10 Ibid.

11 1998 Report, pp. 65–66.

12 Ibid., pp. 73–78.

13 Conclusions of G7 Finance Ministers, 8 May 1998, paras 13–14.

14 1998 Report, p. 8. Other related issues such as tax competition in relation to consumption taxes and the treatment of cross border savings instruments fall outside the scope of the report. For an interesting overview see J.M. Weiner and H. Ault, 'The OECD's Report on Harmful Tax Competition', *National Tax Journal*, 1998, 11, pp. 601–608.

and undermines taxpayer confidence in the integrity of tax systems'.[15] From this base the report proceeded to articulate a strategy for the identification of harmful tax practices and a programme of action to counter them.

As noted above, a major focus of the OECD initiative is on tax havens – jurisdictions perceived as having a significant and increasingly negative impact on the revenues available to other countries.[16] Several significant difficulties confronted the authors of the 1998 report as they sought to articulate a strategy to deal with the alleged negative consequences of the activities of such jurisdictions. Of these, perhaps the most fundamental was the absence of an internationally agreed definition of a tax haven. This difficulty had, by way of illustration, been identified but not satisfactorily resolved in the 1987 OECD study *Tax Havens: Measures to Prevent Abuse by Taxpayers*.[17] That no subsequent international consensus on this matter had emerged is acknowledged in the 1998 Report which notes that the concept 'does not have a precise technical meaning ...'.[18]

Notwithstanding this fact, the report proceeded to provide the Forum with guidance through which tax havens could be identified for OECD purposes. The approach adopted is reflected in para. 52 which reads, in relevant part, as follows:

The necessary starting point to identify a tax haven is to ask (a) whether a jurisdiction imposes no or only nominal taxes (generally or in special circumstances) and offers itself, or is perceived to offer itself, as a place to be used by non-residents to escape tax in their country of residence. Other key factors which can confirm the existence of a tax haven ... are: (b) laws or administrative practices which prevent the effective exchange of relevant information with other governments on taxpayers benefiting from the low or no tax jurisdiction; (c) lack of transparency and (d) the absence of a requirement that the activity be substantial, since it would suggest that a jurisdiction may be attempting to attract investment or transactions that are purely tax driven (transactions may be booked there without the requirement of adding value so that there is little real activity, i.e., these jurisdictions are essentially 'booking centres'). No or only nominal taxation is a necessary condition for the identification of a tax haven. As noted ... above, if combined with a situation where the jurisdiction offers or is perceived to offer itself as a place where non-residents can escape tax in their country of residence, it may be sufficient to identify a tax haven. In general, the importance of each of the other

---

15 1998 Report, p. 8.

16 For example, 1998 Report, pp. 17, 22.

17 See, *supra*, note 5, pp. 21–22.

18 1998 Report, p. 20.

key factors referred to above very much depends on the particular context. Even if the tax haven does impose tax, the definition of domestic source income may be so restricted as to result in very little income being taxed.[19]

It will suffice for present purposes to note that the use of specific criteria in the definitional process constitutes a (welcome) retreat from a heavy reliance within OECD circles on the reputation or 'smell' test[20] (though this element has not been entirely abandoned).[21] Unfortunately, however, certain of the key criteria, such as 'lack of transparency' and 'lack of effective exchange of information'[22] are neither self-defining nor afforded sufficient substantive treatment elsewhere in the report to permit the ready identification of the minimum standards envisaged. This is an issue to which this paper will return below.

The 1998 Report also initiated a process for determining which countries and territories were to be classified as tax havens for these purposes. This matter was assigned to the new Forum on Harmful Tax Practices which, in Recommendation 16, was mandated to establish a list of such jurisdictions. The list, as originally conceived, was intended to 'enable Member countries to co-ordinate their responses to the problems posed by tax havens and to encourage these jurisdictions to re-examine their policies'.[23]

Chapter 3 of the report, entitled 'Counteracting Harmful Tax Competition', addresses numerous measures, variously described, which could be used to counter practices deemed objectionable. Specific recommendations were subject to a threefold division: those concerning domestic legislation, those concerning tax treaties and those requiring intensification of international co-operation. In addition, the report identified a series of topics (including possible non-tax measures) where further study might result in the emergence of new recommendations directed at harmful tax competition. This dimension of the OECD initiative is discussed later in this paper.

Recent Developments

Developments in the implementation of the OECD initiative have been numerous and varied. Many are summarised in the 2000 Report. For the

---

19 1998 Report, pp. 22–23.

20 For example, Avi-Yonah, *supra*, p. 1659, note 6.

21 See, for example, 1998 Report, p. 21.

22 Several of the tax haven criteria are also utilised in the identification of harmful preferential tax regimes in OECD member countries. See 1998 Report, pp. 25–35.

23 1998 Report, p. 57.

purposes of this paper perhaps the most significant relate to the identification of specific jurisdictions deemed by the OECD to meet the tax haven criteria as reflected in the 1998 Report and the clarification of the consequences of such a listing.

The 35 countries and territories so listed[24] are:

Andorra
Anguilla – Overseas Territory of the UK
Antigua and Barbuda
Aruba – Kingdom of the Netherlands
Commonwealth of the Bahamas
Bahrain
Barbados
Belize
British Virgin Islands – Overseas Territory of the UK
Cook Islands – New Zealand
The Commonwealth of Dominica
Gibraltar – Overseas Territory of the UK
Grenada
Guernsey/Sark/Alderney – Dependency of the British Crown
Isle of Man – Dependency of the British Crown
Jersey – Dependency of the British Crown
Liberia
The Principality of Liechtenstein
The Republic of the Maldives
The Republic of the Marshall Islands
The Principality of Monaco
Montserrat – Overseas Territory of the UK
The Republic of Nauru
Netherlands Antilles – Kingdom of the Netherlands
Niue – New Zealand
Panama
Samoa
The Republic of the Seychelles
St Lucia
The Federation of St Christopher and Nevis
St Vincent and the Grenadines
Tonga
Turks & Caicos – Overseas Territory of the UK
US Virgin Islands – External Territory of the USA
The Republic of Vanuatu

---

24 2000 Report, p. 17.

Several factors are important for present purposes. First, prior to the publication of the 2000 Report six jurisdictions – Bermuda, the Cayman Islands, Cyprus, Malta, Mauritius and San Marino – made what are known as 'advance commitments' to comply with the principles of the 1998 Report and to remove all harmful tax practices by December 2005. In recognition of this fact they were omitted from the list 'even if they presently meet the tax haven criteria'.[25] Second, the listing of the 35 jurisdictions in question, as endorsed by the OECD Council on 16 June 2000, is 'not intended to be used as the basis for possible co-ordinated defensive measures'.[26] Rather, a further list of 'unco-operative tax havens' was to be developed within the OECD by 31 July 2001. In the intervening period listed jurisdictions were provided with an opportunity to make a commitment to the progressive elimination of those of their tax practices deemed to be harmful. This 'scheduled commitment' process is examined in greater detail below. The consequence of a failure to take such a step was directly addressed in the OECD Council Recommendation of 16 June 2000. This instructed the Committee on Fiscal Affairs to:

3. Include automatically on the OECD List of unco-operative Tax Havens any jurisdiction identified in the 2000 Report as meeting the tax haven criteria if the jurisdiction does not by 31 July 2001 commit to eliminate harmful tax practices in accordance with the 1998 Report in a manner satisfactory to member countries.[27]

Some jurisdictions had, at the time of writing, made the required commitment.[28] Yet others may follow. Such countries and territories, if any, as appear on the eventual list of unco-operative tax havens, and any that may subsequently be added, can expect to be subject after 31 July 2001 to co-ordinated action within the context of an evolving framework for a common OECD approach to restraining harmful tax practices. As the 2000 Report notes: 'The Committee on Fiscal Affairs will be working within the next six months to a year to consider these possible measures, finalise its recommendations, and adopt an implementation strategy and timetable'.[29]

As noted above, the 2000 Report has been endorsed by the OECD Council. It was been warmly welcomed by G7 leaders at their meeting in Okinawa, Japan. In a statement issued on 21 July 2000, the OECD initi-

---

25 Ibid.

26 Ibid.

27 2000 Report, p. 30.

28 For example, the Isle of Man, the Netherlands Antilles and the Republic of Seychelles.

29 2000 Report, p. 24.

ative on harmful tax practices was addressed in conjunction with certain of the activities of the Financial Action Task Force on Money Laundering and the offshore financial centres dimension of the work of the Financial Stability Forum. The statement reads:

We will take steps to encourage jurisdictions to make the necessary changes and provide technical assistance where appropriate. Where jurisdictions fail to meet certain standards and are not committed to enhancing their level of compliance with international standards, we will also take measures to protect the international financial system from the effects of these failures.[30]

While this process has been supported, often at the highest political levels, by the world's richest countries, it has proved to be a source of 'profound disquiet' in other circles[31] with associated calls for dialogue and compromise. Commonwealth Finance Ministers, for example, have called 'with some urgency, for greater regional and multilateral dialogue at both the political and technical levels on the implications of the OECD proposals, with a view to developing multilateral approaches to take forward the work on all aspects of global tax issues'.[32]

Within this context a multilateral meeting was hosted by the Government of Barbados (a listed state) in early January 2001 in association with the Commonwealth Secretariat and the OECD. These high-level consultations, chaired by the Prime Minister of Barbados, were attended by representatives of more than 40 countries and territories.[33] Sufficient common ground among the participants emerged in relation to the 'broad principles' of transparency, non-discrimination and effective exchange of information to justify establishing a working group to be co-chaired by Australia and Barbados.[34] Its twofold remit was as follows:

♦ First, to take the three principles noted above and to find a mutually acceptable political process by which these principles could be turned into commitments. This process, if successful, would replace the OECD's process in the context of its Memorandum of Understanding.

♦ Second, to examine how to continue the dialogue begun in Barbados.

---

30 G7 Statement, Okinawa, 21 July 2000, para. 26.

31 See, for example, 'Harmful Tax Competition', Statement by Law Ministers and Attorneys-General of Small Commonwealth Jurisdictions, Jersey, 17 May 2000.

32 Commonwealth Finance Ministers Meeting, St Julians, Malta, 19–21 September 2000, Communiqué, para. 21.

33 B. Zagaris, 'Consultations in Barbados on OECD Harmful Tax Competition Initiative Yield Progress', *International Enforcement Law Reporter*, 2001, 17, pp. 50–54.

34 See, for example, Task for Joint Team, Barbados Advocate (Bridgetown), 10 January 2001, pp. 1–2.

The Group was to examine how the recently created Global Forum on taxation could evolve into a truly inclusive Global Forum, which would promote global co-operation on tax matters. It would also identify further relevant tax issues for consideration by such a Forum.[35]

Since that time the group has met on two occasions – in London on 26–28 January and in Paris on 1–2 March 2001. No fixed consensus as to the way forward has so far emerged from this process. Consequently the remainder of this paper has been prepared on the assumption that the core elements of the OECD Initiative are still in play.

Scheduled Commitments

Process Issues

The process of preparing the list of jurisdictions considered to meet the tax haven criteria established by the OECD involved the preparation by study groups of specific jurisdictional reports, certain bilateral and other contacts with countries and territories on an initial indicative list, and discussion within the Forum.[36] As the OECD has noted: 'During the process of consultations, a number of the jurisdictions under review indicated an interest in the possibility of co-operating with the OECD by committing to the elimination of harmful tax practices. The extent of the interest in co-operation was not fully foreseen at the time that the 1998 Report was presented to Ministers'.[37]

In the light of these developments it was decided, *inter alia*, to elaborate a special procedure in respect of such countries and territories included on the list of tax havens which, by 31 July 2001, had made a commitment, in a manner and form acceptable to the OECD, to the elimination of harmful tax practices. Any such jurisdiction would not, for an initial period of one year, be included in the planned list of unco-operative tax havens. Such a 'scheduled commitment' or 'co-operative' jurisdiction would also be 'eligible for successive renewals of its status by making a new public commitment to move to the next stage of the plan of progressive changes'.[38] By virtue of being classified as 'co-operative', and for so long as such a designation subsists, any such jurisdiction would not be subject to the 'co-ordinated defensive measures', examined in greater

---

35 Commonwealth Secretariat Press Release, 9 January 2001, Barbados, p. 2.

36 2000 Report, pp. 10–11.

37 2000 Report, p. 18.

38 2000 Report, p. 19.

detail below. The report notes, however, that OECD member countries reserve the right to apply defensive measures on a unilateral basis.[39]

At the core of the 'scheduled commitment' process as envisaged in the 2000 Report is a 'public political commitment' to the progressive elimination of harmful tax practices by 31 December 2005. In its words:

The procedure for making a scheduled commitment is that a jurisdiction submits a written statement of the commitment of its government. ... The statement is to be in the form of a letter to the Secretary-General of the OECD, and signed by an authorised official. This letter is to be accompanied by an annex setting forth the specifications to which the jurisdiction is agreeing, as discussed with the Forum.[40]

It was anticipated that within six months of the making of such a commitment the jurisdiction in question would develop with the Forum an acceptable plan 'describing the manner in which the jurisdiction ... intends to achieve its commitment, the timetable for so doing, and milestones to ensure steady progress, including the completion of a concrete and significant action during the first year of the commitment'.[41] The jurisdiction was also to agree to a 'standstill' provision[42] and to participate in an annual review process with the Forum. As an inducement to secure compliance with such undertakings, the 2000 Report notes that 'a jurisdiction would be placed on the list of unco-operative tax havens if any harmful aspects of its regime remain after the deadline for their elimination. Also, if the milestones and timetable are not met and there is at any time evidence that the jurisdiction is not acting in good faith in accordance with its commitments, the Committee will place the jurisdiction on the List of unco-operative Tax Havens'.[43]

---

39 2000 Report, p. 26.

40 Ibid., p. 19.

41 Ibid.

42 In the Framework for a Collective Memorandum of Understanding (hereafter Collective MOU) the 'stand-still' concept is defined as follows:

Each Party will refrain from

(i) introducing any new regime that would constitute a harmful tax practice under the OECD 1998 Report on Harmful Tax Competitions.

(ii) with respect to any existing regime related to financial and other services that currently does not constitute a harmful tax practice under the OECD Report, modifying the regime in such a way that, after the modifications, it would constitute a harmful tax practice under the OECD Report; and

(iii) strengthening or extending the scope of any existing measure that currently constitutes a harmful tax practice under the OECD Report.

43 2000 Report, p. 19.

Following further consideration and dialogue on this matter, the decision was taken to introduce certain 'process enhancements' which were set out in an electronic fax from the co-Chair of the Forum on Harmful Tax Practices to the listed jurisdictions. Under this revised scheme the individual commitment process, outlined above, remained available on a somewhat revised basis. In particular, 'the Forum has dispensed with the earlier format of the commitment that envisioned a letter sent by the jurisdiction to the Secretary-General of the OECD. Instead, a jurisdiction can make the individual commitment by issuing a press release accompanied by an annex setting forth the terms of the commitment'. The publication of that annex is regarded as essential.

The letter from the co-Chair of the Forum also introduced a new option, participation by listed jurisdictions in a collective Memorandum of Understanding (MOU) with the OECD as such, rather than with its individual member states. As the letter explains: 'A jurisdiction can become a party to the Collective MOU by a press release announcement. Neither a physical signature nor a letter to the OECD is necessary'. Annexed to that communication is a text entitled 'Framework for a Collective Memorandum of Understanding on Eliminating Harmful Tax Practices'. In addition to clauses on duration and termination, the MOU includes a common schedule for the achievement by listed jurisdictions of specified standards and expectations in relation to such matters as transparency, information exchange, not attracting business without substantial domestic activity and 'standstill'. The deadline for the completion of this process is set at 31 December 2005. Under the heading of 'Collateral Issues' the text also details commitments on the part of the OECD in relation to the listing of unco-operative jurisdictions and resort to co-ordinated defensive measures.[44]

Both the envisaged options for the making of the requisite commitments, unilateral action and participation in the Collective MOU, give rise to issues of interest from the perspective of public international law. By way of illustration, while the designation of an international instrument as a MOU is, generally speaking, an indication of the intent of the parties to

---

44 The Collective MOU is worded, in relevant part, as follows:

List of unco-operative Tax Havens: The OECD will refrain from including the name of a Party on any List of unco-operative Jurisdictions during the duration of the MOU, provided that the Party is proceeding in good faith to satisfy the terms of the MOU.

Defensive Measures: The OECD will refrain from recommending that any common framework of defensive measures (within the meaning of the 1998 Report) be implemented against a Party during the duration of the MOU, provided that the Party is proceeding in good faith to satisfy the terms of the MOU.

enter into an arrangement which, in contrast to a treaty, is not legally binding,[45] it still may, in certain circumstances, give rise to legal consequences. For example, in a recent work one well-recognised authority has noted the potential relevance of the international law principle of estoppel, or preclusion, in the context of MOUs between states. In his words: 'The exact scope of the international law doctrine is far from settled, but in general it may be said that where a clear statement or representation is made by one state to another, which then in good faith relies upon it *to its detriment*, the first state is estopped (precluded) from going back on its statement or representation. If two states choose to record the settlement of a dispute between them in an MOU rather than in a treaty ... they are clearly estopped from denying that the terms of the settlement are binding'.[46] Among issues which are relevant in the current context is the impact, if any, on the legal position of potential listed jurisdiction participants of the facts that the instrument is multilateral rather than bilateral, and that it envisages participation by the OECD rather than its individual members.[47]

Interesting and potentially significant though the above process issues are,[48] the emergence of the MOU is of perhaps even greater significance in its articulation of the standards of conduct expected of co-operative tax havens. It is to that crucial matter that this paper now turns.

Standards

As noted above, the Collective MOU makes a significant contribution to an understanding of the scope and ambition of the tax havens element of the OECD initiative. This it does by setting out in some detail the substantive content of the broad principles of transparency, effective exchange of information, non-discrimination and standstill to which listed countries and territories were being asked to commit themselves. These are described in the MOU as 'international standards'.

---

45 An examination of the form and content of the text in issue here suggests that an arrangement which is not legally binding is in contemplation.

46 A. Aust, *Modern Treaty Law and Practice*, Cambridge University Press, Cambridge, 2001, p. 46.

47 Several associated issues also require clarification, For example, what impact, if any, these 'process enhancements' were intended to have on the annual review process through which determinations were to be reached concerning the progress recorded in the fulfilling of scheduled commitments. See 2000 Report, p. 19.

48 As noted above, the procedures through which listed jurisdictions might make the anticipated commitments is currently under discussion in the Working Group established at the Barbados meeting in January 2001.

In the course of the High Level Consultations held in Barbados in early January 2001 a spirited exchange of views took place as to the source and nature of these standards. The underlying perspective of the OECD delegations was that the principles in question enjoyed a wide acceptance in the international community and that their appropriate interpretation was as reflected in the text of the MOU. Doubts as to the soundness of this perspective were voiced by the representatives of several non-member countries and territories. The strength of this latter perspective can be illustrated by reference to the treatment of elements of two of the central principles as set out in the text – transparency and effective exchange of information.[49]

Transparency

As was noted above, 'lack of transparency' is a factor common to the identification of tax havens and harmful preferential tax regimes for the purposes of the 1998 Report.[50] Part of that broad concept, as envisaged by the MOU, is the complex area of the availability of beneficial ownership information. In particular, the MOU envisages that, by 31 December 2002:

Each Party will ensure that its regulatory or tax authorities have access to information regarding beneficial owners of companies, partnerships and other entities organised in its jurisdiction, including collective investment funds, and to information on the identity of the principal (as opposed to agent or nominee) of those establishing trusts (settlors) and foundations under their laws and those benefiting from trusts and foundations.

The issue of the identification of beneficial ownership is perhaps most strongly associated at the international level with the work of the FATF in relation to the establishment of anti-money-laundering standards.[51] Of particular relevance is Recommendation 11, by virtue of which '[f]inancial institutions should take reasonable measures to obtain information about the true identity of the persons on whose behalf an account is opened or a transaction conducted ...'. Further detail of expectations in this regard is provided in an Interpretative Note to Recommendations 11 and 15–18. Importantly, in the course of 2000 the OECD Committee on Fiscal Affairs committed itself to this standard and indicated that it would

---

49 Some support for this questioning view is to be found in the 2000 Report, p. 7, which speaks of contributing 'to emerging international principles of transparency, fairness, and disclosure'.

50 1998 Report, pp. 23–24, 27–29.

51 For an examination of the work of the FATF see W. Gilmore, *Dirty Money*, Strasbourg: Council of Europe Publishing, 2nd ed, 1999, Ch. IV.

'rely on the work of the Financial Action Task Force in ensuring the implementation of these measures by Member countries'.[52]

It is, however, open to serious doubt if compliance with the above FATF standard, which emerged in the specific and limited context of client identification for credit and financial institutions, would be regarded as relevant to, let alone satisfaction of, the conditions set by the MOU.[53] Rather it would seem that the intention is to address the related but broader issue of access to beneficial ownership information in relation to the registration of corporate and other legal entities.

In this regard, there is a growing awareness at the international level of the problems which can arise from inadequate regulation in this sphere. By way of illustration, in 1996 the FATF amended its 40 Recommendations so as to encourage countries to 'take notice of the potential for abuse of shell corporations by money launderers' and to 'consider whether additional measures are required to prevent unlawful use of such entities'.[54] More recently a greatly increased emphasis has been placed on this issue by various governments and intergovernmental organisations.[55]

Action has been at its most robust in the framework of the FATF's recent and controversial initiative directed against 'Non-Co-operative Countries or Territories' (NCCTs). This is a somewhat similar 'name and shame' exercise which is directed, in the main, towards inducing jurisdictions which offer financial services to improve their co-operation in the fight against the laundering of the proceeds of criminal activity. A 'black list' of NCCTs was drawn up in the course of 2000,[56] following an evalu-

52 *Improving Access to Bank Information for Tax Purposes*, OECD, Paris, 2000, p.14.

53 An argument could be made that the satisfaction of these FATF standards is implicitly required by the MOU under the separate heading of 'access to bank information' to be satisfied by 31 December 2003.

54 FATF Recommendation 25.

55 For example, para. 57 of the conclusions of the Tampere Special European Council of October 1999 stated, in relevant part: 'Common standards should be developed in order to prevent the use of corporations and entities registered outside the jurisdiction of the Union in the hiding of criminal proceeds and in money laundering'. The issue has been revisited since by EU countries. The ECOFIN and Justice and Home Affairs Council, meeting in Luxembourg in October 2000, called on the Commission 'to submit to it an additional report examining in particular the possibility of establishing minimum transparency criteria for various types of legal entities (such as trusts, trust funds and foundations) for the purpose of identifying the beneficial owners more easily'. Doc. 12128/00 (Presse 381–G), para. 5.

56 See *Financial Action Task Force on Money Laundering. Annual Report: 1999–2000*, 22 June 2000, FATF, Paris, Annex A. The 15 jurisdictions listed were: Bahamas, Cayman Islands, Cook Islands, Dominica, Israel, Lebanon, Liechtenstein, Marshall Islands, Nauru, Niue, Panama, Philippines, Russia, St Kitts and Nevis, and St Vincent.

ation conducted on the basis of 25 criteria.[57] Two directly relate to the lack of identification of the beneficial owners of legal and business entities.[58]

While these criteria 'are consistent with the international anti-money-laundering standards set out in the Forty Recommendations of the FATF'[59] there can be little doubt that, in this sphere at least, the NCCT formulation goes beyond the requirements of those Recommendations as currently drafted. Indeed, the weight of evidence clearly points to a growing appreciation of the need to develop relevant standards. For example, in July 2000 G7 Finance Ministers, in their report to Heads of State and Government meeting in Okinawa, called upon the FATF to consider the scope for revising its Recommendations in order to better address the unlawful use of corporate structures. In so doing they welcomed the OECD's forthcoming review of this subject.[60] It is understood that the report in question is in the course of preparation by the OECD Steering Group on Corporate Governance and is due to be presented to Ministers at their meeting in May 2001. It will address, *inter alia*, factors which limit the ability of appropriate national authorities to access beneficial ownership information relating to corporate vehicles and identify options available to improve such access at a domestic level and to share the same on an international basis. It is anticipated that this report will help to inform opinion within the current FATF review of the adequacy of its package of anti-money-laundering measures where the issue of the registration and regulation of legal or business entities or arrangements is likely to be a focus of particular attention.

In the light of the above, it is difficult to resist the conclusion that there is, at present, no fixed international standard in respect of access to beneficial ownership information in the sense contemplated by the MOU. That said, it is equally clear that there is a growing appreciation within the international community of the urgent need both to establish and enforce such a standard.

Exchange of Information
Lack of effective exchange of information is also a factor common to the identification of tax havens and harmful preferential tax regimes for the purposes of the 1998 Report.[61] In classifying this as a particularly harmful

57 See *Financial Action Task Force on Money Laundering: Report on Non-Co-operative Countries and Territories*,14 February 2000, FATF, Paris. Text available at www.oecd.org/fatf.

58 See criteria 13 and 14.

59 FATF Annual Report, *supra*, note 55, p. 19.

60 'Actions Against Abuse of the Global Financial System', 21 July 2000, Okinawa', para. 5(c).

61 For example, 1998 Report, pp. 23, 27.

characteristic of a tax haven the Report notes: 'The most obvious consequence of the failure to provide information is that it facilitates tax evasion and money laundering'.[62] It should not be thought, however, that the
concern is by any means exclusively with international co-operation in
relation to such criminal matters. For example, having noted that
progress had been recorded by certain tax havens in relation to criminal
co-operation, the Report continues:

*Nevertheless, these tax haven jurisdictions do not allow tax administrations
access to bank information for the critical purposes of detecting and preventing
tax avoidance which, from the perspectives of raising revenue and controlling
base erosion from financial and other service activities, are as important as
curbing tax fraud.*[63]

In the light of the above, it was to be expected that the MOU would contain extensive provision on the co-operation issue. This it does in some
detail. Thus, by 31 December 2001 '[e]ach Party will have in place a legal
mechanism that allows information to be provided to the tax authorities
of OECD countries upon request for the investigation of criminal tax
matters'. A similar legal mechanism is to be in place by 31 December
2005 to facilitate the provision, upon request, of information for the
determination, assessment, collection and enforcement of all other tax
matters (hereafter referred to as "civil tax matters")'. The terms 'criminal'
and 'civil' tax matters are not otherwise defined in the text.

Several points of interest emerge from the treatment of co-operation in
criminal tax matters in the MOU. First, and most fundamentally, it
appears to be based on the assumption that there exists an international
standard requiring co-operation in this sphere. While it is true that over
the last 25 years or so a clear trend has emerged to facilitate the provision
of co-operation in criminal tax matters[64] the stage has not yet been reached
where it is possible to say that refusal to assist in relation to fiscal offences
is beyond the bounds of formally sanctioned international conduct.[65]

---

62 Ibid., p. 24.

63 Ibid.

64 For example, an Additional Protocol of 1978 to the European Convention on Mutual
 Assistance removes the right, originally contained in Article 2(a) of the 1959 text, to refuse
 co-operation on the sole ground that the request concerns a fiscal offence.

65 Even some modern multilateral texts continue to sanction the use of the fiscal exemption.
 See, for example, Article 18(1)(d) of the 1990 Council of Europe Convention on laundering,
 search, seizure and confiscation of the proceeds of crime. Similarly, the fiscal offence
 exemption has been circumscribed but not eliminated by Article 18(22) of the 2000 UN
 Convention against Transnational Organized Crime. But see criterion 25 of the FATF's
 NCCT initiative.

Second, while mutual legal assistance (or judicial assistance) is an ortho-dox and widely accepted mechanism for the provision of co-operation in criminal tax matters[66] the use of such a procedure is not specifically men-tioned among the 'various approaches' detailed in the MOU. These appear to contemplate the direct involvement of the tax authorities of the requesting OECD country in the relevant channels of communication. While OECD tax administrations will, no doubt, have a strong prefer-ence for administrative assistance permitting direct contact with either the holders of relevant information in a tax haven or with the appropriate regulatory authorities in such country or territory, it would be both sur-prising and a significant departure from established international practice if reliance on mutual legal assistance in criminal matters agreements or arrangements was regarded as an unacceptable basis for the satisfaction of this requirement of co-operation for MOU purposes.

A third and final issue arises out of the articulation of a condition in the MOU that information in the criminal tax sphere 'must be provided with-out the requirement that the conduct being investigated would constitute a crime under the laws of the Party, if it occurred in its jurisdiction'. This requirement to abolish double criminality in the context of tax offences responds to a well-recognised practical difficulty. As a recent OECD report has remarked: 'where there are marked differences in the definitions of tax crimes, application of a "double incrimination" standard in the tax area can significantly hinder effective exchange of information between treaty part-ners on criminal tax matters'.[67] Such problems would be particularly acute in relationships with zero tax jurisdictions. It can also be said that the inter-national trend in the sphere of mutual legal assistance would seem to be towards the gradual diminishing of the significance of this traditional, and normally discretionary, ground for the refusal of co-operation.[68] However, it is also clear that there is not yet an international consensus favouring the abolition of this doctrine. Such a position has not even been reached with-in the membership of the OECD. Thus, in 2000 the Committee on Fiscal Affairs limited itself to encouraging member states 'in the context of their bilateral tax or mutual assistance treaties, to search for solutions to this issue so that they can in practice exchange bank information' and agreed to review progress 'at the end of 2002 and thereafter periodically'.[69]

---

66 For example, *Tax Information Exchange Between OECD Member Countries*, 1994, OECD, Paris, p. 24.

67 *Supra*, note 51, p. 15, note 7.

68 For example, W. Gilmore (ed.), *Mutual Assistance in Criminal and Business Regulatory Matters*, Cambridge University Press, Cambridge, 1995, p. xvii.

69 For the position in the UK, see C. Murray and L. Harris, *Mutual Assistance in Criminal Matters*, Sweet & Maxwell, London, 2000, pp. 69, 97–98.

In short, the language of the MOU in relation to criminal tax co-operation could perhaps be characterised as an attempt to reflect 'international best practice'. It certainly cannot at present be said to reflect an existing minimum standard even for OECD members.

As noted above, the MOU also calls for a legal mechanism to be put in place by 31 December 2005 to permit the exchange of information upon request in relation to 'civil' tax matters. In this context it should be noted that international co-operation of this kind is of relatively recent origin and has emerged in the face of rules of national law antagonistic to its development. While this process has been fostered in a variety of institutional settings, the OECD has constantly been at the forefront of developments. In a practical sense, the most influential of its products has been Article 26 of the OECD Model Tax Convention on Income and Capital,[70] a provision which has gradually evolved over time and to which refinements continue to be made.

However, for various reasons Article 26 could not, without amendment, be used as a basis for securing the *effective* exchange of information with some, at least, of the countries and territories on the tax havens list.[71] This can be illustrated by reference to the limitations on the obligation to exchange information contained in Article 26(2).

Paragraph 2 directs itself to three situations: where there is lack of reciprocity; where there is a risk of the disclosure of business and professional secrets; and where disclosure would be contrary to public policy. As has been pointed out elsewhere: '[i]f any of these conditions prevail, the exchange is no longer mandatory. Thus the requested State has the discretionary power to refuse to supply information, even though it may equally accede to the request'.[72] These grounds for the refusal of assistance can, either alone or in combination, result in significant restrictions in the scope of the obligation to co-operate. In the present context, for example, where there may well be significant differences in the tax laws and national administrative practices of OECD and tax haven jurisdictions, the operation of the principle of reciprocity, as reflected in Article 26(2)(a) and (b), is likely to have a particularly acute impact. As one leading authority has explained: 'Under that rule an obligation to investigate exists for both States only to the extent that the measures involved are allowed under the law, and are usual in the administrative practice, of both States. What is decisive in each instance is the *lower of the two levels*

---

70 The text can be consulted on the OECD website: www.oecd.org.

71 For example, *supra*, note 5, p. 46.

72 *Supra*, note 65, p. 25.

of intensity of investigation'.[73] Thus the greater the differences in national approach the greater the limitations.[74]

It is no doubt for these reasons, among others, that both the MOU and the 2000 Report envisage the participation of those jurisdictions which have made the required commitments in multilateral discussions. This dialogue is to include the 'development of a model vehicle for exchange of information (for example an OECD Model Tax Information Exchange Agreement or a multilateral agreement').[75]

Looked at in this light, what the relevant MOU provision seeks to accomplish might be characterised as the setting of a framework within which such dialogue will take place. It is of interest to note, however, that in so-doing the MOU uses in some respects a best practice rather than the existing OECD minimum standards approach. This is perhaps most clearly seen in the requirement that 'the Party will provide the information without regard to whether or not the Party has an interest in obtaining the information for its own domestic tax purposes'. In its recent study, *Improving Access to Bank Information for Tax Purposes*, five OECD members were identified as using a domestic tax interest requirement.[76] However, OECD members have agreed unanimously[77] to re-examine such requirements 'with a view to ensuring that such information can be exchanged by making changes, if necessary, to their laws, regulations and administrative practices'.[78] The Committee on Fiscal Affairs has suggested that the necessary changes be brought about by 2003.

Suffice it for present purposes to note from this brief examination of the treatment of the issues of access to beneficial ownership information and effective exchange of information that the MOU cannot be said to confine its ambition solely to a plan to achieve existing international minimum standards of conduct by tax haven jurisdictions. Some at least of its elements could be more appropriately described as reflecting either standards of an evolving or aspirational nature or of perceived 'best practice'.

---

73 Klaus Vogel, *Double Taxation Conventions*, Kluwer, The Hague, 3rd ed., 1997, p. 1441.

74 For example, *supra*, note 65, p. 51.

75 2000 Report, p. 20.

76 *Supra*, note 51, pp. 82–83.

77 Ibid., p. 3.

78 Ibid., p. 14. The UK took this step in s.146 of the Finance Act 2000, c.17.

Co-ordinated Measures Against Unco-operative Tax Havens

A central feature of the 1998 Report was the emphasis placed on the need for enhanced measures to counteract harmful tax competition. To this end it formulated a range of Recommendations concerning: (1) the more effective use of measures currently found in the domestic legislation of member countries; (2) action to be taken in the context of tax treaties; and (3) the possible intensification of international co-operation. Furthermore, the Report identified a series of topics, including the possibility of having resort to non-tax measures, which required further consideration of their potential to supplement the framework for action.[79] This work was to be carried forward by the Forum.

While the Report acknowledges the continued relevance of unilateral and bilateral measures taken by states in this sphere, it places particular stress on the need to develop co-ordinated multilateral responses to what it perceives as a global problem. This dimension to the approach of the OECD is further emphasised and developed in the 2000 Report which details an evolving framework for implementing a common approach to restraining harmful tax practices. Paragraph 35 of the 2000 Report sets out the then state of development of the consideration of the possible range of elements to which recourse might be made within the context of this common framework. Furthermore, '[t]he Committee on Fiscal Affairs will be working within the next six months to a year to consider these possible measures, finalise its recommendations and adopt an implementation strategy and timetable'.[80] The evolving nature of this process is apparent elsewhere in the Report as, for example, in the statement that the Committee 'also intends to continue to explore what other defensive measures can be taken, including non-tax measures'.[81]

As was noted above, it is anticipated that the Committee on Fiscal Affairs will invite members of the OECD 'to adopt such of the measures recommended by the Committee to the extent possible and appropriate within their national systems, to be implemented against unco-operative Tax Havens as of 31 July 2001'.[82] Similar action is envisaged against any 'scheduled commitment' or 'advance commitment' jurisdiction which is

---

79 See generally 1998 Report, pp. 37–62.

80 2000 Report, p. 24.

81 Ibid., p. 26.

82 Ibid., p. 24.

determined not to have met relevant milestone or timetable undertakings or is deemed no longer to be acting in good faith.[83] It is also possible that entirely new jurisdictions may be classified as unco-operative and thus become liable for consideration within the common framework.[84]

The analysis of this critical feature of the initiative taken by the OECD, in so far as it relates to states considered to be unco-operative tax havens, is far from straightforward from the perspective of public international law. The complexity arises in part from the fact that important elements are still evolving. Furthermore, neither the 1998 nor the 2000 Report appears to have been written with a legal audience in mind. Perhaps for that reason neither contains an explicit legal justification for the action contemplated. Similarly, there is a lack of standardisation in the use of certain terminology – a factor which tends to further obscure the underlying legal basis for the initiative. By way of illustration, while the 2000 Report talks of 'co-ordinated defensive measures', the 1998 text uses a range of terms ('countermeasures', 'enforcement measures', 'counteracting measures' and 'defensive measures') seemingly interchangeably. A similar tendency is evident in the News Releases of and public statements made on behalf of the OECD in this context.[85] While such terms may be capable of use as synonyms in political or economic discourse, this is not the case within the context of general international law where certain of the above have a broadly settled technical meaning.

Within the international system there are several circumstances in which resort to economic measures are undoubtedly lawful. Of these the most obvious and well accepted is when economic sanctions are authorised or imposed by a competent organ of the international community (as with measures ordered by the Security Council under Chapter VII of the UN Charter). Sanctions in this sense are not relevant to the current debate. No such action has been taken by the UN Security Council and the OECD has not held itself to possess such authority. As a senior official of the Financial, Fiscal and Enterprise Affairs Directorate of that institution has explained: 'The OECD does envision co-ordinated defensive measures, but it is the member countries, not the OECD, which will apply

---

83 For example, ibid., p. 18, note 14 and p. 19.

84 For example, ibid., p. 20.

85 For example, 'OECD Moves Forward in Countering Harmful Tax Practices', OECD News Release, Paris, 24 November 1999 ('co-ordinated countermeasures'); 'Statement by Mr. Makhlouf, Chairman of the Committee on Fiscal Affairs', OECD, Paris, 26 June 2000 ('co-ordinated sanctions').

those measures. All the OECD does is provide a framework in which co-operation can take place'.[86]

As has been noted elsewhere, 'one frequent but less firmly established usage speaks of sanctions in describing the measures, particularly in an economic context, taken by a State acting alone or jointly with others in reply to the behaviour of another State which, it maintains, is contrary to international law'.[87] In this sense sanctions are part of the law of counter-measures (sometimes known as measures of reprisal).

The nature and extent of the right to resort to countermeasures has generated extensive discussion in academic circles and has been the subject, on several occasions, of judicial clarification.[88] Most recently, the issue was treated in some detail by the International Court of Justice in the *Case concerning the Gabčíkovo-Nagymaros Project*.[89] The noted Australian scholar, Professor Crawford, in his capacity as Special Rapporteur of the International Law Commission on the subject of state responsibility, has summarised the position taken by the Court in these words:

The Court, in a bilateral context in which no issue of prohibited countermeasures were at stake, endorsed four distinct elements of the law of countermeasures: (a) the countermeasure must be taken in response to an unlawful act; (b) it must be preceded by a demand for compliance by the injured State; (c) the counter-measure must be proportionate, in the sense of 'commensurate with the injury suf-fered, taking account of the rights in question', and (d) the countermeasure must have as its purpose 'to induce the wrongdoing State to comply with its obligations under international law, and that the measure must therefore be reversible.[90]

Three points should be emphasised concerning the above formulation. First, the Court was dealing with countermeasures adopted in a bilateral context. Recourse to the use of such measures on a collective basis raises further issues of legal complexity which were not explored.[91] Second, it is

---

86 Interview, 19 October 2000 with J. Owens, available at www.oecdobserver.org/news/fullstory. Site visited 17 November 2000.

87 J. Combacau, 'Sanctions', *Encyclopedia of Public International Law*, Vol. 9, 1986, p. 338.

88 See, for example, Restatement of the Law (3rd): The Foreign Relations Law of the United States, 1987, American Law Institute Publishers, St Paul, Minn., Vol. 2, pp. 380–384; K. Partsch, *Reprisals, supra*, note 86, pp. 330–335.

89 *ICJ Reports*, 1997, p. 7, at pp. 55–57.

90 International Law Commission, Third Report on State Responsibility, by Mr. James Crawford, Special Rapporteur (hereafter ILC Report), UN doc. A/CN.4/507/Add.3 (18 July 2000), p. 3.

91 See generally International Law Commission, Third Report on State Responsibility by Mr. James Crawford, Special Rapporteur: UN doc. A/CN.4/507/Add.4 (4 August 2000) (hereinafter ILC Report 2).

broadly accepted that certain categories of conduct are prohibited as countermeasures such as recourse to the threat or use of force contrary to the UN Charter. This issue was not addressed by the Court in 1997. It will suffice to note that the International Law Commission is currently considering whether resort to extreme economic and political coercion could ever be so categorised.[92] Third, other rules of international law in force between the injured and the target state may restrict or abrogate the right to have recourse to such measures.[93] Notwithstanding these restraining or complicating factors, there is no doubt that when countermeasures can properly be resorted to, the initiating state has a broad, but not unlimited, right to suspend the performance of its legal obligations towards the responsible state.

While the term 'countermeasures' has been used within the context of the OECD initiative, the legal concept has not been specifically invoked. Nonetheless, there are elements in the 1998 and 2000 Reports which, in the abstract, raise the possibility that the underlying legal justification for the measures currently in contemplation may be found, at least in part, in this doctrine. For example, a central thrust of the OECD initiative is to induce unco-operative tax havens to comply with international standards. In the words of the 1998 Report: 'Countries should remain free to design their own tax systems as long as they abide by internationally accepted standards in doing so'.[94] Similarly, in other parts of the main reports one finds wording which echoes central elements of the legal regime of countermeasures such as proportionality.[95]

There is, however, no direct evidence that the OECD Secretariat or member states regard the threat to impose co-ordinated economic measures against unco-operative tax havens as deriving legal validity, even in part, from prior internationally wrongful acts committed by such jurisdictions. Indeed, given the analysis of aspects of the principles of transparency and effective exchange of information contained in this study, it would be surprising if such a justification were to be proffered.

---

92 See, ILC Report, pp. 13–16, 30–31.

93 As has been pointed out elsewhere: 'No doubt a bilateral or multilateral treaty might renounce the possibility of countermeasures being taken for its breach, or in relation to its subject matter. This is the case, for example, with the European Union treaties, which have their own system of enforcement. Under the WTO, special permission has to be obtained for retaliatory measures, and this again would exclude any residual right to take countermeasures under general international law for breaches of the WTO and related agreements'. ILC Report, pp. 26–27.

94 1998 Report, p. 15.

95 2000 Report, p. 24.

In these circumstances the somewhat different question of the nature and extent of the closely associated right of retorsion necessarily arises. For present purposes retorsion may be taken to denote a measure not affecting the legal rights of another state taken in response to an unfriendly or objectionable act by that state. Here the central point of contrast with the doctrine of countermeasures is that the latter consists of acts which would otherwise be illegal.[96] As Professor Crawford has explained, the 'distinction is that between "unfriendly" but not unlawful reactions to the conduct of another State (retorsion) and those reactions which are inconsistent with the international obligations of the State and are justified, if at all, as legitimate countermeasures. While the distinction may sometimes be difficult to draw in practice, especially in the context of collective action, it is crucial for the purposes of State responsibility'.[97] In the practice of states, economic relations have been the primary sphere of application of this doctrine in the post-World War II period.

While the concept of retorsion is rooted in the assumption that one state may respond to the acts of another by recourse to measures that do not violate its legal obligations with respect to that member of the international community with a view to inducing it to adopt an alternative posture or policy, the important question is whether or not the international legal order places any limits on the extent of such freedom of action. Put another way, the issue is whether or not general international law contains rules distinguishing between permissible and impermissible acts of retorsion.

This is one of the most complex and controversial issues confronting the modern law of nations; one which revolves around the legitimacy or otherwise of economic and political coercion.[98] While a comprehensive review of this matter lies beyond the scope of this paper, it would be of value to outline certain of the essential elements of that debate.

There exists no consensus among states or in the scholarly literature as to the existence of a general legal limitation on the right to have recourse

---

96 See, for example, I. A. Shearer (ed.) (1994). *Starke's International Law*, 11th ed., Butterworths, London, p. 472.

97 ILC Report 2, p. 13.

98 See, for example, M. Shaw, *International Law*, Cambridge University Press, Cambridge, 4th ed., 1997, p. 783. See also D. Bowett, 'International Law and Economic Coercion', *Virginia Journal of International Law*, 1976, 16, pp. 245–259; R. Lillich, 'Economic Coercion and the "New International Economic Order": A Second Look at Some First Impressions', ibid., pp. 233–244; T. Farer, 'Political and Economic Coercion in Contemporary International Law', 1985, 79, *American Journal of International Law*, pp. 405–413.

to differing forms of economic and political pressure as an instrument of national policy. Among those who argue in favour of such a prohibitory norm there exists a variety of views as to both its source and nature.[99] Of these the form of analysis which has perhaps attracted the greatest level of support is that the legal limits to the use of economic and other types of pressure are to be found in the general international law principle of non-intervention.[100] While this doctrine is most commonly associated with practices involving the threat or use of armed force, it is widely acknowledged that it has a broader scope. As a study prepared by the Planning Staff of the British Foreign and Commonwealth Office in 1984 noted: 'Many commentators describe intervention in which force, or the threat thereof, is not used as no more than interference. But, apart from force, there are other means, of which economic coercion and propaganda are two examples, of violating a state's absolute sovereignty over its domestic affairs. To define as intervention only those instances of interference in which armed force is used or threatened thus seems artificially restrictive.[101]

The rule of non-intervention had its origins in the practice of the states of Latin America in the nineteenth and first half of the twentieth centuries. That process of gradual evolution culminated in the inclusion of specific and wide ranging regulation of the subject in Chapter IV of the Charter of the Organization of American States.[102] Of special relevance for present purposes are the following provisions:

Article 19

No State or group of States has the right to intervene, directly or indirectly, for any reason whatever, in the internal or external affairs of any other State. The foregoing principle prohibits not only armed force but also any other form of interference or attempted threat against the personality of the State or against its political, economic, and cultural elements.

Article 20

No State may use or encourage the use of coercive measures of an economic or

---

99 See, for example, S. Neff, 'Boycott and the Law of Nations', *British Year Book of International Law*, 1988, 59, pp. 113–149; O. Y. Elagab, *The Legality of Non-Forcible Counter-Measures in International Law*, Clarendon Press, Oxford, 1988, pp. 190–213.

100 See, for example, E. Jimenez de Arechaga, 'International Law in the Past Third of a Century', *Recueil des Cours*, 1978, 159, pp. 111–116; B. Simma (ed.), *The Charter of the United Nations*, Oxford University Press, Oxford, 1994, pp. 112–113.

101 Is Intervention Ever Justified?, Foreign Policy Document No. 148, Annex 1, para. 7, 1984.

102 H. Caminos. 'The Role of the Organization of American States in the Promotion and Protection of Democratic Governance', *Recueil des Cours*, 1998, 273, pp. 196–208.

political character in order to force the sovereign will of another State and obtain from it advantages or any kind.

Throughout the United Nations era the General Assembly has come to recognise the general legal relevance of this principle in a succession of declarations and resolutions. By way of illustration, the Declaration on Principles of International Law Concerning Friendly Relations and Co-operation Among States in Accordance with the Charter of the United Nations (G.A. Res.2625 (XXV) (1970)), which was adopted by consensus, contains extensive treatment of this issue.[103] It reads, in part, thus:

No State or group of States has the right to intervene, directly or indirectly, for any reason whatever, in the internal or external affairs of any other State. Consequently, armed intervention and all other forms of interference or attempted threats against the personality of the State or against its political, economic and cultural elements, are in violation of international law.

The same Resolution also declares, *inter alia*, that 'No State may use or encourage the use of economic, political or any other type of measure to coerce another State in order to obtain from it the subordination of the exercise of its sovereign rights and to secure from it advantages of any kind'. It also proclaims that 'Every State has an inalienable right to choose its political, economic, social and cultural systems, without interference in any form by another State'.

This UN General Assembly Resolution was afforded a position of considerable importance in the reasoning of the International Court of Justice in the *Case Concerning Military and Paramilitary Activities in and Against Nicaragua.*[104] In the course of its judgement the Court affirmed that the principle of non-intervention formed part of modern customary international law. It stated:

The principle of non-intervention involves the right of every sovereign State to conduct its affairs without outside interference; though examples of trespass against this principle are not infrequent, the Court considers that it is part and parcel of customary international law. As the Court has observed: 'Between independent States, respect for territorial sovereignty is an essential foundation of international relations' (ICJ Reports 1949, p.35), and international law requires political integrity also to be respected. Expressions of an opinio juris regarding the existence of the principle of non-intervention in customary international law are numerous and not difficult to find. Of course, statements

---

103 G. Arangio-Ruiz, 'Friendly Relations Resolution', Vol. II, *Encyclopedia of Public International Law*, 1995, pp. 485–490.

104 ICJ Reports, 1986, p. 14.

whereby States avow their recognition of the principles of international law set forth in the United Nations Charter cannot strictly be interpreted as applying to the principle of non-intervention by States in the internal or external affairs of other States, since this principle is not, as such, spelt out in the Charter. But it was never intended that the Charter should embody written confirmation of every essential principle of international law in force. The existence in the opinio juris *of States of the principle of non-intervention is backed by established and substantial practice. It has moreover been presented as a corollary of the sovereign equality of States. A particular instance of this is General Assembly resolution 2625 (XXV), the Declaration on the Principles of International Law concerning Friendly Relations and Co-operation among States.*[105]

The World Court also took the opportunity to provide some clarification of the content of the principle (though in doing so it concentrated on those aspects especially relevant to the resolution of the actual dispute before it). In this regard it emphasised the importance of the notion of coercion. A prohibited intervention must be one:

bearing on matters in which each State is permitted, by the principle of State sovereignty, to decide freely. One of these is the choice of a political, economic, social and cultural system, and the formulation of foreign policy. Intervention is wrongful when it uses methods of coercion in regard to such choices which must remain free ones. The element of coercion which defines and indeed forms the very essence of prohibited intervention, is particularly obvious in the case of an intervention which uses force either in the direct form of military action or in the indirect form of support for subversive or terrorist armed activities within another State.[106]

Elsewhere in its judgement, however, the Court had occasion to consider in brief an argument advanced by Nicaragua that certain economic measures taken against it by the USA, culminating in the unilateral imposition of a trade embargo in 1985, constituted a prohibited form of intervention in its internal affairs.[107] The Court disagreed.[108] This determination has led some commentators to conclude that customary international law does not prohibit economic coercion.[109] Others have argued that,

---

105 Ibid., p. 106.

106 Ibid., p. 108.

107 Ibid., pp. 69–70.

108 Ibid., pp. 126, 138.

109 See, for example, C. Cameron, 'Developing a Standard for Politically Related State Economic Action', *Michigan Journal of International Law*, 1991, 13, p. 249; R. Porotsky, 'Economic Coercion and the General Assembly: a Post-Cold War Assessment of the Legality and Utility of the Thirty-Fife-Year Old Embargo against Cuba', *Vanderbilt Journal of Transnational Law*, 1995, 28, p. 919.

properly construed, the conclusion of the court does not have that absolute character.[110] This perspective is well expressed by the distinguished Canadian jurist, Professor R. St J. MacDonald, who has remarked that the court 'simply held that the above facts did not constitute a violation of the principle'.[111] This latter view finds further support in, among others, the subsequent practice of the UN General Assembly.[112]

Even if one accepts that the legal norm of non-intervention extends to economic measures, difficulties remain in determining whether or not in any particular case the threshold between lawful economic pressure has been crossed and improper economic coercion has commenced.[113] A further factor of importance concerns the implications which flow from resort to economic measures on a collective or co-ordinated basis, as in this instance, rather than unilaterally.[114]

Conclusions

In his opening address to the High Level Consultations held in Barbados in January 2001, OECD Deputy Secretary General Kondo remarked:

Globalisation can pose problems, not just for individuals, but for governments as well. New opportunities are opened up for individuals and enterprises to engage in illegal activities, such as hard core cartels, bribery, money laundering and tax abuses, which distort trade and investment flows.[115]

Few would disagree with the sentiment that countering the 'dark side of globalisation'[116] presents significant challenges for the international community and that 'offshore' financial centres have an important role to play in so doing.[117]

---

110 Neff, *supra*, note 99.

111 R. MacDonald, 'The Nicaragua Case: New Answers to Old Questions?', *Canadian Yearbook of International Law*, 1986, p. 138.

112 See, for example, General Assembly Resolution 53/10 on the 'elimination of coercive economic measures as a means of political and economic compulsion', reproduced in (1999) 38 International Legal Materials, pp. 759–760. See also 'Economic measures as a means of political and economic coercion against developing countries', UN doc. A/48/535, 25 October 1993.

113 See, for example, Lillich, *supra*, note 97, pp. 238–240.

114 For example, C.C. Hyde and L.B. Wehle, 'The Boycott in Foreign Affairs', *American Journal of International Law*, 1933, 27, pp. 4–5.

115 Speech, Monday 8 January 2001, typescript, p. 2.

116 Ibid.

117 For example, UNODCCP, *Financial Havens, Banking Secrecy and Money-Laundering*, United Nations, New York, 1998.

That said, however, this overview of the tax havens aspects of the OECD initiative on harmful tax competition gives rise to certain concerns as to both process and substance. For example, it has been demonstrated that central elements of the conduct expected of listed jurisdictions cannot readily be classified as constituting generally accepted international standards; indeed, in some respects they appear to go beyond what might be termed existing minimum standards for OECD members in their relationships *inter se*. Viewed in this light there is considerable scope for a truly inclusive global forum on tax issues, of the kind contemplated in the remit for the working group established at the Barbados meeting, to contribute to the formulation of such standards and to the subsequent monitoring of their implementation by relevant members of the international community.

To some, resort to co-ordinated economic measures in order to induce compliance with standards of an evolving or aspirational nature on the part of countries and territories which have had no participation in their formulation will be viewed as objectionable in principle. Such a strategy is also controversial when viewed in terms of public international law. For that reason an authoritative clarification of the legal position would be of considerable value. One possibility would be to seek, through the UN General Assembly, an Advisory Opinion on this general issue from the International Court of Justice in The Hague.[118] In the light of such a clarification a proper and much-needed debate could be conducted as to the overall acceptability of and limits to a name, shame and punish strategy at the international level in the opening years of the twenty-first century.

---

118 UN Charter, Article 96(1); Statute of the International Court of Justice, Article 65.